Knowledge management systems
Theory and practice

K nowledge management systems

Theory and practice

Edited by Stuart Barnes

THOMSON

™

LEARNING

Australia • Canada • Mexico • Singapore • Spain • United Kingdom • United States

Knowledge management systems: theory and practice

For more information, contact Thomson Learning, Berkshire House, 168–173 High Holborn, London, WC1V 7AA or visit us on the World Wide Web at: http://www.thomsonlearning.co.uk

British Library Cataloguing-in-Publication Data
A catalogue record for this book is available from the British Library

ISBN 1-86152-616-4

First edition published 2002 by Thomson Learning

Typeset by Dexter Haven Associates, London

Printed in Great Britain by The Alden Press, Oxford

Contents

Contributors   x
Figures and tables   xii

Introduction   1
Stuart Barnes

Features of the book   3
Structure of the book   4
References   10

PART 1: EXPERIENCES IN KNOWLEDGE MANAGEMENT SYSTEMS PRACTICE

1   **Knowledge management systems: issues, challenges
     and benefits**   15
     Maryam Alavi and Dorothy E. Leidner

     Introduction   15
     Knowledge, knowledge management and knowledge
     management systems   16
     Methodology   18
     Study findings   19
     Discussion   26
     Conclusion   29
     Acknowledgement   29
     References   30
     Appendix: knowledge management questionnaire   32

2   **Sharing tacit knowledge: a case study at Volvo**   36
     Dick Stenmark

     Introduction   36
     The problem with externalizing tacit knowledge   37
     The tacitness of professional interests   38
     A new perspective on retrieval systems   40

The site and research method   41
Field results   42
Discussion   44
Conclusions   46
Acknowledgements   47
References   47

**3   Knowledge management in virtual organizations:
     experiences at Sigma   49**
     Birgit Lemken, Helge Kahler and Markus Rittenbruch

Introduction   49
Virtual organizations   50
Challenges to knowledge management   52
Sigma – a team-oriented virtual organization 54
The interaction of technology and culture   60
Conclusion   61
References   62

**4   Managing information overload in the health sector:
     the WaX ActiveLibrary system   64**
     *Claire O'Brien, Rudolf Hanka, Iain Buchan and
     Heather Heathfield*

Introduction   64
The WaX ActiveLibrary   66
The knowledge content in WaX   71
Evaluating WaX   74
Conclusions   79
References   80

**5   Knowledge management in the professions: a study of IT
     support in law firms   82**
     Petter Gottschalk

Introduction   82
Aspects of the research   83
Initial field study   85
The research model   86
Research methodology   87
Research results   88
Discussion   91
Conclusions   92
Acknowledgement   93
References   93

PART 2: DESIGNING ENTERPRISE KNOWLEDGE MANAGEMENT
SYSTEMS ARCHITECTURES

**6 A multi-layer architecture for knowledge management
systems** 97
Ulrich Frank

Introduction 97
Knowledge management systems and information systems 98
The architecture 101
Knowledge management as a permanent process 108
Conclusions 110
References 110

**7 Managing knowledge in decentralized heterogeneous
corporations** 112
Ulrike Baumoel, Reinhard Jung and Robert Winter

Introduction 112
Management holdings 113
The data-warehousing process 116
Reference models 119
Management middleware 121
Conclusion 126
Acknowledgements 126
References 126

**8 Web-based knowledge management support for
document collections** 128
Mark Ginsburg and Ajit Kambil

Introduction 128
Critical issues in the design of KMSS 129
Challenges of designing a Web-based document KMSS 130
Annotate: a Web-based document KMSS 134
Annotate system architecture 138
Evaluating the Annotate system 140
Conclusions 142
Acknowledgement 143
References 143

9   Enterprise information infrastructures for active, context-sensitive knowledge delivery   **146**
Andreas Abecker, Ansgar Bernardi, Knut Hinkelmann and Michael Sintek

Introduction   146
KnowMore knowledge services at a glance   148
Realization of the KnowMore system   152
Discussion   157
Acknowledgement   159
References   159

10   Combining data from existing company sources: architecture and experiences   **161**
Jari Vanhanen, Casper Lassenius and Kristian Rautiainen

Introduction   161
Architecture   163
Experiences   170
Conclusions   175
References   175

PART 3: IMPLEMENTING KNOWLEDGE MANAGEMENT SOLUTIONS

11   Knowledge management: the human factor   **179**
Jacky Swan, Maxine Robertson and Sue Newell

Introduction   179
Defining KM – the case for research   180
Knowledge management in the literature   181
The human factor: a survey of KM practice   184
Discussion   187
Conclusions   192
References   192

12   Fundamentals of implementing data warehousing in organizations   **195**
Pat Finnegan and David Sammon

Introduction   195
Implementing data warehousing   196
Data-gathering   197
Data warehousing in the companies studied   197
Organizational prerequisites for data
warehousing implementation   201
Conclusions   208
References   208

13   **Barriers to adoption of organizational memories: lessons**
     from industry   **210**
     Karma Sherif

     Introduction   210
     Research method   211
     Research findings   214
     Lessons learnt   219
     Conclusion   220
     References   220

14   **Understanding knowledge management solutions:**
     the evolution of frameworks in theory and practice   **222**
     C.W. Holsapple and K.D. Joshi

     Introduction   222
     Representative frameworks   222
     A synthesized framework   229
     A collaborative KM framework   236
     Summary and conclusion   239
     References   240
     Appendix: Delphi panelists (name and affiliation)   242

     Index   243

Contributors

Andreas Abecker, Knowledge Management Group, Kaiserslautern, Germany

Maryam Alavi, Robert H. Smith School of Business, University of Maryland at College Park, USA

Stuart J. Barnes, School of Information Management, Victoria University of Wellington, New Zealand

Ulrike Baumoel, Institute of Information Management, University of St Gallen, Switzerland

Ansgar Bernardi, Knowledge Management Group, Kaiserslautern, Germany

Iain Buchan, Centre for Clinical Informatics, University of Cambridge, UK

Pat Finnegan, Executive Systems Research Centre, University College Cork, Ireland

Ulrich Frank, University of Koblenz-Landau, Koblenz, Germany

Mark Ginsburg, MIS Department, Eller School of Business, University of Arizona, Tucson, USA

Petter Gottschalk, Department of Technology Management, Norwegian School of Management, Sandvika, Norway

Rudolf Hanka, Centre for Clinical Informatics, University of Cambridge, UK

Heather Heathfield, IT Perspectives Ltd, Manchester, UK

Knut Hinkelmann, University of Applied Sciences, Solothurn, Olten, Switzerland

Clyde W. Holsapple, University of Kentucky, USA

K.D. Joshi, Washington State University, USA

Reinhard Jung, Institute of Information Management, University of St Gallen, Switzerland

Helge Kahler, Institute of Computer Science, University of Bonn, Germany

Ajit Kambil, Andersen Consulting, USA

Casper Lassenius, Helsinki University of Technology, Finland

Dorothy E. Leidner, INSEAD, Fontainebleau, France

Birgit Lemken, Plenum Systeme, Wiesbaden, Germany

Sue Newell, School of Management, Royal Holloway, University of London, UK

Claire O'Brien, Centre for Clinical Informatics, University of Cambridge, UK

Kristian Rautiainen, Helsinki University of Technology, Finland

Markus Rittenbruch, Institute of Computer Science, Bonn University, Germany

Maxine Robertson, Warwick Business School, Warwick University, Coventry, UK

David Sammon, Executive Systems Research Centre, University College Cork, Ireland

Karma Sherif, Information Systems and Quantitative Science Department, Texas Tech University, Lubbock, Texas, USA

Michael Sintek, Knowledge Management Group, Kaiserslautern, Germany

Dick Stenmark, Volvo Information Technology, Gutenberg, Sweden

Jacky Swan, Warwick Business School, Warwick University, Coventry, UK

Jari Vanhanen, Helsinki University of Technology, Finland

Robert Winter, Institute of Information Management, University of St Gallen, Switzerland

F igures and tables

Figures

1.1	Respondents by global location	19
1.2	Respondents by position within their organizations	19
1.3	Respondents by industry	20
1.4	Initiators in organizations with, or developing, KMS	23
1.5	Estimated average budgets of KMS in organizations	24
3.1	Polycentric network	51
3.2	Knowledge types	54
3.3	Ariadne's Thread, Sigma's regional structure	58
4.1	Overloaded with paperwork	65
4.2	WaX ActiveLibrary interface, as used during the evaluation	67
4.3	Time taken to reach the required page of information	78
5.1	Research model	87
6.1	Overview of the architecture	102
6.2	Levels of abstraction within a particular view, and their relationship to corresponding aspects of an IS	103
6.3	Excerpt from the object model on the meta-level, with focus on the organizational perspective	105
6.4	Visualization of a process specification within an editor (below) and partial description of corresponding instances	106
6.5	Interfacing KMS and IS by generating (standardized) schema level representations for IS	108
7.1	Business architecture of the information age	114
7.2	The data warehouse architecture	118
7.3	A modified data warehouse architecture serving as a management middleware	121
7.4	Schematic hierarchy of reference models	122
7.5	Business engineering map	123
7.6	Exemplary integration of knowledge scorecards into the BE-Map	124
7.7	Example of an integrated knowledge scorecard	125

8.1	Annotate query interface with a social filter selected	136
8.2	Retrieval layer alterations in the Annotate system	137
8.3	The icon legend	138
8.4	The document is now a hybrid object of data (original author work) and multiple instances of meta-data	139
8.5	The search, retrieval and document interfaces	141
8.6	A simple Schelling diagram	141
8.7	A more complex Schelling diagram with multiple equilibria	142
9.1	A typical purchasing workflow	149
9.2	The KnowMore system offers context-sensitive information supply	150
9.3	Changes in the process status result in refined information support	151
9.4	The three-layered OM architecture	152
9.5	Example of a KIT specification	154
9.6	KIT processing by worklist handler and information/knowledge agent	156
9.7	The KnowMore implementation is a Web-enabled client–server architecture	157
10.1	The LUCOS toolset	163
10.2	EMIX	166
10.3	The measurement design tool (MeTo)	167
10.4	Two ViCA panels and navigation from a chart to another panel	170
10.5	The LUCOS toolset installation	172
10.6	A project control panel in ViCA	172
10.7	The visualization panels	173
11.1	ProQuest references to KM and the learning organization	182
13.1	Barriers to OMIS adoption	215
14.1	KM evolution framework	233

Tables

1.1	Perspectives on KM	21
1.2	Capabilities needed for KM	22
1.3	Key concerns related to KM	22
1.4	Percentage of KMS with various technologies/tools	25
1.5	Importance of knowledge domain	25
1.6	Perceived benefits of existing KMS	26
4.1	WaX library: East Sussex Primary Care Information Service	72
5.1	Characteristics of respondents and organizations	88
5.2	Definitions of KM	88

5.3   Items for measurement of dependent and independent
      constructs   89
5.4   Multiple regression between use of IT and predictors   89
5.5   Responses for different law-firm sizes   91
8.1   Waterfall model of the intranet document life cycle   131
11.1 Comparison of core issues in the the learning
      organization and KM in PQD articles, 1993–8   183
11.2 1993 Learning organization thematic categories   183
11.3 1998 KM thematic categories   183
11.4 Response frequencies and relationship to critical
      variable of KM practices   187
12.1 Data warehousing experience in the organizations
      studied   201
12.2 Organizational prerequisites   208
14.1 Pillars of knowledge management (adapted from
      Wiig, 1993)   223
14.2 Knowledge conversion framework (adapted from
      Nonaka, 1994)   224
14.3 Core capabilities and knowledge-building activities
      (adapted from Leonard-Barton, 1995)   224
14.4 Organizational KM model (adapted from Arthur
      Andersen and APQC, 1996)   225
14.5 Model of the knowing organization (adapted from
      Choo, 1996)   226
14.6 Intellectual capital model (adapted from Petrash, 1996)   226
14.7 Model of knowledge transfer (adapted from Szulanski,
      1996)   227
14.8 KPMG knowledge-management process (adapted from
      Alavi, 1997)   227
14.9 Intangible assets (adapted from Sveiby, 1997)   228
14.10 A framework of knowledge management stages
      (adapted from van der Spijkervet, 1997)   229

I ntroduction   Stuart Barnes

In contemporary business environments, organizations are faced with tremendous competitive pressures. The global economy, combined with issues of rapid technological change and the increased power of consumers, places huge demands on firms to remain flexible and responsive (Drucker, 1988; 1995; Teece, Pisano and Shuen, 1997). Globally, common influences include rapid political changes, regional trade agreements, low labour costs in some countries, and frequent and significant changes in markets (Dam, 2001). In addition, there are changes in the nature of the workforce (which is older, better-educated and more independent), government deregulation and reduction of subsidies, and shifts in the ethical, legal and social responsibilities of organizations (Mazarr, 2001; Naisbitt, 1994). Furthermore, technology is playing an increasingly important role in business in this environment; increased innovation and new technologies are providing vast improvements in cost-performance and an important impetus to strategy.

In the past, a variety of techniques was developed to enhance a firm's ability to react to and cope with such pressures, including business process re-engineering (Hammer and Champy, 1993), total quality management (Edwards Deming, 1986), downsizing (Trimmer, 1993), outsourcing (Bettis, Bradley and Hamel, 1991) and empowerment (Lipnack and Stamps, 1997). However, the power of such methods often appeared limited and transient.

For all these strategic programmes, one fundamental question has been pervasive: how organizations create and sustain competitive advantage. Recently, however, strategic management theorists have begun to rethink ideas about competitiveness. From traditional ideas of organizational capability and competition based on the structure–conduct –performance paradigm (Collis and Montgomery, 1995; Porter, 1985), the focus has shifted to the internal resources of the firm as a key determinant of competitive advantage (Barney, 1991; Grant, 1991a; Lank, 1997). This new approach is often referred to as the resource-based view of the firm.

The resource-based view of the firm recognizes the importance of organizational resources and capabilities as the principal source of achieving and sustaining competitive advantage. According to this approach, there is a distinction between resource and capability (Lee, Kim and Yu, 2001). Corporate resources – including equipment, skills, patents and financial capital – are basic inputs into gaining and maintaining competitive advantage. Organizational capability is the capacity of a firm in acquiring and utilizing its resources to perform tasks and activities for competitive gain (Grant, 1991b). Thus, while resources are the main source of an organization's capabilities, capabilities are the principal source of its competitive advantage.

Within the resource-based perspective, information and knowledge have become increasingly recognized as competitive differentiators. In the knowledge-based view, organizational knowledge – such as operational routines, skills or know-how – is acknowledged as the most valuable organizational asset (Spender, 1996). Knowledge-sharing among employees, with customers and with business partners has a tremendous potential pay-off in improved customer service, shorter delivery-cycle times and increased collaboration within the company or with business partners. Some knowledge also has an important value as a commodity: it can be sold to others or traded for other knowledge.

Moreover, in this new perspective, the capability to manage knowledge strategically is seen as the most significant source of competitive advantage (Grant, 1991b). As a consequence, the field of knowledge management (KM) has been born, and has flourished. Interestingly, KM has captured the imagination of both academics and practitioners alike across a broad range of fields; as ideas about knowledge and management have converged, contributions have been made by disciplines such as information systems (IS), strategy, organization theory and human resources (Alavi and Leidner, 2001). Although the term 'knowledge management' was first used in the mid-1980s, it was not translated into commercial reality until the 1990s. Now, KM is recognized as a long-term strategic field.

In business, a deluge of organizational initiatives has appeared, typically based on the use of modern information technologies for managing organization-wide knowledge resources. KM began to emerge most strongly between 1995 and 1997, after the proliferation of the Web-browser (Maurer, 1998). The browser simplified the development of KM applications because it let developers build to a standard interface. The resulting knowledge management systems (KMS) are at the core of enterprise KM approaches. The leading vendors of commercial KMS include Autonomy, Business Objects, Cognos, Hewlett Packard, Hummingbird and Invention Machine, in a market worth around $8.5 billion for KM software and services in 2002 (Carnelley *et al.*, 2001). Some companies have also developed bespoke KMS solutions. An estimated 80 per cent of the largest global corporations now have KMS projects (Lawton, 2001). Recent examples include the US Central Intelligence Agency, Intel and Shell Oil.

As we shall see in the following chapters, KMS are diverse. They are not a single technology, but instead a collection of indexing, classifying and information-retrieval techniques coupled with methodologies designed to achieve results for the user. The key underpinning technologies enable: content and workflow management, which categorizes knowledge and directs it to workers who can benefit from it; search functionality, allowing users to look for relevant knowledge; and collaboration, to share knowledge (Purvis, Sambamurthy and Zmud, 2001; Woods and Sheina, 1999). If designed and implemented correctly, the potential return from leveraging an organization's knowledge resources can be enormous (Davenport and Prusak, 1998), particularly in areas such as enhancing customer-relationship management, research and discovery, and business processes, as well as group collaboration for design and other purposes (Lawton, 2001).

While compelling, approaches to KM and the use of KMS have not been without problems. Part of the difficulty stems from the very nature of knowledge: defining 'knowledge' is not a simple undertaking. Typically, it is now recognized that there are many types of knowledge present in an organization – contained in the 'organizational memory' (Walsh and Ungson, 1991). Whilst there are various typologies, in its simplest form there are two main types of knowledge – tacit and explicit (Nonaka and Takeuchi, 1995). Explicit knowledge may be expressed and communicated relatively easily; tacit knowledge tends to be personal, subjective and difficult to transmit (or sometimes even to recognize). Thus, while some explicit knowledge may lend itself to codification and commodification in KMS, tacit knowledge is very strongly embedded in the mind of the individual and highly context-sensitive. People are the sole creators and consumers of knowledge. A key challenge of KMS, therefore, has been to make appropriate tacit knowledge explicit and portable (Swan, 2001).

The complexity of knowledge in organizations has further translated into complexity in designing and implementing enterprise-wide approaches to KM, utilizing appropriate KMS but also taking adequate account of human and organizational factors. Two of the main reasons for the failure of KM projects are the lack of strategic priorities and the need to manage knowledge, rather than documents or systems (Ruggles, 1998); KMS are an important enabler, but their value can only be realized by appropriate strategies, policies, procedures, processes, structures and cultures that recognize the complexity of managing organizational knowledge (Garvin, 1993; Purvis, Sambamurthy and Zmud, 2001; Zack, 1999).

Features of the book

This book explores the application of IS to the management of organizational knowledge. This text has arisen from extensive investigation into the impacts of KM upon business, which has typically been highly dependent upon recent technological developments. It has also arisen from a personal review of the available literature on this and related topics, based on the authors' own experience, and in the context of recent developments in the field.

While the book will hopefully be of interest to executives concerned with some of the many complex and inter-related issues associated with managing organizational knowledge using IS, its primary audiences are senior undergraduates and masters students studying for degrees in business-related subjects or management information systems (MIS). Students who are about to begin research in this area should also find the book of particular help in providing a rich source of material reflecting leading-edge thinking.

The collected papers in this book illustrate the wide variety of business opportunities afforded by KM systems. They describe and discuss the important issues that follow in the wake of organizational decisions to embark upon the development of electronic KM solutions. The authors of this text have written recent and emerging research, and have been chosen because their work sits well within the framework of the book and brings a good balance of theory and practical issues.

In the development of this book, articles were solicited from authors worldwide. In this, the purpose was two-fold. Firstly, we wanted the content to have a worldwide appeal. KMS are a potentially global phenomenon. It was desirable that the selection of authors should reflect this. Secondly, the purpose was to present the different perspectives represented by writers from different parts of the globe. In all, nine countries are represented, a total of 33 contributors, largely from Europe and North America.

It is, of course, impossible to cover all aspects of this emerging topic. The focus is on attempting to cover some of the more recent and possibly more important aspects, and from a MIS perspective. The implications are that whilst technological aspects are covered in some detail, especially in section 2, the book is typically presented in a mode accessible to the manager or MIS/business student. Moreover, the book makes use of a considerable number of recent case studies to illustrate, consolidate and exemplify the important concepts or issues under discussion.

Structure of the book

The book is organized into three sections. The rationale for this structure is to provide a formal introduction to KMS practice, before examining some key concepts and issues in both design and implementation of KMS.

Part 1: experiences in knowledge management systems practice

The first section provides an overarching introduction to the field. In particular, it examines the nature of and rationale for KMS, the implications and benefits for organizations, and the current state of KMS usage in organizations today. It recognizes the very practical nature of the field, and aims to provide a number of useful examples of KMS in practice in a variety of organizational and industrial contexts. As we shall see, it is strongly supported by recent surveys, case studies and other empirical evidence.

Part 2: designing enterprise knowledge management systems architectures

The second section takes a more conceptual stance. In particular, it explores the complexity of designing appropriate enterprise KMS architectures. The section provides an introduction to a variety of tools, techniques, models and frameworks for understanding corporate KMS design. The applicability of these conceptual building-blocks is wide-ranging, and touches on a variety of KMS and organizational types. In each case, specifications for a KMS are followed through with examples of theoretical or actual prototype KMS designs. Some designs have been partially tested in practice, and relevant experiences are duly noted.

Part 3: implementing knowledge management solutions

The final section attempts to assist in bridging the gap that is becoming apparent between KMS theory and practice. Good and bad KMS designs alike can fail at the points of implementation and use. Here we analyze some of the problems associated with realizing a variety of KMS designs in practice. Uppermost in the discussion are management, organizational and social factors that influence the successful assimilation of enterprise knowledge platforms. The section draws on theory to demonstrate some of the key issues associated with implementing KMS, and evidence to support and consolidate the arguments given.

Chapter summary

In order to elaborate further on the content of the book and the range of issues covered, each part will now be described in somewhat greater detail.

As indicated above, Section 1 is entitled 'Experiences in knowledge management systems practice', and aims to provide a solid grounding in and understanding of the contemporary KMS environment in organizations. The first chapter is entitled 'Knowledge management systems: issues, challenges and benefits'. This chapter examines the state of the art in KMS development in organizations around the globe. Many organizations are developing IS designed specifically to facilitate the sharing and integration of knowledge, but because KMS are just beginning to appear in organizations, little research and field data exists to guide the development and implementation of such systems, or to guide expectations of the potential benefits of such systems. This study provides an analysis of the nature, current practices and outcomes of KMS as they are evolving in 50 organizations. The findings suggest that interest in KMS is very high across a variety of industries, the technological foundations are varied, and the major concerns revolve around achieving the correct amount and type of accurate knowledge and garnering support for contribution to KMS.

The second chapter examines how organizations can approach the issue of turning tacit knowledge tangible. In particular, 'Sharing tacit knowledge: a case study at Volvo' explores the development and use of a system to share tacit knowledge of professional interests. Typically, our interests as professionals in a modern corporate setting govern our activities more than any formal job role description. However, it is often difficult to describe precisely what we are interested in or what makes a certain book or document interesting. It is, on the other hand, very easy to determine whether or not a given document is interesting just by giving it a quick glance. Based on Polanyi's theories of tacit knowledge, chapter 2 claims is that this is because we use tacit knowledge when making these decisions. By studying how an agent-based retrieval prototype was used, it deduces that technology such as recommender systems may be used to capture our interests and thus make tacit knowledge available to the organization, without having to make it explicit. Such a solution has three advantages. Firstly, instead of using a few keywords to describe an interest, one can give an example in the form of a document. Secondly, an incentive to define an interest exists, since it is rewarded in form of more accurate information retrieval. Thirdly, since knowledge no longer requires externalization, there is less risk that users will feel that they are being made obsolete.

Picking up on the changing nature of modern organizational forms, chapter 3 looks at 'Knowledge management in virtual organizations: experiences at Sigma'. A key concept that has emerged from the synergies between new technological developments and changing paradigms of corporate culture is the virtual organization (VO). Although numerous aspects are considered important in the definition of a VO, it essentially involves virtual business (or v-business) relationships in which partners share complementary resources and technologies to achieve a common goal, such as creating a product or service (e.g. see Barnes and Hunt, 2001). Confronted with a continuously changing competitive environment – due to issues such as globalization, rapid technological change and shifts towards mass customization and improved customer service – this new and flexible organizational model has provided an attractive proposition to organizations entering the twenty-first century. Preserving and fostering knowledge is of vital interest to the network-like VO. The decentralized and geographically distributed organizational structure inhibits knowledge flow. This chapter explores the particular conditions of KM in VOs, using a case study of a German service company. It analyzes how technical and organizational aspects influence knowledge-sharing and transfer, focusing on the introduction of a Web-based KMS. The system, SigSys, initiated a process of externalizing tacit knowledge and aimed to introduce new modes of knowledge transfer in organizational culture. The findings suggest that in fluid VOs, sustained KM means the establishment of an organizational memory that is flexible and adaptable to changing requirements. The chapter also underlines the importance of a strong organizational culture that emphasizes knowledge-sharing by the use of various communication channels.

Chapter 4 examines a very different area of KMS application, focusing on the health sector. KMS that support doctors' decision-making by providing both clinical knowledge and locally directed information have been under discussion since the mid-1990s. 'Managing information overload in the health sector: the WaX ActiveLibrary system' details a specific case in which such a KMS has been developed and used in practice. WaX ActiveLibrary, a modern version of such a system, has been piloted in several regions in the UK, and formally evaluated in 17 general-practice (GP) surgeries based in Cambridgeshire. The evaluation has provided evidence that WaX ActiveLibrary significantly improves GPs' access to relevant information sources, and by increasing appropriate patient management and referrals may also lead to an improvement in clinical outcomes. The chapter also suggests that use of WaX for locally-owned, primary-care-led knowledge distribution, rather than top-down directives from secondary care, is what attracts many GPs to the system. At the same time, information managers in secondary care and health authorities see WaX as a tool for disseminating their own protocols and regulations to manage demand for services. Current users of WaX include both primary-care-based and health-authority-led information services.

The final chapter of the first section explores another knowledge-intensive industry, law firms. Evidence suggests that the use of advanced knowledge technologies has the potential to transform these organizations considerably in the future. The chapter examines the potential use of KM in Norwegian law firms, utilizing both a case study of the largest law firm in Norway and a more extensive survey of the industry. The research suggests a strong belief in the potential benefits from KM in law organizations. Further, firm culture, firm knowledge and the use of IT are identified as potential predictors of IT support for KM in law firms. Interestingly, the extent to which law firms use IT to support KM is most significantly influenced by the extent to which they use IT in general; IT infrastructure and experiences appear to be key prerequisites to the development of KMS projects.

Section 2, 'Designing enterprise KMS architectures', goes beyond the specific examples of KMS in section 1 to examine how such KMS may be designed. It explores the complex inter-relationship between organization and technology, and provides conceptual frameworks and ideas for designing successful KMS architectures. As a starting point, chapter 6 reflects upon ideas about knowledge as a corporate asset – and as subject of organizational learning – and develops a number of requirements for KMS design. It then goes about designing an appropriate KMS to fulfil these requirements, using enterprise-modelling techniques. The proposed KMS features a high level of formal semantics, and the proposed architecture consists of various layers. Overall, the KMS provides a medium to foster discourses between people with different perspectives. The architecture also allows re-use of generic knowledge and enhancement with domain-specific knowledge. Furthermore, it includes an interface level layer that helps with the semantic integration of KMS and traditional IS.

The following chapter, 'Managing knowledge in decentralized heterogeneous corporations', provides conceptual discussion of KMS architectures in a specific organizational setting. One of the current major business trends is gaining market power by mergers and acquisitions, and selling off those business units considered inefficient or which no longer represent core competencies. Chapter 7 aims to conceptualize a KMS architecture that on the one hand enables a speedy integration of decentralized and heterogeneous business units and on the other hand facilitates their sale. Such a 'management middleware' is developed on the basis of the data-warehouse (DW) concept. The core of management middleware is a pool in which specific decision-relevant information and knowledge of the entire corporation is stored. In contrast to a data warehouse, the pool is not a read-only data store, but a read–write information or knowledge junction that allows for information input by decentralized units and, at the same time, allows access to information stored by headquarters or other units. Only a two-way information centre supports the creation of management information and simultaneously enables decentralized but integrated decision-making and corporate management. In the proposed architecture, the decentralized business units own data marts that contain specific decision-relevant information adapted to their individual decision problems.

While much progress has been made on designing IS to support decision-making, the art and design of KM systems to preserve, index, formalize and leverage knowledge in organizations is still new.

Knowledge is fundamentally more complex than information or data, and systems supporting KM have a broader range of design issues. Chapter 8 reviews approaches to KM support systems, and proposes the need to design systems that carefully map their features to target organizations and user groups. The chapter presents a useful framework – the 'waterfall model' – to conceptualize key aspects of enterprise document management. Moreover, the research examines the development of a specific KMS, Annotate, which has been developed according to these specifications. In particular, the system has been designed to support the KM of document collections in federated organizations that lack common vocabularies and central authority. Some initial field testing and evaluation of the Web-based system gives a preliminary indication of the problems and opportunities associated with this type of KMS architecture. Incentives to contribute knowledge, authentication, anonymity and the impact of other policy choices are seen as important influences on system use and effectiveness.

Chapter 9 examines another approach to the design of enterprise KMS architectures that provide meaningful knowledge to users. Proactive and context-sensitive information delivery, the ability to deal with heterogeneity in manifold aspects, and self-adaptiveness are crucial requirements for innovative enterprise information infrastructures supporting comprehensive corporate KM. This chapter illustrates the services offered by the KnowMore system, a prototypical realization of the first two of these core design principles. A sketch of the system architecture is provided, along with some principal considerations for implementing the KMS.

Finally, Section 2 is brought to a close with chapter 10, 'Combining data from existing company sources: architecture and experiences'. Performance measurement is becoming increasingly important in many companies. When implementing measurement systems, companies face problems with combining and utilizing knowledge from different sources. Useful data can be found in various applications, such as spreadsheets, project-management software and version-management systems. To combine and utilize these sources is often a manual and arduous task without proper tool support. This chapter describes an open architecture for designing and implementing a measurement system using data warehousing. A number of applications are also presented, based on this architecture. Furthermore, there is discussion of experiences gained from industrial environments in which the system has been used to instrument software-development projects and the customer-support process.

Following on from the previous section, section 3 examines some important issues involved with the implementation of KMS designs. In particular, 'Implementing knowledge management solutions' utilizes a mixture of theory and evidence to demonstrate core enablers and inhibitors to KMS adoption. Central to the debate are social and organizational factors. The section begins with 'Knowledge management: the human factor'. This chapter argues that KM research is limited because of its focus primarily on hard IS. Insufficient attention has been given to the importance of people-management issues and the complex, multi-faceted nature of knowledge itself. The results of a survey of KM practice in a wide sample of UK firms is presented in support of these assertions, highlighting the need to develop a more critical view of the impact of IT and IS on knowledge-creation and sharing.

Focusing on a specific set of KMS technologies, chapter 12, 'Fundamentals of implementing data warehousing in organizations', explores the core prerequisites for successful DW projects. DW can offer great potential for organizations. Nevertheless, implementing it is often fraught with complexity and organizational difficulties. This chapter presents the results of a study of four large, well-known, mature users of DW technology. Collectively, these organizations have experienced numerous problems and solutions associated with implementation. These experiences are distilled from the research findings, and presented as an organizational-prerequisites model for implementing success-ful DW. The model can be used by organizations to pinpoint areas of potential difficulty in a DW project, and to assess the likelihood of DW project success.

Moving on to another set of core KM technologies, chapter 13 presents a qualitative study of the adoption of Lotus Notes to facilitate knowledge-creation and sharing in four different organizations. The KMS in these cases targets the acquisition and dissemination of information required for problem-solving and decision-making. The ease of retrieving information and the ability to re-use that information in different contexts are decisive factors in determining the effectiveness of the systems. Data collected from four companies suggests that there are inherent barriers within organizations that constrain both the develop-ment and maintenance of these repositories. This chapter focuses on identifying these barriers and suggests ways of coping with them.

Finally, the book is brought to a close with an overarching analysis and synthesis of the KM concept in theory and practice. 'Understanding KM solutions: the evolution of frameworks in theory and practice' takes a broad view of the KM phenomenon. In an effort to bring some clarity to the KM concept, and to bridge the gap between theory and practice, it explores the salient characteristics of KM that need to be addressed in any organizational solution. The chapter draws on a number of key frameworks, models and perspectives that have been used to help understand this emerging phenomenon, both in the academic and practitioner domains. The summary and comparative analysis culmi-nates in a synthesized KM framework. Using a Delphi process involving critiques and suggestions from an international panel of KM researchers and practitioners, the framework is refined and extended to create a strong, collaborative end result. The final framework gives a relatively unified view of KM phenomena, and serves as a strong conceptual foundation for understanding, designing and implementing appropriate KM solutions in organizations.

As you will now be aware, the topic of KMS is both diverse and complex. It is not simply concerned with technology, but incorporates many other aspects, such as strategic management, organizational design and human resources. Such an interdisciplinary perspective is critical if the subject is to be understood fully. Recent examples of KMS offerings that overestimate technology and underestimate users exemplify this point; more than half of all KMS projects are believed to fail due to inadequacy of methodology (Lawton, 2001). For this reason, as you have seen, we take a broad management viewpoint encapsulating both management and technology issues. The issues debated here are far too important to be left to technologists; although technology is an important enabler, the vision, strategy and management of the transition to knowledge-based organizations lies squarely in the hands of managers. To reap the real rewards of KMS, management competence is crucial.

References

Alavi, M. and D.E. Leidner (2001) 'Knowledge management and knowledge management systems: conceptual foundations and research issues', *MIS Review*, 25, 6.

Barnes, S. and B. Hunt (2001) *E-Commerce and V-Business*, Butterworth-Heinemann.

Barney, J. (1991) 'Firm resources and sustained competitive advantage', *Journal of Management*, 17, 99–120.

Bettis, R.A., S.P. Bradley and G. Hamel (1991) 'Outsourcing and industrial decline', *Academy of Management Executive*, 6, 7–16.

Carnelley, P., E. Woods, D. Vaughan *et al.* (2001) *Ovum Forecasts: Global Software Markets*, Ovum.

Collis, D.J. and C.A. Montgomery (1995) 'Competing on resources: strategy in the 1990s', *Harvard Business Review*, July–August, 118–128.

Dam, K.W. (2001) *The Rules of the Global Game*, University of Chicago Press.

Davenport, T.H. and L. Prusak (1998) *Working Knowledge*, Harvard Business School Press.

Drucker, P.F. (1988) 'The coming of the new organization', *Harvard Business Review*, January–February, 45–53.

Drucker, P.F. (1995) *Managing in a Time of Great Change*, Truman Tally.

Edwards Deming, W. (1986) *Out of Crisis*, Cambridge University Press.

Garvin, D.A. (1993) 'Building a learning organization', *Harvard Business Review*, July–August, 78–91.

Grant, R.M. (1991a) 'The resource-based theory of competitive advantage: implications for strategy formulation', *California Management Review*, 33, 114–135.

— (1991b) 'Prospering in dynamically-competitive environments: organizational capability as knowledge integration', *Organization Science*, 7, 375–387.

Hammer, M. and J. Champy (1993) *Re-engineering the Corporation*, Harper Business.

Lank, E. (1997) 'Leveraging invisible assets: the human factor', *Long-Range Planning*, 30, 406–412.

Lawton, G. (2001) 'Knowledge management: ready for prime time?' *IEEE Computer*, 34, 12–14.

Lee, J.H., Y.G. Kim and S.H. Yu (2001) 'Stage model for knowledge management', in *Proceedings of the Hawaii International Conference on System Sciences*, Maui, Hawaii.

Lipnack, J. and J. Stamps (1997) *Virtual Teams*, John Wiley and Sons.

Maurer, H. (1998) 'Web-based knowledge management', *IEEE Computer*, 31, 122–123.

Mazarr, M.J. (2001) *Global Trends 2005*, Palgrave.

Naisbitt, J. (1994) *Global Paradox*, Breadly.

Nonaka, I. and H. Takeuchi (1995) *The Knowledge-Creating Company*, Oxford University Press.

Porter, M.E. (1985) *Competitive Advantage: Creating and Sustaining Superior Performance*, Free Press.

Purvis, R.L., V. Sambamurthy and R.W. Zmud (2001) 'The assimilation of knowledge platforms in organizations: an empirical investigation', *Organization Science*, 12, 117–135.

Ruggles, R. (1998) 'The state of the notion: knowledge management in practice', *California Management Review*, 40, 80–89.

Spender, J.C. (1996) 'Making knowledge: the basis of a dynamic theory of the firm', *Strategic Management Journal*, 17, 45–62.

Swan, J. (2001) 'Knowledge management in action: integrating knowledge across communities', in *Proceedings of the Hawaii International Conference on System Sciences*, Maui, Hawaii.

Teece, D.J., G. Pisano and A. Shuen (1997) 'Dynamic capabilities and strategic management', *Strategic Management Journal*, 18, 509–533.

Trimmer, D. (1993) *Downsizing*, Addison-Wesley.

Walsh, J. and G. Ungson (1991) 'Organizational memory', *Academy of Management Review*, 16, 57–91.

Woods, E. and M. Sheina (1999) *Knowledge Management: Building the Collaborative Enterprise*, Ovum.

Zack, M.H. (1999) *Knowing and Strategy*, Butterworth-Heinemann.

Part 1

Experiences in knowledge management systems practice

1 Knowledge management systems: issues, challenges and benefits

Maryam Alavi and Dorothy E. Leidner

Introduction

Information technologies designed to assist managerial and professional workers evolved over several decades from systems focusing on processing vast amounts of information and disseminating it to managers organization-wide (management information systems, or MIS), to systems focusing on providing tools for *ad hoc* decision analysis to specific decision-makers (decision-support systems, or DSS), to systems designed to provide updated, often real-time, relevant information to senior and middle managers (executive information systems, or EIS). These systems each contributed to individual and organizational improvements in varying degrees, and continue to be important components of an organization's IT investment. An emerging line of systems targets professional and managerial activities by focusing on creating, gathering, organizing and disseminating an organization's 'knowledge', as opposed to 'information' or 'data'. These systems are referred to as knowledge management systems.

The concept of coding and transmitting knowledge in organizations is not new: training and employee development programmes, organizational policies, routines, procedures, reports and manuals have served this function for years. For example, the McDonald's restaurant operating manual captures almost every aspect of restaurant management, including cooking, nutrition, hygiene, marketing, food production and accounting. By capturing, codifying and disseminating this knowledge, the company reduces the level of required know-how for its managers while improving the effectiveness and efficiency of its operations (Peters, 1992). What is new and exciting in the KM area is the potential to use modern information technologies (e.g. the Internet, intranets, browsers, data warehouses, data filters and software agents) to systematize, facilitate and expedite company-wide KM.

The existing body of work on KMS consists primarily of general and conceptual principles (Davenport, 1997b) and case descriptions of such systems in a handful of bell-wether organizations (Alavi, 1997; Baird, Henderson and Watts, 1997; Bartlett, 1996; Henderson and Watts Sussman, 1997; Sensiper 1997; Watts, Thomas and Henderson, 1997). Since KMS are only just beginning to appear in organizations, little research and insight exists to guide the successful development and implementation of such systems, or to frame expectations of the benefits and costs. Nor is it yet clear if KMS will experience widespread development and implementation across a variety of industries, or if they are destined, although highly touted, to find themselves seen as a passing fad. The current exploratory fieldwork aims to contribute an understanding of the perceptions of KM and KMS, both from the perspective of individuals in organizations with KMS as well as those without. More specifically, the study identifies the technologies being used to build KMS, the knowledge domains being incorporated into it, the champions of KMS initiatives, the desired benefits and expected costs, and the major concerns.

The organization of the chapter is as follows: knowledge and KMS are defined, then the study's methodology is described. The subsequent section presents the findings, while a final one discusses the implications.

Knowledge, knowledge management and knowledge management systems

To define KMS, it is necessary first to define knowledge and KM. Knowledge is a broad and abstract notion that has defined epistemological debates in Western philosophy since the classical Greek era. These have been expressed from a variety of perspectives and positions, including the rationalist one (advanced by philosophers such as Descartes in the seventeenth century), the empiricist perspective (advanced by Locke and others in the eighteenth century) and the interactionist perspective (advanced by Kant and others in the nineteenth century). For a discussion of the history of knowledge and epistemology, see Polanyi (1958, 1962). Since this study has an applied (rather than a theoretical or philosophical) orientation, we have adopted the following working definition of knowledge, based on the work of Nonaka (1994) and Huber (1991): 'Knowledge is a justified personal belief that increases an individual's capacity to take effective action'.

Action in this context refers to physical skills and competencies (e.g. playing tennis or carpentry), cognitive/intellectual activity (e.g. problem-solving) or both (e.g. surgery, which involves both manual skills and cognitive elements, in the form of knowledge of human anatomy and medicine). The definitions of knowledge found in the IS literature further distinguish between knowledge, information and data. For example,

Vance (1997) defines information as data interpreted into a meaningful framework, whereas knowledge is information that has been authenticated and thought to be true. Maglitta (1995) suggests that data is raw numbers and facts, information is processed data, and knowledge is 'information made actionable'.

While each conceptualization makes inroads into an understanding of the differences between the three terms, they fall short of providing a means readily to determine when information becomes knowledge. The problem appears to be the presumption of a hierarchy, from data to information to knowledge, with each varying along some dimension, such as context, usefulness or interpretability. What we consider key to an effective distinction between information and knowledge is not found in the content, structure, accuracy or utility of the supposed information or knowledge. Rather, knowledge is information possessed in the mind of an individual: it is personalized or subjective information related to facts, procedures, concepts, interpretations, ideas, observations and judgments (which may or may not be unique, useful, accurate or structurable). We are basically positing that knowledge is not a concept radically different to information, but rather that information becomes knowledge once it is processed in the mind of an individual ('tacit' knowledge in the words of Polanyi [1966] and Nonaka [1994]), which then becomes information (or what Nonaka refers to as 'explicit knowledge') once it is articulated or communicated to others in the form of text, computer output, spoken or written words, or other means. The recipient can then cognitively process and internalize the information so that it is converted back to tacit knowledge. This is consistent with Churchman's (1971) conceptualization of knowledge and his statement that 'knowledge resides in the user and not in the collection [of information]'.

Two major points emerge from this conceptualization:

- Since knowledge is personalized, for one person's knowledge to be useful for another individual, it must be communicated in such a manner as to be interpretable and accessible to the other individual.
- Hoards of information are of little value: only that information which is actively processed in the mind of an individual through a process of reflection, enlightenment and learning can be useful. KM, then, refers to a systemic and organizationally specified process for acquiring, organizing and communicating both tacit and explicit knowledge of employees so that other employees may make use of it to be more effective and productive in their work.

The major challenge of managing knowledge is less its creation and more its capture and integration (Davenport, 1997a; Grant, 1996). Indeed, knowledge is of limited organizational value if it is not shared. The ability to integrate and apply specialized knowledge of organizational members is fundamental to a firm's ability to create and sustain competitive advantage (Grant, 1996). Traditionally, knowledge creation and transfer has occurred through various means such as face-to-face interactions (planned or *ad hoc*), mentoring, job rotation and staff development. However, as markets and organizations become more global and move to virtual forms, these traditional means may prove to be too slow, less effective and in need of being supplemented by more efficient electronic methods. On the other hand, as Brown and Duguid (1991) note, knowledge will not necessarily circulate freely through a company just because the technology to support such circulation is available.

Indeed, studies on such technologies as Lotus Notes have not shown a change in information sharing and communication patterns; rather, members of organization who tended to communicate regularly and frequently without Notes communicated regularly and frequently with it, those who communicated less regularly and less frequently before the implementation continued to communicate less regularly and less frequently afterwards (Vandenbosch and Ginzberg, 1997). Hence, in the absence of an explicit strategy better to create and integrate knowledge in the organization, computer systems that facilitate communication and information sharing have only a random effect at best. As a result, companies, particularly those that compete on the basis of services and expertise (e.g. management consulting and professional services firms), are beginning to implement IS designed specifically to facilitate the codification, collection, integration and dissemination of organizational knowledge (Alavi, 1997; Bartlett, 1996; Sensiper, 1997). It is these systems that are referred to as KMS.

Popular claims for KMS include that it offers organizations the ability to be flexible and respond more quickly to changing market conditions, and the ability to be more innovative, as well as improving decision-making and productivity (Harris, 1996; Sata, 1989). To develop an understanding of the current practices and outcomes of KM, as well as the form and nature of KMS that are evolving in organizations, we undertook a descriptive study of perceptions and practices of KMS in 50 organizations from a variety of industries. We hope that the findings of this study will lead to insights that guide early KMS initiatives in organizations and reduce failures and false starts. In addition, we anticipate that the results will help guide further research endeavours in this emerging area.

Methodology

We invited a non-random sample of 109 participants in an executive development programme conducted at a northeastern US university to participate in this study (see Alavi and Leidner, 1999). The participants in the programme represented a cadre of vanguard organizations from 12 countries that in the authors' view represented those with significant IT investments. Thus, they would be likely to have KMS under consideration, development or already in operation. These participants were attending a two-week residential executive development programme on the management of IT. The participants were chief information officers (CIOs), IS managers, and general and functional area executives. The participants were asked to respond to the study questionnaire on an individual basis during the first three days of their programme. The questionnaire, which appears in the appendix which follows this chapter, contained 13 questions requiring brief answers or multiple-choice selection. The respondents estimated that it took approximately 30 minutes to complete the questionnaire. A total of 50 usable responses were received, a response rate of 45.8 per cent. The questionnaire tapped into the respondents' conception and perceptions of KMS, their perceptions of the current levels of KMS activities in their firms, their expectations of potential benefits, and their concerns.

Study findings

Figures 1.1 to 1.3 depict the sample of respondents by their location, their position within their organizations and their industry. As can be seen in the three figures, the respondents represent a range of countries, organizational positions and industries. Twelve different countries are represented: Australia, Canada, Germany, Israel, Luxembourg, the Netherlands, Saudi Arabia, South Africa, Spain, Switzerland, the UK and the US. Thirty-two organizations from the US represent the large majority of responses. Ten US and four non-US respondents report having KMS in their organizations. Three US and five non-US respondents reported that their organizations were currently developing KMS.

Figure 1.1   Respondents by global location

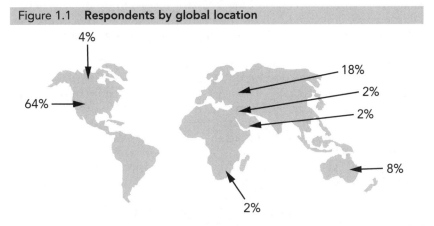

Figure 1.2   Respondents by position within their organizations

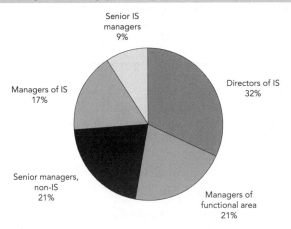

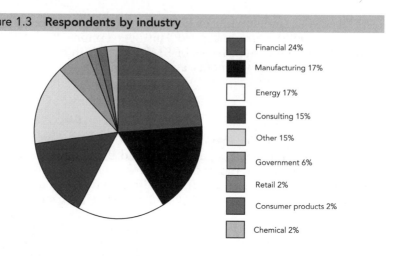

Figure 1.3 **Respondents by industry**

Financial 24%

Manufacturing 17%

Energy 17%

Consulting 15%

Other 15%

Government 6%

Retail 2%

Consumer products 2%

Chemical 2%

All respondents, regardless of whether they currently had or were developing a KMS in their organizations, responded to questions concerning their perceptions of KM, the capabilities they believed necessary for effective KM, and the key concerns they had about it. The results are summarized in tables 1.1 to 1.3, and discussed below.

Perspectives on knowledge management

One of the objectives of the study was to ascertain the meaning managers ascribe to the concept of KM. Three perspectives emerged: an information-based one, a technology-based one and a culture-based one (see table 1.1).

In terms of the information-based perspective, managers reported perceiving KM to be about characteristics of information, such as that it should be readily accessible, real-time and actionable. Some spoke in terms of free text and concepts being the information foundation of KM. Several managers mentioned their view that KM was concerned with reducing the overload of information by 'filtering the gems from the rocks'. There was an apparent concern with the extraordinary amount of information that can now easily be gathered and disseminated via IT. The managers expressed a desire to obtain competitive advantage from information itself (as opposed to associating competitive advantage with any particular IT). Lastly, some managers thought very specifically of KM as being a 'corporate yellow pages' or a 'people-to-people information archive'. In other words, they viewed KM as a means of keeping track not so much of knowledge itself, but of who held the knowledge and how to locate them.

Knowledge was not distinguished from information or data; rather, the words were evidently used interchangeably. However, the managers were implicitly making distinctions among the terms. For example, one manager stated 'one person's knowledge is another's data'. This view is consistent with the view that knowledge resides in the individual and that there are no inherent 'objective' attributes that distinguish between the two constructs.

In terms of the technology-based perspective, the managers associated KM with various other systems (including data warehousing, enterprise-wide systems, executive information systems, expert systems and intranets), as well as various tools (e.g. search engines, multimedia and decision-making tools). More generally, participants associated KM with IT infrastructure and, more specifically, with the integration of cross-functional systems worldwide. A clear view of a new type of technology specifically dedicated to KM did not emerge. Indeed, this is consistent with the fact that KM systems can be accomplished with different technologies, the most effective of which are likely to depend upon an organization's size and existing technical infrastructure.

Lastly, in terms of the culture-based perspective, managers associated KM with learning, primarily from an organizational perspective, communication and intellectual property cultivation. Some suggested that the information/technology component of KM was only 20 per cent of the concept; the cultural and managerial aspects accounted for the bulk of it. However, the responses were nebulous in specific cultural implications, perhaps indicating a root concern about concrete ideas on how to address these issues.

Table 1.1   Perspectives on KM

Information-based	*Technology-based*	*Culture-based*
Actionable information	Data mining	Collective learning
Categorization of data	Data warehousing	Continuous learning
Corporate yellow pages	Executive information systems	Intellectual property
Filtered information	Expert systems	cultivation
Free text and concepts	Intelligent agents	Learning organization
People information archive	Intranet	
Readily accessible information	Multimedia	
	Search engines	
	Smart systems	

The responses were examined on the basis of whether the responding individual was from an organization with a KMS or not. However, there did not appear to be any major differences in the perceptions of KMS for the two groups, with the exception that individuals from organizations without KMS tended to offer technology-based responses slightly more frequently than individuals from organizations with KMS.

Required KM capabilities
When asked what capabilities related to KM their organizations needed, the managers also tended to offer three perspectives (see table 1.2). In terms of information, they suggested the need for access to customer information, client information, competitor information, and product or market information. All of this information is external, and had historically not been provided by most computer systems. Several internal knowledge domains were also desired, including activity-based costing, human resource information and up-to-date financial reports. The technology capabilities desired included wider bandwidth, a consistent suite of e-mail and Web-based products, search engines, intelligent agents, navigational tools, global IT infrastructure, interoperability of existing data systems, and fast retrieval. Lastly, the managers reported

a need for practical guidelines on how to build and implement KMS, and how to facilitate organizational change to promote knowledge sharing.

Table 1.2	Capabilities needed for KM	
Information-based	*Technology-based*	*Culture-based*
External	Integrated databases	Teamwork
• Client information	Interoperability of existing	Practical guidelines
• Competitive information	systems	Knowledge-sharing
• Customer information	Larger bandwidth	
• Market information	Global IT infrastructure	
	Intelligent agents	
Internal	Consistent suite of e-mail	
• Activity-based costing	and Web products	
• Financial information	Navigational tools	
• Human resources information	Fast retrieval	
• Product/services information		

Key issues concerning KM

When asked about managers' key concerns regarding KM, the primary issues raised were cultural, managerial and informational (as shown in table 1.3). With the cultural issues, the managers were concerned over the implications for change management, the ability to convince people to volunteer their knowledge, and the ability to convince business units to share their knowledge with other units (particularly when each business unit was responsible for showing a profit). The managerial concerns related to the business value of KM and the need for metrics upon which to demonstrate the system's value. There was apprehension over how to determine who would be responsible for managing the knowledge, and over the bringing together of the many players involved in developing KMS, including technical staff, corporate librarians, documentation staff, archivists, database administrators and the professionals with the knowledge. Concern was also expressed over how to implement KMS effectively.

Table 1.3	Key concerns related to KM
Information	Building vast amounts of data into a usable format
	Avoiding overloading users with unnecessary data
	Eliminating wrong or old data
	Ensuring customer confidentiality
	Keeping information current
Management	Change management implications
	Getting individuals to volunteer knowledge
	Getting business units to share knowledge
	Demonstrating business value
	Bringing together the many people from various units
	Determining responsibility for managing the knowledge
Technology	Determining infrastructure requirements
	Keeping up with new technologies
	Security of data on the Internet

Generally speaking, the respondents expressed concern that senior managers might perceive KM as just another fad, and that the concept suffered from immaturity. In particular, managers from organizations that had not yet implemented KMS expressed a need to understand better the concept and to be convinced that KM 'worked' before pursuing future developments.

The concerns related to information were primarily associated with a desire to avoid overloading already taxed users with yet more information. The concern was as much about the new information that would now be available as it was about eliminating 'old or wrong data' or knowledge that was no longer valid. This supports Courtney, Croasdell and Paradice's (1997) assertion that 'omitting the unimportant may be as important as concentrating on the important' in determining what knowledge to include in KMS. Concern was expressed about customer and client confidentiality now that much information would be gathered and widely available in organizations.

Lastly, several managers expressed concerns over technological issues. These issues related to technical infrastructure and the security of data on the Internet. More specifically, the study highlighted the importance of configuring an effective technical infrastructure and architectural requirements in the face of highly dynamic technology.

Characteristics of KMS

For those respondents whose organizations had or were developing KMS, questions were asked about the initiator, the team members on the KMS project, the budget, the types of knowledge included, and the tools used. As is apparent in figure 1.4, senior general managers most commonly champion KMS. This finding would be expected, given that KM, as a concept, is not directly tied to technology; rather, emerging technologies provide a means of enabling more effective KM. In terms of the KMS development teams, virtually all respondents providing information on the teams responsible for developing their organization's KMS indicated that they were comprised of directors from the business

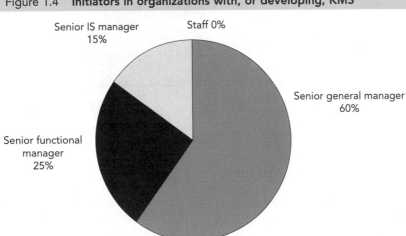

Figure 1.4   **Initiators in organizations with, or developing, KMS**

Senior IS manager 15%

Staff 0%

Senior general manager 60%

Senior functional manager 25%

units as well as IS managers and staff. Less consistency emerged about the individual responsible for the KMS. In some cases, respondents reported that the CIO was responsible for leading the KMS development team; in other cases, respondents indicated that a business unit director reporting to the CIO was responsible for the team.

Figure 1.5 shows the estimated average budgets associated with KMS development. The lowest reported budget for a KMS was $25,000. The highest reported figure was $50,000,000. The wide range of estimated budgets may be attributed to several factors, including the size of the organization, the current level of infrastructure, and the scope of the KM initiative. In some firms, KM is a company-wide initiative involving the upgrading of the technical infrastructure, deploying workstations to professional staff desktops, developing and implementing large intranets, and implementing large-scale communication and groupware tools. On the other hand, with the appropriate technology and information infrastructure in place, the average KMS development budget is substantially lower. For example, in a professional services firm that had already installed Lotus Notes, the cost of a KM system for the project engagement teams was limited to the cost of developing several Notes templates that the team then used to populate with the customer and project-related knowledge created and shared through the engagement process. At the other extreme, the estimated budget of KMS in another professional services firm was $50,000,000. This figure included the cost of content development, training and overhaul of the technical infrastructure of the entire firm (including hardware, software and network acquisition and development).

Figure 1.5   Estimated average budgets of KMS in organizations

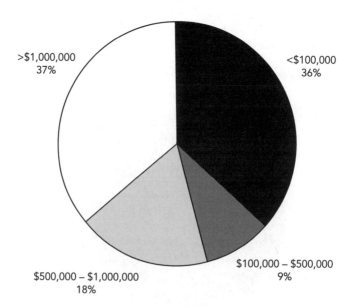

Table 1.4 shows the technologies being used in KMS development. The intranet seems to be the primary means of displaying and distributing knowledge in organizations with 90 per cent of the organizations using browser tools. The other two most common tools are e-mail and search/retrieval tools.

Table 1.4 Percentage of KMS with various technologies/tools

Browser	90	
E-mail	84	Note: multiple items
Search/retrieval tools	73	could be specified
Information repositories	52	when applicable
Web server	42	
Agents/filters	36	
External server services	31	
Videoconferencing	23	

Table 1.5 shows the importance of various types of information that may be included in KM systems. Questions were answered on a seven-point scale, with seven representing the highest score. Respondents in organizations without KMS were also asked to rate the importance of the various domains of knowledge in their organizations even if they did not have technology designed to provide such knowledge. The most important knowledge domain for firms with and without KMS is customer service. The second and third domains for firms with KMS were business partners and internal operations. For firms without KMS, the second and third highest domains were marketing/sales and business partners. For both groups, knowledge on suppliers was indicated as the least important domain of knowledge to be included in systems, perhaps reflecting the large percentage of service-oriented firms (54 per cent) in our sample. Overall, external sources of information tended to be rated highly.

Table 1.5 Importance of knowledge domain

	Firms with, or building, KMS	*Firms with no KMS*
Customer service	5.14	6.15
Business partners	4.83	5.00
Internal operations	4.62	4.95
Competition	4.57	4.90
Marketing/sales	4.57	5.30
Suppliers	4.56	4.26
Human resources	3.94	4.72

Note: maximum value = 7

Perceived benefits of existing KMS

The respondents who reported that their organizations currently had or were developing KMS expressed the idea that the KMS was designed to achieve both process results and organizational outcomes (see table 1.6). The process improvements involved many specified benefits, including shortening the proposal time for client engagements, improving project management, increasing staff participation, saving time (generally), enhancing communication, making the opinions of plant staff more visible, reducing problem-solving time, better serving clients, and providing better measurement and accountability. These process improvements can be thought of as either relating to communication enhancements or efficiency gains. The process improvements, then, in the minds of the managers, led to cost reduction of specific activities, increased sales, personnel reduction, higher profitability, lower inventory levels, ensuring consistent proposal terms for worldwide clients, and marketing-related outcomes (i.e. better-targeted marketing, locking in customers, and what one respondent termed 'proactive marketing' – approaching clients 'for solutions to problems they don't even face'). Thus, the perceived organizational benefits of KMS can be thought of primarily as being of a financial, marketing and general nature (see table 1.6).

Table 1.6 **Perceived benefits of existing KMS**	
Process outcomes	*Organizational outcomes*
Communication • Enhanced communication • Faster communication • More visible opinions of staff • Increased staff participation	Financial • Increased sales • Decreased cost • Higher profitability
Efficiency • Reduced problem-solving time • Shortening proposal times • Faster results • Faster delivery to market • Greater overall efficiency	Marketing • Better service • Customer focus • Targeted marketing • Proactive marketing
	General • Consistent proposals to multinational clients • Improved project management • Personnel reduction

The data suggest that these practitioners did not value KM for the sake of knowledge as an end in itself, but only when it was perceived to lead to desirable organizational benefits. This finding is consistent with King's (1993) view that knowledge should make a difference in some way '...materially, aesthetically or spiritually' (p.80).

Discussion

Several observations can be drawn from the data. In this section, we examine several salient points that emerge quite clearly from the practitioner survey report.

The increasing ubiquity of KMS
KMS are not just for consulting and professional services firms. Traditionally, such firms have been considered knowledge-intensive,

and therefore interested in KM and KMS. For example, almost all of the 'big five' accounting and consulting firms (Arthur Andersen and Andersen Consulting (now Accenture), Deloitte & Touche, Ernst & Young, KPMG Peat Marwick and PriceWaterhouseCoopers) have created internal KMS over the past few years. Our survey showed, however, that interest in KMS goes far beyond professional services firms. A broad range of organizations from a variety of industries are now looking into this area, feeling that they can potentially benefit from KMS.

The organizational complexity of KMS
KMS are multi-faceted. That is, effective ones involve far more than just technology, encompassing broad cultural and organizational issues. In fact, effective resolution of both cultural and organizational issues were identified as major concerns in the deployment of KMS. This result is consistent with the IT management literature, which advocates organizational and behavioural change management as critical success factors in the implementation of IS (Alavi and Joachimsthaler, 1992). Company-wide KMS usually require profound cultural renovations because, traditionally, organizations have rewarded their professionals and employees on the basis of individual performance and know-how. In many organizations, a major cultural shift would be required to change employees' attitudes and behaviour so that knowledge and insights are willingly and consistently shared. An effective way to motivate knowledge sharing is through the organizational reward and incentive mechanisms. Both McKinsey and PriceWaterhouseCoopers (a management consulting and a professional services firm, respectively) use this mechanism to promote knowledge sharing among their consulting and professional staff. At McKinsey, for example, both the number and internal frequency of use of a consultant's publications (a measure of knowledge sharing) is an important input to the consultant's promotion decisions. Similarly, PriceWaterhouseCoopers enhanced the appeal of knowledge sharing by revising the professional's performance reviews to reward them for knowledge-sharing activities (Hildebrand, 1994).

Measuring KMS benefits
It is important to try to develop metrics to assess the benefits of KMS. Although none of the organizations participating in our survey had conducted (or were planning to conduct) formal cost–benefit analysis for their KMS, the respondents felt that development of meaningful metrics for measuring the value, quality and quantity of knowledge is a key factor in the long-term success and growth of KMS. To this end, KM initiatives should be directly linked to explicit and important aspects of organizational performance (e.g. customer satisfaction, product/service innovations, time to market, cost savings, competitive positioning and market shares). In other words, organizations need to find leverage points where enhanced 'knowledge' can add value, and then develop KMS to enable significant benefits through delivery of the required knowledge.

Technological architectures for KMS

An integrated and integrative technology architecture is a key driver for KMS. No single dominant technology tool or product for KMS emerged in our survey. KMS seem to require a variety of technological tools in three areas: database and database management, communication and messaging, and browsing and retrieval. The need for seamless integration of the various tools in these three areas may lead to the dominance of the Internet and Internet-based KMS architectures. For example, the knowledge domains identified as valuable both by organizations with and without operational KMS in this sample (e.g. customers and business partners) had an external focus. Thus, the Internet and Internet-based technologies and service providers can play a key role in development of KMS by providing cost-effective access to external knowledge domains. At KPMG Peat Marwick, a participant organization in our survey, some of the files from external sources (e.g. the Gartner Group's weekly analyst report files and customer data files) are imported to the firm over the Internet using file transfer protocol (FTP).

Since access to internal organizational knowledge sources was also rated relatively high and desirable by our sample, we predict that organizational intranets will also play a dominant role in support of internal KM activities, due to cost-effective technical capabilities, including: access to legacy systems; platform independence; access to multimedia data formats; a uniform and easy-to-use, point-and-click interface; and the capability for easy multimedia publication for knowledge sharing.

The nature of information and knowledge

Knowledge in the context of KMS is perceived to constitute a new form of information not previously addressed in other systems such as MIS, DSS and EIS. The respondents in the survey implied a distinction between information and knowledge, although they seem to have used the words interchangeably. This distinction was implicit in their discussions of a potential to create cognitive overload due to an over-supply of information, and the desirability of providing access to people with knowledge (e.g. corporate yellow pages), rather than the information itself. This is consistent with the view held by some of the participants who linked KM to organizational learning processes. If we view learning broadly as the process of internalizing and converting information to knowledge, these two perspectives seem to support the view that information is the raw material of knowledge, and that more information does not necessarily lead to enhanced knowledge creation and sharing. This insight is very important for the designers of KMS for the following reason: simply delivering or 'pushing' information (even pre-filtered information) to the user's desktop may not be an effective KM strategy, due to the scarcity of user attention required for processing this information and converting it to knowledge. That is, in addition to the provision of the necessary information (the raw material for knowledge creation), the individuals should also be motivated to convert it to knowledge (i.e. to learn and internalize the information). Hence, knowledge is created and shared on the basis of 'pull' by individuals and not a centralized technology-enabled 'push' of information to desktops (Manville and Foote, 1996).

Conclusion

The study presented here provides a description of emerging issues and practices of KMS. While the respondents were not drawn from a random sample of organizations or industries, and the number was relatively small, their views do represent a range of industries, organizational levels and nationalities. The study was not intended to build or test theory, but does offer some insights into needed and relevant research in the area of KMS.

One useful line of enquiry entails an exploration of the KMS-culture fit. Much has been made of technology-structure alignment, but the success of KMS may be more related to organizational culture than to organizational structure, as evinced by the concerns of our respondents on getting knowledge sharing accepted in their organizations.

Another useful line of research would consider methods of making users active contributors to KMS. The very label 'user' is somewhat inappropriate in the context of KMS, as users are both contributors and beneficiaries of the system. Involving users in design is not sufficient: they must be involved consistently in the maintenance of KMS.

A third potential line of research suggested by our study would uncover the decision-making process for determining what knowledge to include in KMS. Since a major concern of our respondents was avoiding too much information, it is worth asking at what point knowledge may stifle rather than enhance performance.

Finally, an important line of research will consider the issue of KMS benefits. Given the primarily external focus of information contained in KMS, it is likely that outcomes experienced should involve enhancing relationships with external entities such as customers and business partners. Studies that include the views of an organization's external entities might shed light on the actual benefits of KMS.

The research on these topics (i.e. determining the relevant knowledge domains and obtaining business pay-offs from KMS) may benefit from a focus on the possible links between knowledge and a firm's strategy and an explicit re-examination of competitiveness from a knowledge-resource perspective.

To make information resources productive, they should be converted into actionable knowledge. Such a process introduces challenges relating to knowledge creation, capture, sharing and maintenance. Our study suggests that KM benefits will only be realized by organizations that are not only technologically adept, but that make the long-term investment to align cultural, managerial and organizational elements for KM.

Acknowledgement

This chapter is reprinted with the permission of Communications of the AIS. An earlier version also appeared as Alavi and Leidner (1999).

References

Alavi, M. (1997) 'KPMG Peat Marwick U.S.: One Giant Brain', Case 9–397–108, Harvard Business School.

Alavi, M. and E. Joachimsthaler (1992) 'Revisiting DSS implementation research: a meta-analysis of the literature and suggestions for researchers', *MIS Quarterly*, 16 (1), 95–116.

Alavi, M. and D. Leidner (1999) 'Knowledge management systems: emerging views and practices from the field', *Proceedings of the Hawaii International Conference on Information Systems*, Maui, Hawaii.

Baird, L., J. Henderson and S. Watts (1997) 'Learning networks: an analysis of the Centre for Army Lessons Learned', *Human Resource Management Journal*, 36 (4), 385–96.

Bartlett, C. (1996) 'McKinsey & Company: Managing Knowledge and Learning', Case 9–396–357, Harvard Business School.

Brown, J.S. and P. Duguid (1991) 'Organizational learning and communities-of-practice: toward a unified view of working, learning and innovation', *Organization Science*, 2 (1), 40–57.

Churchman, C.W. (1971) *The Design of Inquiring Systems: Basic Concepts of Systems and Organizations*, Bencis Books.

Courtney, J., D. Croasdell and D. Paradice (1997) 'Lockean inquiring organizations: guiding principles and design guidelines for learning organizations', *Proceedings of the Americas Conference on Information Systems*, Indiana, http://hsb.baylor.edu/ramsower/ais.ac.97/papers/courtney.htm.

Davenport, T.H. (1997a) *Knowledge Management at Ernst and Young*, http://knowman.bus.utexas.edu/E&Y.htm.

— (1997b) *Some Principles of Knowledge Management*, http://knowman.bus.utexas.edu/kmprin.htm.

Grant, R.M. (1996) 'Prospering in dynamically-competitive environments: organizational capability as knowledge integration', *Organization Science*, 7 (4), 375–87.

Harris, D.B (1996) 'Creating a Knowledge Centric Information Technology Environment', http://www.htca.com/ckc.htm.

Henderson, J.C. and S. Watts Sussman (1997) 'Creating and exploiting knowledge for fast-cycle organizational response: the Centre for Army Lessons Learned', *Boston University Working Paper Series*, no 96–39.

Hildebrand, C. (1994) 'The greater good', *CIO*, November 15, 32–40.

Huber, G. (1991) 'Organizational learning: the contributing processes and the literatures', *Organization Science*, 2 (1), 88–115.

King, J. (1993) 'Editorial notes', *Information Systems Research*, 4 (4), 291–8.

Maglitta, J. (1995) 'Smarten up!', *Computerworld*, 29 (23), 84–6.

Manville, B. and N. Foote (1996) 'Harvest your workers' knowledge', *Datamation*, July, 78–81.

Nonaka, I. (1994) 'A dynamic theory of organizational knowledge creation', *Organization Science*, 5 (1), 14–37.

Peters, T. (1992) Knowledge management structures I: taking knowledge management seriously, in *Liberation Management*, Alfred A. Knopf, 382–439.

Polanyi, M. (1958) *Personal Knowledge*, University of Chicago Press.

— (1962) *Personal Knowledge: Toward a Post-Critical Philosophy*, Harper Torchbooks.

— (1966) *The Tacit Dimension*, Routledge and Kegan Paul.

Sata, R. (1989) 'Organizational learning – the key to management innovation', *Sloan Management Review*, Spring, 63–74.

Sensiper, S. (1997) 'AMS knowledge centres', Case N9–697–068, Harvard Business School.

Vance, D.M. (1997) 'Information, knowledge and wisdom: the epistemic hierarchy and computer-based information system', *Proceedings of the Americas Conference on Information Systems*, Indiana, http://hsb.baylor.edu/ramsower/ais.ac.97/papers/vance.htm.

Vandenbosch, B. and M.J. Ginzberg (1997) 'Lotus Notes and collaboration: plus ça change', *Journal of Management Information Systems*, 13 (3), 65–82.

Watts, S.A., J.B. Thomas and J.C. Henderson (1997) 'Understanding 'strategic learning': linking organizational learning, sense-making, and knowledge management', *Proceedings of the Academy of Management Meeting*, Boston.

Appendix:
knowledge management questionnaire

Instructions:
Please answer the questions to the best of your knowledge. There is no right or wrong answer. I am interested in your opinion on the issues.

1. How would you describe your industry? (Circle the best answer.)

   Extremely   Extremely
   stable   competitive/unpredictable

   1   2   3   4   5   6   7

2. In a professional (as opposed to a personal) context, what things first come to mind when you think of the concept of 'knowledge management'? (Please list words or phrases.)

   _____
   _____
   _____
   _____

3. What would you consider the most needed KM capability (products/services) in your organization?
   Type of KM capability

   a. _____
       _____

   b. Don't know.

4. What questions/issues/concerns are on your mind regarding KM?

   _____
   _____
   _____
   _____

5. In general, knowledge sharing and learning are valued in my company culture.

   Strongly   Strongly
   Disagree   Neutral   Agree
   1   2   3   4   5   6   7

6. Please circle as many answers that are applicable:

   a. We have completed at least one KM project in my company
       (If more that one, how many? __)
   b. We have not completed a KM project, but we are in the process of working on one.
   c. We have not started on any KM projects, but we are considering it.
   d. We do not have a project and are not even considering KM.
   e. I had never heard of KM before.

Please elaborate on your answer(s) above.

_____
_____
_____
_____

Note: if you circled choice a and/or b above, please answer the questions in part A below. If you circled choice c, d, and/or e above, please answer the questions in part B.

Part A (Please complete this section if you circled a and/or b for question 6).

7. In your opinion, what specific and tangible business results are targeted by the KM project(s) in your company?

    a. _____
    b. _____
    c. _____
    d. _____
    e. Don't know.

8. In your estimation, what is the average development budget of KM projects in your company?

    a. _____
    b. Don't know.

9. Rate the importance of the following knowledge domains for your company. (Circle a number between 1 and 7).

	Very low		Neutral			Very High	
Marketing/Sales	1	2	3	4	5	6	7
Customer Service	1	2	3	4	5	6	7
Competition	1	2	3	4	5	6	7
Internal company operations	1	2	3	4	5	6	7
Human resources	1	2	3	4	5	6	7
Suppliers	1	2	3	4	5	6	7
Business Partners	1	2	3	4	5	6	7
Other (specify) _____	1	2	3	4	5	6	7

10. The KM project(s) in my company was initiated by:

    a. Senior level general management (CEO, COO, CFO, Senior VP etc.).
    b. Senior functional managers (e.g. director of marketing, or operations).
    c. Director of IS function.
    d. Staff members (specify) _____
    e. Other (specify) _____

11. The KM project leader in my company is (title and functional area):

    _____

12. List the title/functional area of the full-time KM project team members.

a. _____
   _____
   _____
   _____

b. Don't know.

13. Please circle the technical components of your KM system. (Please specify the products for each category from b to j that you circle.)

a. I do not know.
b. Browsers (e.g. Netscape, Microsoft).
c. Search and retrieval tools (e.g. Verity, OpenText).
d. Agents/Filters (e.g. IBM's InfoMarket, General Magic's Telescript).
e. E-mail and groupware systems (e.g. Lotus Notes).
f. Web server/communication software (e.g. Netscape's Collabra).
g. Data repositories.
h. External server services.
i. Videoconferencing.
j. Other (specify):

   _____

You have now completed the questionnaire. Thank you for your time and co-operation.

Part B (Please complete Part B if you circled c, d, and/or e for question 6).

14. In your opinion, what specific and tangible business results should be targeted by the KM project(s) in your company?

a. _____
b. _____
c. _____
d. _____
e. Don't know.

15. In your opinion, what should be the average development budget of KM projects in your company?

a. _____
b. Don't know.

16. Rate the importance of the following knowledge domains for your company. (Circle a number between 1 and 7.)

	Very low			Neutral			Very High	
Marketing/Sales	1	2	3	4	5	6	7
Customer Service	1	2	3	4	5	6	7
Competition	1	2	3	4	5	6	7
Internal company operations	1	2	3	4	5	6	7
Human resources	1	2	3	4	5	6	7
Suppliers	1	2	3	4	5	6	7
Business Partners	1	2	3	4	5	6	7
Other (specify) _____	1	2	3	4	5	6	7

17. In my opinion, KM projects in my company should be initiated by:
    a. Senior level general management (CEO, COO, CFO, Senior VP, etc.)
    b. Senior functional managers (e.g. director of marketing, or operations)
    c. Director of IS function
    d. Staff members (specify) _____
    e. Other (specify) _____

18. In my opinion, the KM project leader should be (specify the title and functional area):

    _____

19. In my opinion, the KM full-time project team members should come from these ranks/functional areas:

    _____
    _____
    _____

You have now completed the questionnaire. Thank you for your time and co-operation.

2 Sharing tacit knowledge: a case study at Volvo

Dick Stenmark

Introduction

Ever since man first shared the knowledge of how to make fire with his fellow human beings, the managing of knowledge has been employed by masters training their apprentices and by parents teaching their children. In recent years, however, the importance of knowledge in business and industry has increased dramatically, and changed from being a resource amongst many to being primary. Being able to manage this asset effectively has thus received the attention of many chief executives, and KM as a concept has become a debated topic.

Without going too deeply into the philosophical debate of what exactly knowledge is, we notice that on an epistemological level knowledge may be split along several dimensions. One categorization is, as suggested by Polanyi (1966), to distinguish between tacit and explicit knowledge. The phrase 'tacit knowledge' refers to knowledge that cannot be easily articulated, and thus only exists in people's hands and minds, manifesting itself through actions; explicit knowledge means knowledge that has been captured and codified into manuals, procedures and rules, and is easy to disseminate. Others have chosen more detailed classification schemas. For example, Choo (1998), based on Boisot's (1995) typology, suggests a differentiation between tacit, explicit and cultural knowledge, and Blackler (1995), elaborating on Collins (1993), speaks of embodied, embedded, embrained, encultured and encoded knowledge. Though many other ways to classify knowledge exist and have been suggested, they all, more or less, build on the premises suggested by Polanyi. While acknowledging the many nuances that exist between the two extremes, we select Polanyi's terminology of tacit and explicit knowledge for the scope of this chapter.

This work is based on an empirical study of how a recommender system is used on a large corporate intranet. The empirical findings have been interpreted using the theories of Polanyi (1966) and Argyris and Schön (1974), and the aim has been to understand how the technology can be used in new and innovative ways in an intranet context, rather than to study the technology *per se*.

It has been claimed that research on KM has thus far been dominated by an IS/IT perspective, resulting in an overemphasis on codification of explicit knowledge, suitable for databases and other traditional IS solutions (Swan, Scarbrough and Preston, 1999). While being part of the IS/IT community, the author agrees with this critique but argues that technology can be used in many different ways. Instead of trying to make tacit knowledge explicit, the argument here is that we should design IT solutions that help us locate and communicate with knowledgeable people.

This text presents three claims: firstly, that our interests as experts and professionals are examples of our tacit knowledge; secondly, that Web documents may be used to visualize and communicate this knowledge; thirdly, that information retrieval systems, such as recommender systems, can be used to exploit such tacit knowledge on an organizational level, without making it explicit.

In the next section we shall explore the duality of tacit knowledge before explaining the relationship between knowledge and interests. The fourth section describes an approach to information retrieval technology, and it is followed by a section in which the research site and the research methodology are discussed. The field results are followed by a discussion.

The problem with externalizing tacit knowledge

An interesting but also troublesome property of tacit knowledge is the inherent tension between its value on the one hand and its elusiveness on the other. Its high value stems from the fact that most of our body of knowledge is made up of things we know but are unable to express. In Polanyi's words, 'We can know more than we can tell' (1998: p.136). Leonard and Sensiper go even further, stating that 'we can often know more than we realize' (1998: p.114). Our explicit knowledge is thus only the tip of an iceberg, which indicates the importance of tacit knowledge, and suggests that it should receive a higher degree of attention.

Unfortunately, tacit knowledge is difficult for organizations to exploit. Since it only resides inside people, it cannot easily be sought electronically. The problem of determining who knows what grows with the size of the organization. The fact that tacit knowledge is not available in an explicit form makes it difficult – if not impossible – to quickly spread or share it within the organization. This circumstance presents problems for today's organizations. In their widespread model of knowledge creation, Nonaka and Takeuchi (1995) suggest that tacit knowledge becomes explicit through the process of externalization, i.e. by a sharing of metaphors and analogies during social interaction.

However, such a process is both difficult and costly, and the fact that the tacit knowledge must be externalized before it can be exploited limits its usefulness. It is even questionable whether it is desirable to try to make (certain) knowledge explicit (Hansen, Nohria and Tierney, 1999).

The troublesome aspect of tacit knowledge is its elusiveness, which derives from at least three sources: we are ourselves not fully aware of it; there is no personal need to make it explicit on the individual level; and there is a potential risk of losing power and competitive advantage by making it explicit.

Firstly, Davenport and Prusak (1997: p.70) observe that tacit knowledge 'incorporates so much accrued and embedded learning that its rules may be impossible to separate from how an individual acts'. A baseball batsman knows how to hit a ball, but cannot describe it explicitly enough for someone else to learn. Such knowledge cannot be represented outside the human body. Choo (1998: p.117) takes a similar stand: 'tacit knowledge is distributed in the totality of the individual's action experience'; tacit knowledge is 'relying on tactile cues registered by the human body interacting with its environment'. In other words, our daily activities are informed by our tacit knowledge, without us thinking of it as, or recognizing it as, knowledge. For example, we know how to ride a bicycle without having to think. The knowledge resides within us, but we can neither document it in a manual nor explain it in words to others. To transfer such skills, the master and the apprentice must – during periods of internship – share experiences through actions.

Secondly, there is really no need for externalization from the individual's point of view. Since we are able to use our tacit knowledge without thinking, we do not need to document it. Should we have to express our tacit knowledge in words, not only would it be a difficult and laborious task, but also a labour from which we would not directly benefit. Rather, it would be for the benefit of someone else in our organization or for the good of our community. Grudin (1987) has argued convincingly that situations in which one person is forced to do the work while another gets the benefit very often result in failure.

A third reason for the evasiveness of tacit knowledge is uncovered by Leonard and Sensiper (1998), who argue that making tacit knowledge explicit is not always beneficial at the individual level; if the tacit knowledge provides an important competitive advantage, there is little reason to share it with the rest of the organization. Taken to the extreme, extensive knowledge sharing by externalization may create a situation in which a member of an organization 'automates away' the reason for his or her existence in the organization.

The tacitness of professional interests

There may be a significant discrepancy between the espoused image of organizational work and the actual reality. In his ethnographic study of how work is conducted at Xerox, Orr (1996) describes the ways in which an organization's view of work contrasts sharply with what it really takes to get a job done. Although there are formal job descriptions, these are seldom enough to account for the actions performed during a working day. Instead, our interests as professional experts often make us elaborate within, and often even outside, our role definitions.

Its everyday meaning is, however, too general to be useful in this discussion – unless we narrow its scope to that of a corporate setting. Suchman (1987) convincingly argues that all of our actions are situated within particular social and physical circumstances, and heavily dependent on tacit knowledge. In an office context, specific professional interests dictate which reports we read and which documents we write, governing much of our daily activity. If we could capture some of that activity and derive our underlying interests, we might be able to communicate part of our tacit knowledge. Such a possibility would be useful to an organization: it would enable this valuable resource to be shared and help us find people who hold relevant knowledge.

Even though we may be unable to produce an exhaustive definition of our interests, we usually have little problem in determining whether or not a given document is interesting. The reason why we intuitively know what we are interested in when we see it may be explained by applying Polanyi's (1966) theory of the proximal and distal terms of tacit knowledge.

Polanyi claims that tacit knowledge has two distinct properties, which he names its proximal and distal terms. The proximal term is the part that is closer to us, while the distal is the part that is further away. Polanyi gives an example, describing how the police help a witness who is unable to describe a criminal to create a reconstructed image by selecting pictures from a large selection of human features such as eyes, noses and hair. By moving from the first, closer image in the memory to the second, more distant picture collection, the witness is able to communicate their awareness of the face.

Similarly, Polanyi refers to an experiment in which a person was presented with a large number of written nonsense syllables, and after certain syllables the individual was given an electric shock. Interestingly, the subject was able to anticipate the shock at the sight of the correct syllables, but on questioning remained unable to identify them. Again, by attending to the distal term – the shock – the test person became aware of the proximal term – the shock association. Tacit knowledge is, argues Polanyi, the understanding of the unity that this proximal/distal pair together constitutes. We become aware of the proximal term only in the presence of the distal term, but remain unable to communicate the former.

Applying Polanyi's theories to our research problem, we see that when projecting our interests (the proximal term) to the document (the distal term) we are able to recognize and express those interests. Through documents, tacit knowledge may be communicated, despite the fact that it is not easily expressible in words. Hansson (1998) argues that tacit knowledge is not at all 'tacit' – it just expresses itself in a form other than spoken language. Indeed, Choo (1998) suggests that rich modes of discourse, including analogies, stories and metaphors should be used to reveal tacit knowledge. Clearly, we need an instrument to help us attend to this other, richer form.

A new perspective on retrieval systems

Recommender systems (e.g. Resnick and Varian, 1997) are able to anticipate those items a user is likely to be interested in, and can, in a hopefully intelligent way, recommend such items. How this 'anticipating intelligence' is implemented varies from product to product and is not relevant to the discussion in this chapter. Academic research and the success of commercial products have shown that such systems work; therefore, we may safely assume this to be true in this particular case.

While implementing and studying the usage of an agent-based Web retrieval prototype, we observed unexpected but interesting user behaviour which led us to do further investigations. Based on these studies, we claim that such systems can provide the mechanism that allows us to solve the three key problems mentioned previously: it helps communicate tacit knowledge; it presents a natural incentive to do so; and, it does not involve externalizing away competitive advantage. By identifying certain documents as interesting, the user could tell an agent-based retrieval system to maintain a dynamic profile that represents some of the user's tacit knowledge without requiring explicitly defined keywords or manually updated records. Since this profile is used to provide the user with information that is more accurate and search results that are more precise, a natural incentive exists for the user to give feedback and thus cultivate the profile. The resulting profile represents part of the user's tacit knowledge, which becomes useable without being made explicit.

Research concerning agent-based retrieval systems has mainly focused on user-to-object or user-to-information objectives, although it has sometimes also addressed user-to-user considerations. Few, however, have yet approached agent-based retrieval systems from a KM perspective; this requires discussion of what knowledge governs the individual activities and how tacit knowledge may be put to use in the community. This chapter contributes to the corpus of knowledge by proposing an interpretation explaining both how tacit knowledge is activated and made tangible in an organizational setting.

The research described herein is thus not about recommender systems *per se* but rather the usage of such technology. However, the way in which the recommender system prototype was implemented helps to explain the findings and hence we will briefly describe some of the main features in the tool used. To speed up the development process we wanted to build on existing software tools. While examining the commercial tools available at the time, it became clear that there were two different perspectives on how content was handled and what role the user played. These two views may be labelled 'push' and 'pull' respectively.

Push-oriented products focus on the content providers and how the site owners can best deliver added value to the customers. Though being able to adapt to user behaviour and learn to recognize user preferences, this is primarily done in order to help the content provider. Further, since every server that should be able to offer this feature must have the appropriate software installed, this solution works best when a single Web server is used. For example, when Amazon uses push-based technology to recommend books or music, it only recommends books and music from the Amazon site. It does not provide references to competitors. However, for an intranet this approach is less useful.

A pull-oriented product, on the other hand, starts with the user's needs and pulls whatever information it can find that matches the user's interests – from any Web server – and delivers it to the user's browser. No modification to or restructuring of existing data is needed and no additional software has to be installed on the Web servers. Given the objectives of the research, a pull-oriented technology was considered more suitable.

The prototype application used in this research, described in more detail elsewhere (Stenmark, 1999), was based on a commercially available agent-technology tool from Autonomy Nordic. This uses neural networks and advanced pattern-matching techniques to identify text patterns in profiles and to look for similar patterns in other profiles or Web documents (Autonomy, 1998).

The system spidered the intranet each night, synthesizing each Web document found to a 0.5 kilobyte digital representation. This 'fingerprint' contains the characteristics of the document. Once the fingerprint signature was created, the reasoning part of the system could perform concept matching (e.g. finding documents relevant to each other), agent creation (e.g. setting up agents that can find relevant documents), and agent retraining (e.g. adapting the agent to a set of relevant documents).

The site and research method

During the autumn of 1998 four months were spent implementing an agent-based recommender system and studying its usage at Volvo Information Technology, an IT service company within the Volvo Group. At the time, Volvo's intranet consisted of some 450 Web servers and had approximately 400,000 documents. Most of the content was official or semi-official information, such as department presentations, project reports, Frequently Asked Questions (FAQs) and online help material.

Approximately 80 users were invited to participate in the study, which ran from August to November 1998, of which 48 agreed. The incentive to participate came from the assumption that the prototype being tested would be able to provide them with more targeted information for a lower user effort. The interested users were invited to a 2-hour introduction meeting, where a number of fundamentals were explained, including the purpose of the research, the concept of agent-based systems, the design of the application and how to operate it, how to register and log in, and how to set up and run individual agents. We also asked the participants to keep informal records of particular incidents that they considered worth noting, and informed them that we would contact them during or after the test to collect their viewpoints. Seven users were unable to attend any of the three introduction meetings, and were instead given the above information via e-mail. Most, but not all, of the 48 users who registered and participated in the test were Volvo IT employees. Their job descriptions varied from technicians and system developers to content providers and administrators. All were experienced computer users with access to intranet-connected PCs.

The research used a grounded theory-inspired approach, meaning that instead of starting by forming hypotheses that may later be tested, the field is approached in an exploratory way, letting empirical findings suggest the theories on which the analysis is built. The research also subscribes to the view that our knowledge of reality is achieved only through social constructions such as language, shared meanings and artefacts such as tools and documents. Thus, the investigation borrows characteristics of what Klein and Myers (1999) refer to as interpretative research. Analysis of this case study involved an iterative process during which the discovered theory has been gradually refined until it comprises all observed individual cases. User experiences and hard data have been collected in several ways including interviewing, question-naires and Web server log file analysis. First, all users were invited to a group interview (although only eight attended). From the results, certain emerging patterns could be seen and a first tentative theory was formed. Second, the remaining 40 users were sent an e-mail questionnaire (of which 12 responded). After re-looping the analytic phase (Strauss and Corbin, 1990), based on user responses and the application log files, seven semi-structured qualitative interviews were conducted which shaped the final conclusions reported herein. The interviews were open-ended and lasted between 28 and 66 minutes.

Field results

In the week immediately following the initial introduction of the system, at which all participating users were provided with a user ID, password and the Web address of the prototype, the usage was high. During the following two weeks, usage declined slightly before settling at a stable level. This level was then maintained throughout the rest of the test. The users typically used the application frequently, sometimes heavily, during several days, then preferring to stay away from the system for a while before returning for another session. The prototype was designed and implemented to support the creation and maintenance of individual agents, the facilitation of networked communities, and the enabling of finding similar agents. The results from these areas will now be reported in turn.

The prototype system offered individual agents that could be set to find intranet documents, and these agents went beyond a keyword-based query towards a richer representation of an interest. To receive customized information, the users were required to identify themselves by logging in. Once given access, the users could create agents, name the agents, and assign them tasks. A task corresponded to a search engine query, but was expressed in natural language. Typically, the best results were achieved when the users cut and pasted a relevant document (or pieces of text thereof) and asked the agents to find similar documents.

Overall, the user reactions were positive. All 27 responding users claimed the prototype was useful or at least potentially useful. The respondents said they believed in this technology and considered it to be 'an extremely important asset' with a 'great potential'. In the words of one user: 'In the future we're going to be bombarded with even more information and this may be the only way to stay ahead'. By automatically monitoring the search index, the agent could detect relevant intranet updates and thus off-load the user from manual searching. This feature was appreciated as it 'saved time not having to search'. Besides the timesaving aspect, the most frequently reported reason for these beliefs was the ease of constructing queries. Seven users explicitly expressed their appreciation of not having to come up with descriptive keywords, since 'they never do fully contain the meaning you have in mind anyway', as one of the respondents explained. However, eight users did not consider the prototype useful in its current state, but they did believe a future version would be likely to deliver expected benefits. For each agent the users had four options: delete it, edit it, find similar agents or check the result. The search results from the agents were displayed in a simple list, similar to those generated by most search engines, and by clicking on the associated hyperlinks the documents were retrieved. When the user had read and verified that one or more of the returned documents were indeed relevant, the user could provide the agent with positive feedback by marking the document(s) and clicking the retrain button. The digital signature of the agent was then merged with the signature(s) of the selected document(s) and the result became the new agent signature, replacing the previous one.

The retraining process was not trivial and despite general claims that these sorts of retrieval agents were welcomed and appreciated, many users experienced mainly negative actual results. A majority of the users (15 of 27) reported what they referred to as 'strange' or 'unexpected' document matches. In the words of one user: '[it is] hard to get something useful out of it. After retraining it with relevant documents it comes up with nothing.' However, the users tended to blame these bad results on their own inability rather than on the application. One user who had received very little useful information suggested: '…the rather shallow results may depend on me not using the right words. Otherwise, I like the idea. Keep improving!'

The system provided a Community feature that was intended to enable users to locate colleagues with similar assignments and organizational roles by matching user-provided job descriptions. New users were expected to create a user profile that described their job role or work responsibilities via free text. If a user already had a curriculum vitae stored elsewhere, it could be copied into this field. The profile, once saved and stored, was then converted to a digital signature, and when clicking on the Community button, the user profile signature was matched with that of other users and the resulting users were listed on the screen. The user could now display the e-mail address or the profile of any colleague found by clicking the corresponding hyperlink, and had the opportunity to contact him or her. The intention was to make the users aware of each other's presence and thus facilitate the emergence of online communities.

Notwithstanding, few users exploited the Community feature. The primary reasons given for this eventuality were either existing knowledge of enough people doing similar jobs or that most users with similar profiles worked at the same department as the respondents. The respondents were not particularly interested in finding like-minded colleagues. As one user suggested: 'What's the use of hooking up with people doing the same stuff I do? ... It would probably be better to team up with those who know stuff I don't know.' Those who tried the Community feature used it only once or, in one case, twice. With one exception, all interviewees considered the Community feature to be working, or to use their words, it delivered what it was supposed to. One user, however, claimed to have been connected to people with whom he had nothing in common. This was not what he had expected and his reaction to this outcome was rather negative: '...this was clearly a bug'.

The Similar Agents feature was a rather late addition to the application. It was tempting to include the feature since it was particularly easy to implement. The original plan was to let users search for and find similar agents and clone them by copying to their own private area. In this way, new and inexperienced users would receive help improving the quality of their agents. However, this functionality was not implemented in time for the study. The only feature offered to the users during the test was the option to find other users with similar agents.

Remarkably, even though the Similar Agents feature generated exactly the same output as the Community feature, it tended to be much more frequently used, and received much more interest. One user commented: 'It's really interesting to see who else is searching for these sorts of things'. Six respondents reported that they were surprised to find certain people sharing their interests, and another four said that the Similar Agents feature returned users whom they had not expected to be interested in a particular topic. However, these comments were not articulated in a negative way, as was the case with the remarks on the Community feature. On the contrary, the users regarded these unexpected results as useful new insights and none questioned their correctness.

Discussion

Rather than invent clever keywords to describe their interests, the users claimed to prefer utilizing examples by pointing to relevant Web documents. This result is perhaps not surprising; the act of recognizing an interesting document utilizes tacit knowledge while the task of selecting descriptive keywords requires a (non-trivial) translation to explicit knowledge. However, to many organizational members the use of keywords is the established way of searching and they have difficulty rethinking such practices. Despite the instructions to use entire documents as query input users continued to type in (a few) keywords. This suggests that the system should more actively encourage and facilitate the use of documents rather than keywords – possibly by letting the user enter a Web address instead of text. This would prevent a user from entering keywords only.

By drawing a parallel to Polanyi's account of the face description and the shock association, we can see that our interests constitute the proximal term of our tacit knowledge. In the presence of the distal term – here represented by the Web document as previously the picture cards and syllables – we are able to attend to the proximal term, our interests. Polanyi explains: 'This is how we come to know these particulars, without becoming able to identify them' (1998: p.138). Using these Web documents we are able to communicate part of our tacit knowledge of interests to the rest of the organization.

This distinction between tacit and explicit knowledge is parallel to the differences between the Similar Agents and Community features; it explains why the Community feature, which is based on explicit knowledge, was not used much whereas the Similar Agent feature, which relies on tacit knowledge, was more deeply explored.

People are often viewed as performing their jobs according to their formal job descriptions though, as shown by Brown (1998), everyday practice provides evidence to the contrary. Brown's account is consistent with the earlier findings of Argyris and Schön (1974) who refer to the world view and values that people believe, suggesting behaviour is based on an 'espoused theory' as opposed to 'theory-in-use'. The organizational structure and the department descriptions – that are not only already known to the members but also experienced as fictitious – depict the espoused theory of work. The Community feature was built upon static profiles provided by the users themselves to mirror the official responsibilities placed upon them by the organization. The users rightly or wrongly assume that they already possess the explicit knowledge that the Community feature will return. Consequently, they dismiss it as of little interest.

The Similar Agents feature differs from that of Community; it does not rely on static profiles provided to describe an official role. Instead, Similar Agents relies on the tacit knowledge of our interests, made tangible through dynamically retrained agents created with a totally different purpose than the static profiles. If the prompt 'enter your profile' connotes a question equivalent to 'what is your official job description?' the agents are instead created for personal benefit only and no official considerations are taken into account. True and real interests govern the choice of topics, which makes these search profiles more 'believable' than the previous job describing ones. The most notable observations from the interviews are that when matching job profiles built on explicit knowledge and espoused theory of work, the user being linked to unexpected colleagues referred to the result as 'strange' in a negative sense. At the same time, the users matching agents built on tacit knowledge and practice commented upon similar results as 'interesting' in a positive sense. The tacit theory-in-use is obviously regarded as more trustworthy.

Nonaka and Takeuchi's (1995) model of knowledge creation and sharing largely ignores the fact that knowledge is a competitive resource not only on the organizational level but also on the individual level. People do not share knowledge without a strong personal motivation, and they would certainly not give it away without concern for what they may gain or lose by doing so. This problematic circumstance is avoided by the approach suggested in this work, where knowledge does not have to be externalized.

Instead, the whereabouts of the knowledge may be identified, made explicit and communicated. In this way, the users' value will increase both for themselves – as they are identified as having certain knowledge – and for the organization – which can use the knowledge. If users no longer perceive a risk of their knowledge being tapped and replaced by a database, their reluctance to contribute is reduced. Davenport, Eccles and Prusak (1992) reason along these lines when they discuss information politics; collective knowledge of the organization is worth managing, but not necessarily worth capturing. Hansen, Nohria and Tierney (1999) take a similar stance when they conclude that the management strategies for knowledge should be informed by the nature of the business. When mainly tacit knowledge is used to solve problems, a face-to-face approach to communicate knowledge should be facilitated, rather than any attempt to store it. Trying to externalize tacit knowledge can lead to serious problems since the nuances and details that are exchanged in physical interactions are lost.

However, the approach suggested here has certain problems that remain to be solved. McDonald and Ackerman (1998) point out that many recommender systems do not distinguish between different levels of knowledge; there is no way of telling whether a user with an interest is an experienced expert or just a curious novice. Further, interests are in themselves rather elusive. Interests may shift over time but that does not imply that the knowledge is gone. For example, a senior C++ programmer with a corresponding interest may develop an interest in Java programming, and eventually focus entirely on this new field. Since the agent would evolve with the programmer's shifting interest, it would then not be possible to identify this user as a C++ expert.

In a future version of this prototype system, an added feature would be the possibility to explicitly search for a specific interest by entering a description and matching it against both agents and user profiles. This will enable the organizational members to find each other based on their tacit knowledge of interests.

To be able to find this sort of knowledge is, however, only a first step; it only helps identifying experts within the organization. Importantly, it does not prevent experts from leaving the organization nor guarantee that they will have time or willingness to share their knowledge on request. Davenport and Prusak (1997: p.81) observe that 'mapping who knows what in an organization creates an essential knowledge inventory, but does not guarantee the ongoing availability of knowledge.' To foster an environment that appreciates, encourages and rewards active knowledge sharing, other measures that fall outside the scope of this text must be deployed.

Conclusions

Despite the fact that externalization of tacit knowledge is difficult, costly, and not always desired, it is the prevailing approach in most IS- or IT-driven KM projects. In contrast, the work described in this text suggests a novel attempt to utilize IT in order to exploit tacit knowledge without making it explicit. The contribution is thus an interpretation that explains how tacit knowledge is activated, and how it may be made tangible.

This chapter has argued that the professional interests of users in a corporate setting are manifestations of tacit knowledge, and that this knowledge governs many of their daily activities. Focusing on a subset of the organizational environment – the intranet – it is suggested that Web documents can be used to communicate this tacit knowledge, which is otherwise so difficult to articulate. The research has also shown that an information retrieval system based on software agent technology can act as a facilitator in the knowledge-managing process by identifying tacit knowledge on an intra-organizational Web.

There are three key benefits with the suggested approach. Firstly, the complex problem of producing an exhaustive definition of one's interests is replaced with the much simpler task of determining whether or not a given document is interesting. Secondly, since a good profile results in more accurate information, a natural incentive to maintain the profile by giving feedback exists. Thirdly, the knowledge is not externalized but allowed to reside within the users, and therefore no loss of competitive advantage is experienced.

Recommender systems may function as visualizers of tacit knowledge without users giving away their competitive advantage. It is also noticeable from the results of the research that profiles based on tacit knowledge identified by practice are considered more trustworthy than the espoused theory-based job descriptions. This is an important implication for future KM systems.

Acknowledgements

Thanks are due to Volvo Information Technology for their support during this research and to Autonomy Nordic for the use of their software. Thanks also to Jan Ljungberg, Magnus Bergquist and Rikard Lindgren at the Viktoria Institute for useful comments that helped improve this text.

References

Argyris, C. and D. Schön (1974) *Theory in Practice: Increasing Professional Effectiveness*, Jossey Bass.

Autonomy (1998) Technology White Paper, http://www.autonomy.com/tech/whitepaper.pdf.

Blackler, F. (1995) 'Knowledge, knowledge work and organizations: an overview and interpretation', *Organization Studies*, 16 (6), 1021–1046.

Boisot, M. (1995) *Information Space: A Framework for Learning in Organizations, Institutions and Culture*, Routledge.

Brown, J.S. (1998) 'Internet technology in support of the concept of "communities-of-practice": the case of Xerox', *Accounting, Management and Information Technologies*, 8, 227–236.

Choo, C.W. (1998) *The Knowing Organization*, Oxford University Press.

Collins, H. (1993) 'The structure of knowledge', *Social Research*, 60, 95–116.

Davenport, T.H., R.G. Eccles and L. Prusak (1992) 'Information politics', *Sloan Management Review*, 34 (1), 53–65.

Davenport, T.H. and L. Prusak (1997) *Working Knowledge: How Organizations Manage What They Know*, Harvard Business School Press.

Grudin, J. (1987) 'Social evaluation of the user interface: who does the work and who gets the benefit?' in *Proceedings of INTERACT '87* (eds H.J. Bullinger and B. Shackel), Elsevier Science Publishers.

Hansen, M.T., N. Nohria and T. Tierney (1999) 'What's your strategy for managing knowledge?' *Harvard Business Review*, March–April, 106–116.

Hansson, H. (1998) 'Kollektiv kompetens', Ph.D. Thesis, School of Economics, Göteborg University.

Klein, H. and M. Myers (1999) 'A set of principles for conducting and evaluating interpretative field studies in information systems', *MIS Quarterly*, 23 (1), 67–94.

Leonard, D. and S. Sensiper (1998) 'The role of tacit knowledge in group innovation', *California Management Review*, 40 (3), 112–132.

McDonald, D.W. and M.S. Ackerman (1998) 'Just talk to me: a field study of expertise location', in *Proceedings of CSCW '98*, Seattle.

Nonaka, I. and H. Takeuchi (1995) *The Knowledge-Creating Company: How Japanese Companies Create the Dynamics of Innovation*, Oxford University Press.

Orr, J. (1996) *Talking About Machines: An Ethnography of a Modern Job*, Cornell University Press.

Polanyi, M. (1966) *The Tacit Dimension*, Routledge and Kegan Paul.

— (1998) 'The tacit dimension', in *Knowledge in Organization* (ed L. Prusak), Butterworth-Heinemann.

Resnick, P. and H.R. Varian (1997) 'Recommender systems', *Communications of the ACM*, 40 (3), 56–58.

Stenmark, D. (1999) 'Using intranet agents to capture tacit knowledge', in *Proceedings of WebNet '99*, Honolulu, Hawaii.

Strauss, A. and J. Corbin (1990) *Basics of Qualitative Research*, Sage.

Suchman, L. (1987) *Plans and Situated Actions: The Problem of Human–Machine Communication*, Cambridge University Press.

Swan, J., H. Scarbrough and J. Preston (1999) 'Knowledge management – the next fad to forget people?' in *Proceedings of ECIS 99*, Copenhagen.

3 Knowledge management in virtual organizations: experiences at Sigma

Birgit Lemken, Helge Kahler
and Markus Rittenbruch

Introduction

As knowledge is one of the key assets of service-oriented enterprises, effective use of knowledge resources is a precondition of gaining advantages in market competition. Especially network-like organizations depend heavily on knowledge sharing, while their decentralized and geographically distributed structure inhibits knowledge flow. Classical organizations keep a part of their knowledge in hierarchical structures and defined procedures. Knowledge is connected to certain hierarchical levels and transferred by reporting procedures. Virtual organizations (VOs) are less structured than traditional ones and therefore lack these knowledge processes. Sustainable KM in the context of VOs demands the establishment of structures that are flexible and adaptive to highly dynamic organizational changes. An organizational culture that emphasizes knowledge sharing by using various communication channels plays a major role in this.

What is meant by knowledge? A satisfying answer is hard to come by. Nonaka and Takeuchi (1995), for example, trace knowledge through the history of Eastern and Western philosophy. Textbooks on epistemology provide more detailed explanations (e.g. Audi, 1998). Certainly, knowledge is based upon information and bound to people (Davenport and Prusak, 1998). We understand knowledge as actively processed information and personal experience. There is not always a sharp distinction between knowledge and information.

This chapter investigates issues concerning sustainable KM in VOs, starting with a short overview of VOs – especially team-oriented ones.

After outlining some issues of KM in the context of VOs, we present our case study of a team-oriented VO. The study was carried out in the context of the projects VIRTO, funded by MSWWF, NRW, Germany and InKoNetz, funded by the European Union initiative ADAPT. Using the example of the case study, we will analyze how technical and organizational aspects influence knowledge processes. In our example, an existing knowledge-sharing tradition was a drawback in the use of knowledge-supporting technology. Particular emphasis is placed on the interaction of technology and organizational culture.

Virtual organizations

During recent years, many new organizational concepts have emerged, reflecting the demands of modern business. A common aspect of the majority of these new organizational forms is that they are partially structured as networks, among them the VO (Davidow and Malone, 1992). A good overview of the different definitions and how VOs relate to networks, joint ventures, strategic alliances, agile enterprises, value-adding partnerships or clan organizations is provided by Strausak (1998).

Within the group of VOs, we find very different business models. Walden Paddlers, for example, is a small enterprise manufacturing and selling kayaks. The company's core business is to organize the work along the entire value chain (Welles, 1993). Virtual enterprises are not restricted to one country: Rosenbluth International Alliance is a global co-operative alliance of independent travel agencies (Miller, Clemons and Row, 1993). The former Coopers & Lybrand was an international audit and business advisory partnership with businesses in about 130 countries (Sieber and Suter, 1997).

The term 'virtual organization' can be traced back to two different sources. Davidow and Malone (1992) coined the phrase in their book, *The Virtual Corporation*. They stress the temporal aspect: a corporation forms to realize a business goal and separates after achieving it. During the 1980s, Mowshowitz (1997) developed a model of the VO in which task requirements and satisfiers are strictly separated; at the very moment a request is received, the satisfiers are assigned to the task. Both models include improved resource utilization and greater flexibility at lower costs as advantages of VOs.

A generally approved formal definition of the VO is elusive. The common understanding covers the co-operation of legally independent partners that contribute their core competencies to a vertical or horizontal integration and appear as one organization to the customer. The organization is often established for a limited time, and participants are usually geographically distributed. Compared to traditional enterprises, they are less rigidly structured (see Paetau, 1999). Decentralized organizations with almost no hierarchies rely heavily on communication and co-ordination of internal processes. Therefore, one of the prerequisites for VOs is the existence of a technical infrastructure to support communication and collaboration.

A special variety of VO is constituted by co-operation of freelancers or very small enterprises. We call this a team-oriented VO. Such an organization bundles the capabilities of its members and sells them as services to the customer. In contrast to multi-level hierarchies in traditional enterprises, the structure is mainly horizontal. It is best characterized as a polycentric network in which project teams form temporary sub-structures – as illustrated in figure 3.1. Local centres may change or remain static.

Figure 3.1   Polycentric network

The customer perceives the organization as a whole, not seeing its virtual characteristics. By combining capabilities, know-how and qualities of diverse sources, it is possible to cover a broader market segment than each of the individuals can do alone. Acquiring projects, managing customer care, and organizational issues like accounting or marketing, are tasks for the VO as a whole. Viewed from inside, the enterprise consists of several project teams that are highly diverse in magnitude, number of members or duration.

Within the team-oriented VO, there are few permanent organizational functions bound to people. Project leaders will only manage their own projects. Work that relates to the whole, e.g. book-keeping, is done in projects within the enterprise or given to an external service provider. The ability to form a project team that perfectly meets the project task is considered one of the key advantages of VOs. Indeed, Jarvenpaa and Shaw (1998: p.35) write, 'The basic building block of VOs is a virtual team'. It is the centre of activity in the organization. Here, projects are carried out, new business strategies and products are developed.

Project teams form only for a limited time while the VO as a whole heads for permanent existence. Former project experiences help to acquire new projects within a business field. Therefore, it is crucial to save and procure information and knowledge acquired in projects, and to make it available for future use. A VO depends on the commitment of each of its members. The relationship of the members to the enterprise and to each other is crucial. Quality of work and motivation are directly connected to the depth of one's personal commitment. Due to their geographical distribution, members work separately. Developing a community feeling is important, though inhibited by geographical distances and communication mediated by technology.

Rittenbruch, Kahler and Cremers (1998) identify three enabling factors for team-oriented VOs:

- Communication and collaboration support. Communication and co-operation procedures require special organizational and technical support.
- The ability to build flexible teams. The organization's flexibility is critical to its ability to react to market demands.
- Mutual trust among the members. Lacking rigid formal obligations, trust is considered a vital requirement for collaboration.

As the support of collaboration and co-ordination is a general demand within team-oriented work, we will not consider it in detail. For an explanation of the basic concepts of groupware, see Ellis, Gibbs and Rein (1991).

Challenges to knowledge management

A virtual enterprise can be regarded as a typical knowledge organization. 'It is the most radical form to realize the customer- or task-oriented integration of information and knowledge within a temporal and fluid configuration' (Krebs, 1998: p.32). While classic enterprises organize parts of their knowledge along organizational structures and hierarchies, virtual enterprises lack this option, as they have a horizontal structure and fuzzy boundaries. Notwithstanding, VOs depend heavily on effective KM. They are competitive by bundling capabilities and competencies, i.e., they sell their know-how.

KM in a team-oriented VO implies some challenges. Work is carried out under great time pressure, leaving no room for additional knowledge-oriented work. The organizational structure is highly dynamic, which inhibits the establishment of a knowledge-oriented infrastructure that supports knowledge sharing. Members compete with each other – even though mutual trust is required for successful collaboration. Knowledge sharing is coupled with the risk of losing competitive advantages. At the start of a project, the knowledge resources of the participants are partly unknown. As teams form only temporarily, there is a high risk of losing knowledge acquired in a project. Recently acquired know-how is difficult to preserve at the end of collaboration. The fuzzy boundaries of the organization and turnover of members are further factors that increase the risk of knowledge loss, especially when people leave the enterprise and take their knowledge with them.

Building a VO can be regarded as the bundling of competencies and know-how to act on the market. Coupling knowledge resources is quite demanding for the participants, as it requires co-ordination, and co-operation. To co-operate the partners must share their knowledge while at the same time ensuring their own business activities. Trust plays an important role in overcoming the tension between competition and co-operation, providing a base of social cohesion (Jarvenpaa and Shaw, 1998). Trust implies a relationship ready for open and risky information exchange. It is a prerequisite and consequence of successful business relationships. Lipnack and Stamps (1997) regard trust as the belief in integrity, fairness and reliability of a person or organization, based on past experience. VOs have to face special difficulties, as the development of trust is restricted by technically mediated communication and temporal work relationships. Trust between people needs personal contact and time to grow.

Cohesion – i.e. forces that attract members to common goals, establishing identity and shared values – is a central factor in making a VO work. Organizational culture is defined as patterns of shared values and beliefs that over time produce behavioural norms adopted in solving problems (Hofstede *et al.*, 1990). Similarly, Schein (1991) notes that culture is a body of solutions to problems that have worked consistently and are taught to new members as the correct way to perceive, think about and feel in relation to those problems. The sum of these shared philosophies, assumptions, values, expectations, attitudes and norms binds the organization together. Moreover, the regulation of organizational processes works better by means of collective values and models than by means of formal structure (Kahler and Rohde, 1996). Organizational culture, therefore, may be thought of as the manner in which an organization solves problems to achieve its specific goals and to maintain itself over time. Importantly, it is holistic, historically determined, socially constructed and difficult to change (Hofstede *et al.*, 1990). Organizational culture is a key to collaboration in VOs as it creates identity and may be used to support knowledge-oriented practices.

The challenge in VOs is that effective KM is more difficult to establish, in that VOs lack the support of traditional enterprises, for example management support or human resources development. VOs need 'to replace the water cooler informal communication' (Liegle and Bodnovich, 1997) with computer-mediated communication. The main tasks of KM in team-oriented VOs are the same as in traditional companies:

- to identify, open up and gather sources of information and knowledge
- to organize these sources and resources and to make them available to the members
- to support knowledge acquisition and development as well as transfer and provision.

As stated by Nonaka and Takeuchi (1995), knowledge appears in two forms: tacit knowledge that is subjective and difficult to transmit; explicit knowledge that is objective and easy to communicate. Knowledge can be transformed between these two states, for example learning transforms explicit knowledge into tacit. There are a lot of technical solutions that contribute to KM. Document management systems provide access to explicit knowledge sources. Electronic mail management (Lindstaedt and Schneider, 1997) offers organization of communications and access to communication histories. Workflow management systems realize process-oriented knowledge through workflow procedures.

A more holistic view of knowledge-oriented tasks is taken by Stein and Zwass (1995), who introduce the concept of the organizational memory information system (OMIS). The OMIS integrates past and present knowledge by making it explicit for future use. The idea behind an 'organizational memory' (see Ackerman, 1994; Bannon and Kuutti, 1996; Walsh and Ungson, 1991) is to cover several forms of knowledge (as illustrated in figure 3.2). As tacit knowledge is difficult to externalize, it is expertise management rather than the managing of facts that is currently growing in importance (McDonald and Ackerman, 1998). However, VOs have fuzzy boundaries and suffer from the fluctuation of members, which limits the option of expertise management.

Figure 3.2   **Knowledge types**

Sigma – a team-oriented virtual organization

Over the last four years, an empirical study was carried out in a team-oriented German service company. The development and structure of this organization, its technical support for information and communication, and how it changed over time are described. Communication processes and knowledge sharing are analyzed with respect to organizational culture.

Methodology
Several empirical methods were used to gain an understanding of the organization as a whole and the viewpoints of individual members. The authors participated in an internal working group called Sigma Information and Knowledge Management (SIK). This group met once a month. The use of SigSys, a bulletin-board system introduced in 1996, was analyzed. As participating users, the authors had access to the system and its discussion groups. The researchers also participated in a working group – set up by Sigma – on organizational culture. This group launched a questionnaire aimed at discovering members' perceptions of the social environment. Finally, semi-structured interviews were carried out. Using a set of predefined questions, the authors conducted 16

narrative, face-to-face interviews and 14 telephone interviews with members of Sigma, each lasting between 20 and 60 minutes. The interviewees represented several functions (e.g. senior management, project managers and project members) and were distributed all over Germany. Interestingly, while participation in working groups and keen observation of the use of SigSys gave insight into organizational matters, the interviews clearly demonstrated the heterogeneity of personal views.

Sigma's history and structure

Sigma was founded in 1992 as a freelance network offering training courses and consulting services. In the beginning, there were approximately 20 members, most knowing each other through former collaboration. During the 1990s, Sigma underwent rapid growth. Today, Sigma consists of about 200 consultants and trainers with home offices in various parts of Germany. The rapid growth led to changing organizational requirements, especially with regard to information distribution and communication. Through the introduction of SigSys, computer-mediated communication took on a role in communication and information sharing. Further, by establishing 11 regional branches, the network developed a more locally oriented structure.

Sigma's management regards the company as a VO built from a network of freelance consultants and trainers. Trainers and consultants join together as teams in order to realize specific projects. Special positions (e.g. manager of a local branch) require a shareholding in the company. The organization has five business divisions that are managed separately. The boundaries of Sigma are open and fuzzy; there are, at any time, newcomers about to join the organization and others only in loose contact or about to leave. Members differ in their level of involvement. While most work full-time for Sigma, others have part-time positions.

Sigma owns an office, located in central Germany, in which most management work is done; other organizational tasks are distributed, for example book-keeping is done by a member in the north of Germany who receives the data via ISDN. Members mostly work from home offices or have a workplace provided by their customer. The 11 regional branches are spread over Germany. These branches are orthogonal to business divisions. The number of members of a local branch varies between 10 and 40. Most branches have no office. Local groups meet between bi-weekly and bi-monthly to exchange news, develop business plans or give talks about their work practice. Once a year, a workshop for all Sigma members is held.

Continuous organizational development is ongoing. One regional branch is founding a legally independent company, while still intending to be part of Sigma's network. Other regional branches are planning to do the same. At the end of 1999, Sigma's financial department was established as a company, and now offers its services to external customers. Moreover, Sigma continues to expand its network by developing partnerships with other companies.

Due to geographical distribution, the use of telephone, fax and computer-based communication are crucial means of communication and collaboration. SigSys was introduced in 1996, and is used by about 150 people. It can be operated via modem or ISDN allowing access to discussion groups that deal with the company and regional or project-related issues. Furthermore, SigSys provides the storage and exchange of binary data in data pools and an e-mail service. At the time the system was introduced, it was regarded both as safer and cheaper than the Internet. However, a Web-based version of SigSys, SigSys-Online, was introduced in early 2000. It was very quickly accepted, and is now the most popular interface.

The flow of information and knowledge

Sigma started as a small network of people who knew each other personally. They had come together sharing ideas and goals about collaboration and working practice. At that time, telephone, fax and meetings were the means to share information. A few people (e.g. project managers) played a central role in information distribution. Information-seekers contacted them to receive desired data. A network of expertise was established, and every member knew whom to ask – or at least whom to ask to get an expert.

The network of expertise was maintained during the growth of Sigma. Newcomers made their way into the organization by personal acquaintance with a Sigma member. The senior member guided the new one and served as a primary contact point. Almost all interviewees told us that they received a friendly and warm welcome when entering the organization, making them enthusiastic to work and share results. However, growth and geographic distribution made it difficult to rely on personal acquaintance for all members. To maintain the principle of personal relationship, regional branches were established, driven by the same goals and ideas as the whole organization. For those members whose activities take place within the region, this solution is very effective. People in a regional branch know each other through regular meetings, and contacts are very close. Typically, individuals regard themselves as part of a branch; belonging to Sigma as a nationwide organization is less important.

The interviews showed that within the various branches different cultures and climates have been established. While, for example, group A is very homogeneous, group B shows a greater variety. The members of branch A stay in close contact by telephone and bi-weekly meetings. All members belong to a small number of projects within the region, though they also work on other projects. The members of branch B belong to several projects with very different backgrounds (e.g. IT vs human resources). The placing of new project tasks raises jealousy and competition. A sub-group and local newcomers attend the monthly group meetings. People who work in nationwide projects rarely belong to a local group. These people regard regional branches as a hindrance to the establishment of a common identity for Sigma as a whole. Some long-term members think that introducing regional branches has done more harm than good, developing a latent competition between the branches and reduced communication between individuals across branches. However, newcomers benefit from local groups, and many members enjoy the opportunity to build contacts on a small scale.

SigSys was developed as a result of management's perception of a lack of information flow within the organization. The bulletin board offers open and closed discussion groups as well as access to binary data pools. It took more than a year to achieve a general acceptance of the system. Due to the top-down – instead of participatory – introduction, there was resistance from organizational members; IT people regarded the system as insufficient compared to other software solutions, while non-IT people had reservations about computer-mediated communication in general. SigSys has some technical limitations that restrict information sharing. Within discussion groups, no threading is provided, which makes it difficult to track a certain topic. The lack of acknowledgement mechanisms makes it hard to use SigSys for time-restricted and formal tasks. A project manager, for example, was building a new team and posted an application request in SigSys. When time became short, she was not sure whether her request had been ignored or had simply not been read. As a consequence, the project manager had to revert back to the telephone to gather the team members. SigSys's data pools are open to related group members. Access rights are very coarse-grained, although it is important to enable a graded control over information (Shen and Dewan, 1992). While Sigma members are open in sharing their data when contacted personally, they have great reservations in sharing their information anonymously.

The use of SigSys is a reflection of the opportunities and drawbacks of the system. The 150 users access the system between once a week and every day. Most of the topics in open groups deal with organizational matters, like announcing meeting dates or deadlines. Some serious discussion topics also move into open groups (e.g. perception and improvement of organizational culture). The interviewees suggested that they usually browse SigSys to see what is going on, but find it difficult to filter out important messages. People who are working part-time within Sigma consider SigSys as a connection line. These individuals usually access SigSys weekly to get an overview about topics and activities although they are aware that only a small part of Sigma's life is represented in the system. The introduction of SigSys-Online did not change the usage pattern. However, members prefer the Web-based version – it is user-friendlier and almost everybody has Internet access. Apart from SigSys, Internet e-mail is used by a lot of members to communicate with project members and customers. Some processes are completely handled electronically, like the book-keeping.

In general, Sigma members know that they need to 'pull' information and know-how. Asked if they push or pull information, apart from some managers, members emphasized the latter. However, as telephone calls are the most frequent way to get information, providing and requesting information are in fact balanced. The mutual exchange of information and knowledge works twofold: the communication partners receive as much information as they provide, and the personal relationship between the partners is enforced. Personal information exchange cannot cover all information that arises within the organization. Someone who does not know about a topic cannot ask about it. The activities of local branches and topics discussed in working groups are not transparent to all members. Therefore, most members criticize the distribution of general information; this was further underlined by the survey of the working group on organizational culture.

Supporting knowledge management

Approximately one year after the introduction of SigSys, members had developed their use of different means of communication (i.e. telephone, fax, SigSys and e-mail) and selecting the appropriate one for a task. SigSys is now considered and accepted as Sigma's communication media. However, it plays a secondary role to personal communication, and has not been successfully used to share knowledge. SigSys-Online did not change this usage pattern, although the Web interface is easier to handle.

The SIK working group was created to take care of information, communication and co-operation. When the authors joined the group it was decided to make the work of the group public to all members. A quarterly information letter was started, containing information about the current work of the group and contributions of Sigma members. The information letter is available on paper and for downloading from the SigSys data pool. It is the first regular and official information distribution in the organization beyond the annual workshop. By making the internal processes of SIK transparent to the Sigma community, a first example of providing information for the whole organization was given.

Newcomers, in particular, suffer from the lack of transparency within Sigma. They depend heavily on the person who brought them into the organization. SIK decided to address this problem using a new IS: Ariadne's Thread (in German, 'Roter Faden'). Ariadne's Thread, a Web-based IS, was created to provide a common information source with a special focus on new members (as shown in figure 3.3). As in the ancient myth, it should guide people through the maze – in this case of procedures and processes. Ariadne's Thread covered information about Sigma's organization and structure, and provided space for the presentation of individuals, projects and regional branches. A list of contact persons

Figure 3.3   Ariadne's Thread, Sigma's regional structure

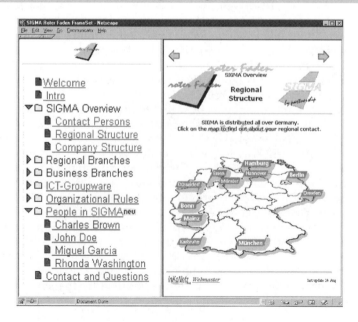

served as a first source of expertise for new members. Members could navigate through the website using a conventional browser and edit HTML pages that were uploaded to the server. Access to the website was password-restricted. To prepare the data for Ariadne's Thread, the co-operation of several groups was needed. SIK members carried out the work. Organizational information was gathered and prepared with the management. Procedures and regulations were written, making partly tacit knowledge explicit. The website was introduced to serve as a knowledge base for Sigma members. Some project groups, as well as individuals and regional groups, took the chance to present their activities.

Motivational factors play a key role in creating necessary incentives for members to provide resources and information to the organization, and thus to form the basis for the development of an information marketplace. Important in this context are the personal profiles provided and maintained by Sigma members themselves. Such self-maintained profiles can also help to avoid fundamental problems, as seen from the discussion on groupware, such as the development of awareness and privacy (see Bellotti and Sellen, 1993; Clement, 1994; McDaniel and Brinck, 1997). We postulate that decisions about the degrees of awareness and privacy needed have to be made by the user.

By providing information about both the organization and its members, Ariadne's Thread aimed at supporting the distribution of information and know-how. Although Ariadne's Thread had been used for about a year, we have to admit that it did not meet our expectations. The content in the organization, group and member areas did not increase after the initial phase. A vicious circle had started. Members visited the site two or three times without discovering new and interesting information. The personal benefit was low and the motivation to contribute to Ariadne's Thread sank. As no editor was responsible for updating organizational information, breaking news never made its way into the site. Instead, this information cycled through informal channels and SigSys. The organizational development of legally independent branches shows that diverging forces are very strong in Sigma. Within these branches, personal communication is dominant. There is no great interest in following what is going on in Sigma besides management information. As it was designed to provide information, Ariadne's Thread offered no communication channels, for example discussion groups, which may also have contributed to the relative failure of the system.

After intensive discussions, SIK decided provisionally to keep SigSys as the organization-wide means of communication. We analyzed the system with respect to its ability to support information and knowledge transfer. Since SigSys is the organization-wide communication tool, we considered it to be important to influence its future development. Suggestions concerning further development included threaded discussion groups, acknowledgement mechanisms and enhanced security and access restrictions. However, instead of a functional enhancement, SigSys was prepared for Web-browser access without any change to its basic functions. Being aware of the shortcomings of SigSys and the need to support project teams, SIK decided to evaluate a Web-based groupware product that provides document management, discussion groups, calendaring, resource allocation and further applications. A test version of the software was installed on a Web server, and all members were invited to participate in the evaluation. Each member can use the system to, for example, manage tasks, appointments and documents. By working with the product and testing it, all members can participate in the decision. This participatory approach is meant to ensure enhanced acceptance by future users.

The interaction of technology and culture

Due to the know-how and capabilities of its members, Sigma is now flourishing. When the company was small, the exchange of information and knowledge was sufficient through personal communication, either by telephone or during meetings. As long as all members knew each other, this form of information and knowledge sharing was adequate. A trustful environment made successful collaboration easy. The rapid growth in members required an organizational restructuring. By establishing regional branches, Sigma tried to preserve its communication culture. This strategy was partly successful, as people in local branches stay in close personal contact. However, a general transparency was missing; information and knowledge cycled in these groups and knowledge islands emerged.

Continuing Sigma's highly communicative tradition, its management decided to introduce SigSys. This is a good example of the interplay between technology and organization (Orlikowski, 1992; Stiemerling, Wulf and Rohde, 1998). Theoretically, SigSys is suitable for information and knowledge transfer. Discussion groups enable people to share information and exchange opinions. What was not foreseen is the fact that the communication style provided by SigSys differs from the former tradition within Sigma. While personal information exchange is always balanced, consisting of mutual contributions, the bulletin board allows the gathering of anonymous information without any reciprocation. Without usage conventions, the system could not serve as a reliable communication medium. Moreover, SigSys competes with Internet e-mail, especially in project work and confidential communication.

According to media richness theory (Daft and Lengel, 1984) a communication medium can be ranked on its ability to handle equivocation and uncertainty. In practice, situation requirements matched against media characteristics as well as social and organizational factors influence media choice (Caldwell, Uang and Taha, 1995; El-Shinnawy and Markus, 1997). Among these requirements are message urgency and content length. The size of the user base is considered critical for a general system acceptance (Grudin, 1994). Our observation of communication media use within Sigma suggests a distinction between one-to-one and group communication. Further, communication means differ in their capability to balance the push and pull of information. In particular, group communication with a high rate of pull access needs trust to work. It also requires particular attention in system design with respect to usage regulations.

Ariadne's Thread was designed as a knowledge base for the whole organization, in which all members could pull information. By making related activities transparent and inviting Sigma members to participate, the involvement of the whole organization should have been initiated. However, as the individual members work under time pressure and with subjective goals, it proved to be difficult to include them in this process. This is a drawback of the lightweight structure of VOs – they often do not provide resources for organizational activities (Rittenbruch, Kahler and Cremers, 1998).

The ability to build flexible teams is one of the enabling factors of VOs. The procedure of establishing a team is often done under time pressure. The current evaluation of Web-based groupware addresses this requirement. The software consists of several functions that are especially useful in the context of project teams. Provided that the participatory evaluation is successful, this application may become Sigma's new communication and collaboration tool.

The Sigma case study clearly demonstrates some mechanisms of knowledge sharing. A living tradition of oral and personal information distribution cannot simply be replaced by introducing computer-mediated communication and IS. As these technical systems provide a more anonymous access, mutual information exchange is not granted. Technical systems are useful when other options are not available, for example to keep in contact at low cost, or to provide information to the whole community (Karsten and Jones, 1998; Whittaker, 1996). Within a VO information and knowledge provision is vital. Besides organizational resources and support, the commitment and contributions of all members are required.

Conclusion

The skeleton of a team-oriented VO consists of information and communication systems embedded into a strong organizational culture that emphasizes the importance of knowledge sharing. To achieve sustainable KM, all members and levels of the organization must co-operate. This becomes possible when everyone is participating in a process of developing common goals, values and procedures. Knowledge sharing requires mutual trust. By providing transparency about ongoing activities and an openness to participation by all members, a trustful environment is created.

As information and knowledge always flow through several channels consisting of different technologies and communication media, KM means to guide the usage of these channels according to conventions to achieve greater coherence. By embedding KM in the organizational culture, procedures and values must be developed that foster information and knowledge sharing. KM can be considered as an evolutionary process driven by a commonly supported strategy and commitment. The introduction of new communication or information technologies capable of enhancing knowledge sharing can be used to initiate a knowledge culture. Importantly, building up a permanent organizational memory requires the inclusion of all members of the organization in its construction. The participatory development of contents, rules and goals creates cohesive forces and becomes part of the organizational culture.

References

Ackerman, M.S. (1994) 'Augmenting the organizational memory: a field study of answer garden', in *Proceedings of the Conference on Computer Supported Co-operative Work*, Chapel Hill.

Audi, R. (1998) *Epistemology: A Contemporary Introduction to the Theory of Knowledge*, Routledge.

Bannon, L. and K. Kuutti (1996) 'Shifting perspectives on organizational memory: from storage to active remembering', in *Proceedings of the 29th Hawaii International Conference on System Sciences*, Maui, Hawaii.

Bellotti, V. and A. Sellen (1993) 'Design for privacy in ubiquitous computing environments', in *Proceedings of the European Conference on Computer-Supported Co-operative Work*, Milan.

Caldwell, B.S., S.T. Uang and L.H. Taha (1995) 'Appropriateness of communications media use in organizations: situation requirements and media characteristics', *Behaviour and Information Technology*, 14 (4), 199–207.

Clement, A. (1994) 'Considering privacy in the development of multi-media communication', in *Proceedings of the Conference on Computer Supported Co-operative Work*, Toronto.

Daft, R.L. and R.J. Lengel (1984) 'Information richness: a new approach to managerial behaviour and organization design', in *Research in Organizational Behaviour* (eds B.M. Staw and L.L. Cummings), JAI Press, 191–233.

Davenport, T.H. and L. Prusak (1998) *Working Knowledge: How Organizations Manage What They Know*, Harvard Business School Press.

Davidow, H.W. and M.S. Malone (1992) *The Virtual Corporation: Structuring and Revitalizing the Corporation for the 21st Century*, Harper Collins.

Ellis, C.A., S.J. Gibbs and G.L. Rein (1991) 'Groupware: overview and perspectives', *Communications of the ACM*, 34 (1), 18–29.

El-Shinnawy, M. and M.L. Markus (1997) 'The poverty of media richness theory: explaining people's choice of electronic mail vs voice mail', *International Journal of Human-Computer Studies*, 46 (4), 443–467.

Grudin, J. (1994) 'Groupware and social dynamics: eight challenges for developers', *Communications of the ACM*, 37 (1), 93–105.

Hofstede, G., B. Neuijen, D.D. Ohayu *et al.* (1990) 'Measuring organizational cultures: a qualitative and quantitative study across twenty cases', *Administrative Science Quarterly*, 35, 286–316.

Jarvenpaa, S. and T.R. Shaw (1998) 'Global virtual teams: integrating models of trust', in *Organizational Virtualness* (eds P. Sieber and J. Griese), Simowa-Verlag, 35–52.

Kahler, H. and M. Rohde (1996) 'Changing to stay itself', *SIGOIS Bulletin*, 17 (3), 62–64.

Karsten, H. and M. Jones (1998) 'The long and winding road: collaborative IT and organizational change', in *Proceedings of the ACM Conference on Computer-Supported Co-operative Work*, Seattle.

Krebs, M. (1998) 'Die virtuelle unternehmung als wissensorganisation: potentiale und grenzen des wissensmanagements', *Arbeitspapiere des FB Wirtschaftwissenschaften*, No. 181, University of Wuppertal.

Liegle, J.O. and T.A. Bodnovich (1997) 'Information technology in virtual organizations: a needs assessment from the perspective of human resource management', in *Proceedings of the Americas Conference on Information Systems*, Indianapolis.

Lindstaedt, S.N. and K. Schneider (1997) 'Bridging the gap between face-to-face communication and long-term collaboration', in *Proceedings of the International Conference on Supporting Group Work*, 331–340.

Lipnack, J. and J. Stamps (1997) *Virtual Teams*, John Wiley & Sons.

McDaniel, S.E. and T. Brinck (1997) 'Awareness in collaborative systems', *SIGCHI Bulletin*, 29 (4), 68–71.

McDonald, D.W. and M. Ackerman (1998) 'Just talk to me: a field study of expertise location', in *Proceedings of the ACM Conference on Computer-Supported Co-operative Work*, Seattle.

Miller, D.B., E.K. Clemons and M.C. Row (1993) 'Information technology and the global virtual corporation', in *Globalization, Technology and Competition* (eds S.P. Bradley, J.A. Hutchinson and R.L. Nolan), Harvard Business School Press, 283–307.

Mowshowitz, A. (1997) 'Virtual Organization', *Communications of the ACM*, 40, 30–37.

Nonaka, I. and H. Takeuchi (1995) *The Knowledge-Creating Company*, Oxford University Press.

Orlikowski, W. (1992) 'Learning from Notes: organizational issues in groupware implementation', in *Proceedings of the ACM Conference on Computer-Supported Co-operative Work*, Toronto.

Paetau, M. (1999) 'Can virtual enterprises build up an own identity?' *Cybernetics and Human Knowing*, 6, 39–54.

Rittenbruch, M., H. Kahler and A.B. Cremers (1998) 'Supporting co-operation in a virtual organization', in *Proceedings of the International Conference on Information Systems*, Helsinki.

Schein, E.H. (1991) 'What is culture?' in *Reframing Organizational Culture* (eds P.J. Frost, L.F. Moore, M.R. Louis, C.C. Lundberg *et al.*), Sage, 243–253.

Shen, H. and P. Dewan (1992) 'Access control for collaborative environments', in *Proceedings of the ACM Conference on Computer-Supported Co-operative Work*, Toronto.

Sieber, P. and B. Suter (1997) 'Ein instrument zur entwicklung von typen virtueller unternehmen – anwendung auf den fall C&L International', Arbeitspapier der Reihe *Informations- und Kommunikationssysteme als Gestaltungselement Virtueller Unternehmen*, No. 16, Bern.

Stein, E. and V. Zwass (1995) 'Actualizing organizational memory with information systems,' *Information System Research*, 6 (2), 85–117.

Stiemerling, O., V. Wulf and M. Rohde (1998) 'Integrated organization and technology development – the case of the ORGTechProject', in *Proceedings of Concurrent Engineering*, Tokyo.

Strausak, N. (1998) 'Resumée of VoTalk', in *Organizational Virtualness* (eds P. Sieber and J. Griese), University of Bern, 9–24.

Walsh, J. and G. Ungson (1991) 'Organizational memory', *Academy of Management Review*, 16 (1), 57–91.

Welles, E. (1993) 'Virtual realities', *Inc.*, 14 (8), 50–58.

Whittaker, S. (1996) 'Talking to strangers: an evaluation of the factors affecting electronic collaboration', in *Proceedings of ACM Conference on Computer-Supported Co-operative Work*, Boston.

4 Managing information overload in the health sector: the WaX ActiveLibrary system

Claire O'Brien, Rudolf Hanka,
Iain Buchan and Heather Heathfield

Introduction

The human brain, a product of evolution, is near to its capability limits; our future evolutionary potential is limited unless we learn to organize knowledge effectively and develop new and efficient methods for knowledge retrieval. Doctors can no longer memorize or effectively apply the vast amounts of scientific knowledge relevant to their clinical practice, and it is widely recognized that medicine has reached a crisis point. Estimates suggest that human knowledge doubles every 33 years (Hanka, 1997) while the expansion of medical knowledge is currently estimated to double every 19 years (Wyatt, 1991). By contrast, our intellectual capacity doubles every 1.5 to 3 million years, and thus has remained practically static over the past hundred thousand years (Hanka, 1997).

One hundred years ago a physician could be expected to know all there was to know about medicine at that time, while narrow specialization only became a common practice early this century, and the process continues. Today a typical doctor will face, during their working lifetime, a several-fold enlargement of the body of medical knowledge upon which to base practice. As our overall knowledge base increases, we have to specialize more and more if we wish to remain near the top of our particular field.

Efficient organization of knowledge is now one of medicine's biggest challenges, a challenge that also offers exciting opportunities. IT has demonstrated over the years that it too is capable of exponential growth and, furthermore, has been achieving this while dramatically reducing its costs. Utilizing IT, it is possible to extract, almost immediately, information that is relevant to a particular user, and to organize it efficiently. However, simply converting existing information resources into an electronic form and distributing or making them accessible to users is far from adequate, and can often exacerbate the problem of information overload. Instead, there is a need for KM tools, which can be expected to transform the way medicine is practised.

Manufacturing industry has for some time now operated the 'just-in-time' methodology that replaces over-stocked stores of components with an efficiently organized supply of the right components at the time they are needed and in the required place. More recently, encouraged by the results of the just-in-time methodology, some large companies have introduced a 'just-in-time staff' concept in order to manage better their human resources.

In both cases the emphasis has shifted from storage to distribution and delivery. In a similar way, we need to develop KM methodologies that will provide the knowledge as and when it is required. Such 'just-in-time knowledge' tools are likely to become essential to many ways of working in the twenty-first century. The changing use of computer infrastructure itself supports this development, with the move from mainframes to personal computers and from local storage to Web technology.

General practice in medicine is a typical example of an activity suffering from information overload (Audit Commission, 1995; Haines and Jones, 1994; O'Brien, 2000; O'Brien and Cambouropoulos, 2000). Leaving aside both basic and specialized medical knowledge, a general practitioner (GP, or family doctor) in Britain is expected to know the contents of numerous health policies, referral protocols, governmental circulars and guidelines, warnings of adverse effects of drugs issued by pharmaceutical companies and so on. A typical collection of such papers forms a column some 26 inches high (Hibble *et al.*, 1998), as illustrated by figure 4.1.

Figure 4.1   **Overloaded with paperwork**

(Reproduced with the permission of Dr A. Hibble)

This, combined with the general expectation that a GP should also advise patients on matters tangentially related to health, such as social services, results in a massive knowledge and information overload. Recognition of this problem, combined with the knowledge that computers are good at handling and organizing data, led to the development of the WaX ActiveLibrary.

The WaX ActiveLibrary

WaX ActiveLibrary aims to provide intuitive support for clinical decision-making by putting key clinical knowledge, evidence-based information, details of services provided locally, outcome measures, information for patients and so forth at the fingertips of GPs in the form of integrated electronic documents. An important objective of this system is to provide relevant information in the right form, at the right time and in an intuitive, non-intrusive manner. Specific objectives of the WaX ActiveLibrary are:

- to provide an efficient information management structure to collect, organize and distribute reliable knowledge, evidence and service information that supports local clinical practice
- to provide a clinician–computer interface for decision-support that is usable without the need for formal training
- integrity of information, authenticity of source and non-repudiation (i.e. the author of information cannot deny ownership).

WaX ActiveLibrary is an IT system that provides users with a library of electronic books with all the searching power, hypertext features and multimedia expected from, say, a CD-ROM product. Furthermore, the library is active in the sense that the user can search across all or selected books in the library, assemble new books on specific topics as a result of searches, update the library by adding new books or updating the existing books, insert notes on the pages of books, author one's own books and communicate with authors of other books via a feedback facility.

Interface design

The first priority in designing the WaX interface was to provide a structure for, and means of navigating through, information that is accessible enough to be useful in clinical practice.

The educational experience of healthcare professionals is based around hierarchically classified paper systems such as libraries of books. It is possible to use current Web browsers to create a 'book-like' presentation of information, but the result is far from optimal. The WaX browser can achieve a more book-like feel, and the format of its files is generally much more portable.

Browsing performance is essential to clinical usefulness; busy clinicians are irritated by anything less than 'near instantaneous' hyperlinking. Optimal performance is achieved when hypertext is browsed directly from a local storage device such as a hard disk. Individual electronic files stored locally on a PC or on a remote WaX ActiveLibrary server represent WaX books. These files can be accessed on a central server, downloaded from it or, if necessary, distributed locally on diskettes or CD-ROMs or attached to e-mails. Downloaded books are periodically checked for validity, and any changes made to them are automatically propagated throughout the network, thus ensuring automatic version control. Today, most GP surgeries in the UK have a connection to the Internet and/or the National Health Service (NHS) private network, NHSnet, so the use of remote ActiveLibraries is the usual mode of operation for several information services based on WaX. However, GP connectivity was not widespread during the evaluation of the system and all WaX books and subsequent updates were distributed on floppy disks that were sent to participating surgeries at regular intervals. The use of graphics and multimedia files can increases the size of the books considerably, and this is overcome by storing multimedia files separately.

The WaX hypertext browsing software was developed to meet a clinical need and has been refined in response to feedback from users. We designed an interface with large icons and 'paper-familiar' terms to facilitate intuitive operation that does not depend upon knowledge of a particular operating system. The interface, as used in the evaluation, is shown in figure 4.2. Its most recent version is further simplified, but retains all essential features.

Figure 4.2   **WaX ActiveLibrary interface, as used during the evaluation**

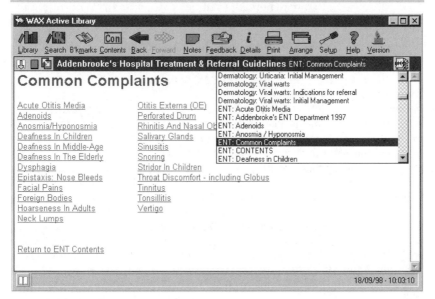

In the WaX browser, information is arranged in chapters of books placed on shelves in a library. Open books can be arranged on a desk area. Each book has an automatically generated 'index' of pages listed alphabetically by title, which the user can scroll through while watching the relevant pages change in real time on screen. The design of the WaX software enables the page-changing to occur at a speed comparable with 'flicking' through pages of a paper book. Users can add their own notes to any page of a WaX book without altering the book's content; these notes are kept in place when the book is updated. Cross-references can be made between books in the library, and many books can be open at one time. A single book, a selection of books, the whole library or selected networked libraries can be searched for words or phrases using the increasingly common notation found in current search systems.

The WaX system includes a complete text editor that enables both individual users and those running an information service to create and edit books, insert hyperlinks to other sources, and add graphics or multimedia files (this is further described in 'Creating WaX books').

A built-in audit trail records the pattern of system use in routine clinical practice, and the feedback facility provides users with a means of communicating back to the author of a page an assessment of its usefulness and impact on clinical practice, and supporting free-text comments. Audit trails and items of feedback are either uploaded to the central WaX server automatically when the user's computer connects to the server, or, in the case of manual updates via diskettes, copied to a disk and sent manually to editors.

Retrieval of information in WaX

The success of knowledge tools depends on the efficiency of information retrieval. Two types of barriers to retrieval efficiency exist, physical and functional. Physical barriers relate to how far the resource is located/retrieved from where the patient care is occurring. Functional barriers relate to the organization of any given knowledge resource once it has been physically accessed.

The physical barrier of distance from the point of care is circumvented by the fact that WaX software is normally installed on PCs held in GPs' consulting rooms. Sometimes WaX is installed in the reception area for secretarial use, or in a practice library. However, there are many situations in which a GP requires access to information outside the surgery, e.g. on a home visit, when a notebook computer is the obvious answer. In this case, when the notebook is connected to the Internet or NHSnet, the automatic check of all downloaded books for their continuing validity – and updates as necessary – is an extremely useful feature.

Functional barriers predict knowledge-resource use better than perceived resource benefits, such as the quality of the knowledge resource (Curley, Connelly and Rich, 1990). For example, searching MEDLINE frequently yields a low ratio of clinical-acceptability-to-retrieval-effort, and it is thus used infrequently in clinical settings. Time and effort are the major barriers to knowledge access: these barriers have largely blocked the integration of knowledge seeking into the usual workflow, and have traditionally limited the usefulness of decision-support applications (Gorman and Helfand, 1995; Tang *et al.*, 1991). WaX ActiveLibrary is therefore designed to balance the requirements of operating within an acceptable time frame and yielding information judged to be relevant, with providing a sufficiently extensive knowledge resource. WaX users can then access information that they know is in the library, rather than search amorphous sources to find out what information exists in the first place.

Knowledge tools require the capture of coded triggers to activate appropriate information displays. They must have vast stores of data and clinical knowledge available electronically, but resources must also be identifiable as relevant to some specific decision tasks. This means that knowledge must be given some structure (Nygren and Henriksson, 1992). Although the text contained within WaX books need not be structured in any systematic manner, each book has a contents page (usually indicating something of the structure of the book), and each page has a title. All page titles are alphabetically listed in the index of a WaX book. The consistent structure of pages making up discrete books allows users to move easily between books compiled by different editors and from different knowledge sources.

The process of simply retrieving passages of unstructured text for visual scanning and interpretation mimics established patterns of patient record use by clinicians, who are making decisions about individual patient care (Curley, Connelly and Rich, 1990). The human mind is good at identifying misspellings, synonyms or related words when looking for something in a text. This is not the case with a computerized search process, in which only limited account is taken of misspellings, synonyms and related terms in finding matches to a query. This problem is commonplace in using the Web, when often several hundreds of hits may be obtained for a particular search, many of which are totally irrelevant.

One solution to the computer-search problem is to use some sort of 'term bank' or semantic model that enables the system to match synonyms or related terms. However, these approaches require complex search algorithms and large amounts of storage. At the moment it is not known how detailed a structure is required to support knowledge tools. Notwithstanding, given the vast amounts of patient data and clinical knowledge that these tools must use, even minimal structuring could require major effort. A simpler solution adopted for WaX was to define a set of likely misspellings, synonyms and so on for each book, and use these for searching. However, even a simple approach like this requires some common assumptions and consistency in order to function usefully.

WaX ActiveLibrary can be searched not only by keywords that occur in the text, but also by concepts, which are meta-tags attached to each page. By using 'concept search', it is possible to retrieve a block of text that deals with, say, pregnancy without the word 'pregnancy' itself appearing in that text. Perhaps even more importantly concept-based searching retrieves only those blocks of text in which pregnancy is discussed, rather than overwhelming the user with all the pages on which the word itself simply happens to be mentioned.

Creating WaX books
Creation of the content in WaX needs to occur at many levels within the NHS, at multiple distributed locations; for example, in the hands of primary care group knowledge officers or hospital administrators, as well as at centralized national information sources. The virtual private network created by WaX, and the ability of books from different sources to co-exist in adjacent libraries and shelves allows and encourages this multiple-point contribution to the knowledge content, although a degree of co-ordination may be necessary, perhaps implemented at the level of a district WaX server, in order to ensure that paper information overload does not become WaX information overload.

If many different people are to take on the role of providing some of the content of WaX books, the editing procedure needs to be as simple as possible, and to encompass a wide range of source documents.

The WaX editor software is based on an editing component from Microsoft's Internet Explorer 4.0, and has an interface with a toolbar of basic word-processing functions familiar to anyone using the Word application. Empty books and pages with the ready-made WaX structure can be generated with a keystroke, and text can be cut and pasted in from documents in other applications or typed in. Formatting from one page can be duplicated using the template function. Hyperlinks can be created between pages in one book and between books and even libraries (with the caveat that WaX material controlled by other people may change or disappear from remote libraries).

Alternatively, any file format that can be converted into HTML pages, and collections of HTML pages representing all or part of a website, can be automatically 'bound' into a WaX book – preserving any existing hyperlinks – using the WaX server software functions. This material can also be edited subsequently via the editor software; thus, page names can be adjusted, concept terms added, and so on. Where archives of documents in other formats are required, the WaX server software can bind a collection of, say, Word documents, preserving their format but adding a book structure with a title page and an alphabetical page list compiled from the document titles.

Integrity and authenticity

The WaX user needs to have both confidence in the 'mission critical' information, such as drug doses or treatment regimes provided in WaX books, and proof that it was supplied by the correct source. Even though the overall level of threat against WaX security is low, certainly much lower than against systems involving identifiable personal health information, we have identified the following primary threats:

- A WaX book's content could be altered, whether by accident or malice.
- WaX software could be maliciously altered, whether by a general virus or by a more targeted attack.
- An incorrect book source (author or publisher) might be claimed.
- A party involved in a dispute might deny the content of a previously published book, or challenge the date on which the information was published.

The first three are familiar from the general computer security environment (Anderson, 1994); the fourth threat might concern a provider of information that subsequently proves to be incorrect, with the provider then claiming that it had published warnings at an earlier date than it had done. Thus, in addition to the integrity and authenticity of books and software, we want a non-repudiation service that covers both content and publication dates. Although the second threat does not introduce a serious risk in our application, it is the main concern with distribution and installation.

One issue is where to draw the fine line between prudence and paranoia when it comes to trusted distribution. The main control mechanism occurs when WaX is first installed: a hash of the installed software and of the catalogue of trusted books can be checked against the value printed on the registration form, and furthermore can be compared with a value published by the distributor. A reasonable level of trust can thus be placed in the WaX software, and consequently in the hash of the cata- logue of all authenticated books that the distribution software contains. The software checks this hash every time it loads the catalogue of WaX books. The user can also initiate this check whenever else it is required. The trust model is based on the WaX-root certifying the publisher, and the publisher certifying the book, taking responsibility for its content to the same extent as in the present world of paper.

The effect of this design is to reduce the problem of the trusted distribution of books to the trusted distribution of the WaX software and of the master catalogue. Under the circumstances, we consider that an appropriate level of effort has been expended on trusted distribution; any more effort than this would cross the line into paranoia.

The knowledge content in WaX

Experiences in implementing WaX, both directly in running a pilot evaluation around Cambridge and in supporting other users in locations across the UK, has highlighted many issues facing the developers of KM tools and the associated information content. Thus different projects have run in parallel, each learning how best to serve the information needs of their local target users, and using different methods for choosing, sourcing, reformatting, checking and testing the knowledge content of their WaX libraries.

Choice of content
The choice of knowledge content is likely to be dependent on who chose to fund and use WaX, and why: is it supporting a knowledge-sharing system owned by primary care, for example, or acting as a demand-management tool for service providers? Ideally, the needs of the target users will dictate the range and scope of content.

Some editors have decided to censor parts of the information content for quality – for example including clinical guidelines only if they are evidence-based. Others have sourced whichever guidelines were described as the users' favourites. Usually a range of material from different levels of the NHS and other agencies is included, so that there may be more than one opinion or guideline covering a particular topic, leaving the end user to exercise the same appraisal and gatekeeping process that is necessary with paper-based information.

Information sources
Sources for national and local WaX books include clinicians, admini- strators and information managers from national, regional and local health service providers, local health authorities and hospital trusts, local GP audit groups, local patient support groups, government departments, charities and professional medical or scientific organi- zations. The shelf-by-shelf 'catalogue' of the WaX library assembled by the East Sussex Primary Care Information Service, shown in table 4.1,

gives an indication of the range of information chosen by and for local users.

Table 4.1   WaX library: East Sussex Primary Care Information Service

1. Primary Care Information Service
    - Primary Care Information Service news
    - Internet links
      o evidence-based Internet sites
      o Health Services Internet sites
      o journals
      o travel medicine
      o trusts, HAs and PCGs

2. Hospitals (inc. private)/community services
    - Brighton Health Care NHS Trust
    - South Downs Health NHS Trust
    - Eastbourne & County Healthcare NHS Trust
    - Eastbourne District Hospital
    - Hastings & Rother NHS Trust
    - Kent & Sussex Weald NHS Trust
    - Mid-Sussex NHS Trust
    - Worthing & Southlands Hospital NHS Trust
    - Worthing Priority Care NHS Trust
    - national NHS allergy clinics
    - other trusts' addresses and details
    - private hospitals and clinics

3. Social services/councils/voluntary organizations
    - Brighton & Hove Council
    - Brighton & Hove Social Services
    - East Sussex County Council
    - Wealden, Lewes & Eastbourne Social Services
    - local voluntary organizations
    - national voluntary organizations

4. Healthcare contacts
4.1 Health authorities and primary care groups
    - East Sussex, Brighton & Hove Health Authority
    - primary care groups
    - Sussex Ambulance Authority
    - West Sussex Health Authority
4.2 Homes and hospices
    - guide to residential and nursing care
    - hospices
    - nursing homes
    - residential homes
4.3 Local healthcare practitioners
    - alternative therapists
    - counsellors
    - dentists
    - GPs
    - opticians
    - pharmacists

4.4 Miscellaneous
    - citizen's advice bureaux
    - community health councils
    - coroner's jurisdictions

5. Guidelines and procedures
5.1 National/international
    - back pain guidelines (RCGP)
    - current medical standards of fitness to drive (DVLA)
    - effective healthcare bulletins
    - management of asthma (BTS)
    - management of COPD (BTS)
    - medical evidence for statutory benefits (Benefits Agency)
5.2 Local
    - child protection procedures (East Sussex)
    - guidelines for referral and treatment (East Sussex)
    - MAAG guidelines (East Sussex)
    - nursing guidelines (East Sussex)
    - public health guidelines (East Sussex)

6. Educational/administrative/professional resources
6.1 Administration
    - reimbursement information for vaccines
    - statement of fees and allowances (Red Book)
6.2 Education
    - postgraduate courses
    - SE Thames Personal Learning Plan
    - SE Thames – postgraduate education
    - SE Thames – regional guide for trainers
    - Sussex Postgraduate Medical Centre – Library Services
6.3 Local medical committees
    - local medical committees (East Sussex)
    - local medical committees (West Sussex)
6.4 Professional resources
    - professional associations
    - talk things through

7. Storage shelf
    - Guy's & St Thomas' Hospital NHS Trust

When sourcing material for the WaX library in our pilot evaluation, we found that some information providers were initially reluctant to provide the required information. However, most eventually saw a benefit to themselves, for example deciding to adopt WaX as a more efficient distribution system for their own communications.

An important consideration that prevents some information providers from giving access to new knowledge sources is the relative ease of comparisons of information once uploaded onto WaX from diverse sources – what we refer to as a 'transparency' barrier. While most WaX users welcome this, some information providers are uncomfortable with the idea that such comparisons might expose disparities in practice.

Reformatting issues

In earlier versions of WaX, the program used a proprietary markup language for text requiring all material uploaded into WaX books to be reformatted using the simple editing interface. Newer versions use HTML pages, so that any file format that can be changed into HTML electronically, and existing Web or intranet pages can automatically be included in WaX books.

When collecting material, some WaX editors found that the sources that they required did not exist amalgamated into written or printed formats, in which case they constructed WaX pages with a standard proforma style – for example to record local service provision with standard headings and entries – and completed the separate fields piece-meal by typing from diverse sources (including telephone enquiries). Thus use of WaX has in these instances led to the assembly of totally new information resources. One primary-care-based information service has worked a clause into the purchaser-provider agreement whereby local service providers are responsible for keeping the WaX editor updated with all changes to their service and contact information.

It is often necessary to involve information providers in re-engineering their use of IT in order that their data can then be used to its maximum potential in the WaX system: for example collecting clinic waiting times in a database program rather than a spreadsheet, so that frequent updates can be compiled automatically into WaX books; or encouraging a charity that maintains a large database of support organizations to use a structured, hierarchical keyword system in order to provide a useful search tool for the WaX version of the material (and consequently for their own use of the database).

There has frequently been resistance from information providers to get involved with our project; often it means that they need to examine more closely how they are using IT and to consider even minor alter-ations to their established procedures. If the encounter with WaX is the first time the information provider has been asked to think about moving into electronic or database formats, then this is perceived as a major barrier and difficulty, but identical issues need to be addressed for other electronic KMS (O'Brien, 2000). For example, if an organization is setting up an intranet for information sharing, then it will be considering some of the same issues and already dedicating staff and resources to making the procedural change.

As more information providers move to sophisticated methods of data capture, storage and distribution, and learn to use intranets and publish Web pages, more WaX books can be produced automatically, and updated with minimal editorial input.

Granularity of information

To be used efficiently, information on screen must be displayed in a form that preserves the context and allows the user to focus quickly on the relevant item, without any need to scroll down or link sideways to follow long tracts of text. Therefore, ideally, each page of a WaX book is shorter than the length of an average screen. When making WaX books from linear documents, it is usually possible to take advantage of the natural paragraph or section breaks in long texts to divide material across several WaX pages. Once such documents are split up in this way, and the pages hyperlinked in a branched or networked relationship, the user requires extra navigation aids in order to understand at a glance the overall structure of the information content.

The editor can provide a diagram of the branching structure to indicate the depth of information content, while pages consisting of a list of hyperlinks, either alphabetical or by broad subject group, indicate the breadth of topic coverage. True algorithmic decision paths can be converted into a series of hyperlinked pages. Page headers or footers can indicate the section or chapter to which the page belongs, and additional hyperlinks can take the user to the next or previous page in a series.

Checking final versions

Some editors have not consulted information providers at all after receiving the material for a new WaX book, and have no established approval system. Some have inserted a disclaimer for responsibility for accuracy at the front of every WaX book. An alternative approach used by the Centre for Clinical Informatics is to present the information provider with the electronic version of their material and ask them to sign it if they are satisfied with the accuracy and format. This process encourages thinking how better to exploit the new medium, and the editor is freer to experiment with novel structures. Setting up a longer-term collaborative approach is also beneficial when the WaX editor needs to be apprised of updates to the information; indeed, it is a mistake to gather lots of material into a WaX library without ensuring that there can be mechanisms for fast communication from information providers of changes, updates and withdrawals.

Evaluating WaX

WaX is being used for health KM and information services in several locations in the UK, after successful pilot projects demonstrated benefits and received long-term funding commitments. The aim continues to be to provide local referral guidelines and directories, local and national patient management guidelines, and health service and other government department information to local GPs, usually within the context of a number of primary care groups.

Our pilot evaluation was conducted with GPs in and around Cambridge in 1998 (O'Brien and Cambouropoulos, 2000). The local health authority wanted to manage demand for the services of three busy departments at Addenbrooke's Hospital NHS Trust in Cambridge by providing GPs with referral guidelines and patient management guidelines for common conditions. Meanwhile, a Cambridge GP had begun a project to rationalize the provision of all types of guidelines to local GPs (Hibble *et al.*, 1998). He had collected some 850 different paper guidelines – defined as any type of material supporting clinical decisions – used by 22 local practices (figure 4.1), and gathered the GPs' views on which were most useful. A selection of the most popular guidelines, both local and national, were obtained and converted into WaX books, and, along with the three sets of Addenbrooke's departmental guidelines similarly converted into WaX, formed the knowledge content for the Cambridge WaX pilot project.

The Cambridge pilot was designed to evaluate formally the usability and usefulness of the system. The software was in its earlier, non-networked version, and thus the WaX books and software were uploaded by our team onto stand-alone computers, with updates being distributed on floppy disk.

The pilot began with a seminar for participating GPs in March 1998. This was followed by installation of the WaX software in 17 participating practices (usually on several computers at each location). Audit trail and feedback files pertaining to the WaX books on each computer were collected at six-week intervals. These files contain, respectively, an automatic audit trail of WaX pages that have been opened on screen, and feedback in the form of text comments and scores of usefulness appended to specific pages by the user.

Methodology

Information is critical to decision-making. However, the process of delivering clinical knowledge for decision-making has received little attention from informatics workers, particularly in the field of evaluation, in which systems have generally been evaluated by decision outcome, rather than the decision process components (Tierney *et al.*, 1987, 1988; Tierney, Miller and McDonald, 1990; Connelly, Sielaff and Willard, 1995). A more appropriate evaluation in this case is one that focuses upon process gains in decision-making, such as more efficient information seeking, as opposed to only outcomes (Heathfield, Pitty and Hanka, 1998).

The evaluation of the Cambridge pilot focused on the usefulness and usability of WaX as an information-seeking tool rather than on an assessment of changes in clinical outcomes. Although the number of WaX users increased as the pilot progressed, the evaluation was based only on the 19 GPs who initially agreed to participate in the pilot (in two of the 17 surgeries there were two such participating GPs); all 19 GPs completed the full six months of the study. Questions addressed in the evaluation included system usage, the usefulness of WaX as a tool for delivering information, the information content of the system, and comparison with paper-based equivalents.

Several instruments were used for evaluation, including audit trail analysis, questionnaires and meetings, as described below.

Pre-study questionnaire

This was completed by GPs at the launch meeting (to ensure compliance), and included questions on:

- demographics
- computer knowledge, experience and attitudes
- use and attitudes towards paper guidelines (including reasons for usage or non-usage)
- the perceived role for WaX
- information desired for inclusion in WaX.

Mid-study questionnaire

This was completed three months into the pilot and was mostly concerned with the content of the WaX books supplied.

Post-study questionnaire

This was completed in the post-study meeting – after six months – and focused on:

- The WaX interface, including ease of use, navigation, use of mouse, and the amount and adequacy of training and technical support.
- The ease and speed of access to WaX, compared to paper guidelines, and the likelihood that guidelines in WaX format would be used.
- The future role of WaX. Will GPs continue to use WaX after the pilot? If not, why not? What changes would users like to see? Is there a willingness to pay for the service?
- Specific questions about the books supplied with WaX. For example, how useful were individual sections? Were they detailed enough? What additional information would GPs like?

WaX Audit Log

The software recorded automatically who used WaX, when, and for which parts of content.

WaX feedback

Users' comments about specific books and pages were entered electronically, on a voluntary basis. Some of these feedback comments resulted in alterations to the format or content of the books during the study.

The formal evaluation ran from 1 April to 30 September 1998. The final questionnaires were collected from users in early October, together with the audit-trail files from their computers. The questionnaires were coded and the data analyzed using SPSS statistical software. Audit-trail data were converted into a Microsoft Access database file. Access was also used to produce statistics concerning the patterns of use.

Results

When the pilot began, 11 of the 19 GPs used the Internet either at home or at work, and 10 used e-mail. By the end of the pilot, e-mail was used at two more sites and the Internet at three more. Thus, while many subjects began the pilot with some experience of computers other than their practice clinical systems, they were by no means all proficient in the use of computers. Interestingly though, a total of 17 out of 19 users

(90 per cent) declared that WaX was easy to learn, including three who did not use a computer at home.

All users reported that they found it either 'very easy' or 'moderately easy' to navigate around the information content in WaX, to find a specific book, and to use the search facilities. All users except one rated the WaX search function either 'very effective' or 'effective'.

Fifteen GPs used WaX in the consulting room when patients were present. Overall, WaX was rated by GPs as an 'excellent' tool for use in consultations or as an information source (Chi-square= 8.22, p<0.05 and Chi-square=12.79, p<0.01 respectively); one GP, for whom WaX was only available on a PC in the practice manager's office, rated the system 'not useful'. A less positive overall rating ('adequate') was given to WaX as a patient management tool or diagnostic aid. This is not surprising, as WaX was not designed to be an aid to diagnosis.

More than half (11) of the users considered themselves familiar with 10 or fewer clinical guidelines. Two users declared familiarity with 30 or more guidelines. However, 53 per cent of GPs used only four or fewer guidelines regularly. Twelve users (71 per cent) said they were 'much more' likely to use a referral guideline in WaX format than on paper, four (23 per cent) thought it 'a bit more' likely, and one user thought that he would use a WaX version 'a bit less' than a paper version. Eleven GPs (65 per cent) thought they were making more appropriate referrals with WaX than before, with four (23 per cent) not having a clear opinion and two (12 per cent) preferring working with paper.

A declared familiarity with, or regular use of, large numbers of paper guidelines did not correlate with rating WaX guidelines as easy to locate or use; those GPs who had incorporated more of the 'paper tower' into their workflow had neither advantage nor disadvantage compared with others when it came to using the alternative electronic source. Nine out of 15 (60 per cent) declared that specific guidelines were easier to locate in WaX than on paper.

All GPs wanted to continue using WaX after the pilot study, either as it stood or with a small modification to the software (15 GPs; 88 per cent), or after a major improvement to the software (two GPs; 11 per cent). Almost half of the users (47 per cent) expressed a willingness to pay £10 or more per month for continued use of the system.

Eighteen out of nineteen GPs considered that WaX had 'an important role to play in the future of general practice', and while 10 out of 19 thought that there were no major barriers to widespread use of WaX, eight believed that there were barriers, several citing as examples the lack of both computer hardware and computer literacy among GPs. Thirteen out of eighteen users thought that tools such as WaX would have additional roles in the context of primary care groups, stating a predicted increase in the number of guidelines, greater need for uniformity, and other consequences of grouping practices and of implementing clinical governance.

When considering new ways to use tools such as WaX, 11 out of 19 GPs did not – and seven did – want assistance with clinical decision-making. In terms of networking, direct communication between WaX and the practice clinical system or the local hospital system would be 'helpful' according to eleven and nine GPs, respectively.

The audit trail revealed that 19 GPs used WaX 350 times during the first month of the pilot (April 1998). This declined to 240 times in May. From then on, the usage steadily increased every month, finally reaching 490 instances in September. The mean number of pages viewed by individual users during the first and second halves of the six-month pilot showed a statistically significant increase from 38.6 pages per user during April, May and June, to 140.1 pages during July, August and September (95 per cent confidence interval of the increase: 8.8 to 194.1 pages). In the second half of the study, GPs were accessing WaX approximately twice a day.

The granularity of WaX books and the functionality of the user interface have been designed so as to minimize the time taken to access required information. As can be seen from figure 4.3, in about 25 per cent of cases this happened within 10 seconds, and in 45 per cent of cases within about 30 seconds.

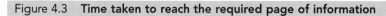

Figure 4.3   **Time taken to reach the required page of information**

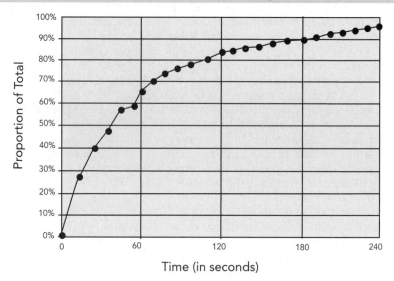

A total of 97 comments were collected via the 'feedback' function in the user interface. They can be divided into three categories:

- 50 specific comments on current information content (24 comments praised the content or system, while 11 criticized the content for inadequacy)
- 25 general requests for additional or new information and new system features
- 22 specific comments on other issues, including book structure, page layout and sensible hyperlinks.

Conclusions

WaX started out as a research concept four years ago. Since then the project has experienced many difficulties in making the transition from a prototype system towards a fully operational KM tool, including the limited resources available, scalability problems, extension from a single-user to a multiple-user system, debugging and platform dependence. The University of Cambridge has subsequently set up a spin-off commercial company, WaX Info Limited, which has developed the software further and is now distributing it to healthcare users in the UK and abroad.

The future success of KM tools such as WaX depends not only on solutions to technical issues, but also on new and innovative professional and organizational infrastructures being put into place in the clinical arena. Clinicians should no longer be perceived as independently contracted individuals who must supply their own knowledge storage and retrieval tools. More recently, they have become production workers, with health-care organizations being pressed to provide the essential production tools to them as 'clinical workers'. Berwick (1996) stresses that we need to change the whole system, not just make changes within it, if we are to succeed in making improvements to clinical care. Our experience in trying to implement a new KMS indicates that it is not only in the clinical arena that practices need to change, but also in the administrative and backup functions, where inefficient technology and data capture infrastructures hamper a progression to efficient use of clinical KM tools.

A review article by Smith (1996) that looked at the information needs of GPs reached several conclusions, one of which was that a significant barrier to the widespread use of KM tools is the psychological needs of clinicians. According to Smith, doctors are looking for guidance, psycho-logical support, affirmation, commiseration, sympathy, judgement and feedback. He argues that this aspect of doctors' information needs is particularly poorly explored, and yet it may well be the most important need and the biggest stumbling block to a technical solution. In our study, specific feedback comments recorded by GPs indicate that they appreciate the guidance and affirmation it provides (e.g. 'useful to confirm I was doing the right thing' or 'it is reassuring to know you are using currently recommended antibiotics in any given situation'). When users begin to edit their own WaX books and share these with colleagues, KM tools such as WaX may also enhance the personal exchange of information and support that currently takes place verbally.

The major users of WaX, the participating GPs, have been uniformly enthusiastic about the system. Other local GPs have subsequently asked to join the scheme, and have provided their own computer hardware. Enthusiasm for WaX among the major providers of information, such as local hospitals, was varied, primarily because they could not immediately see a benefit to themselves.

The feedback of comments from the users of WaX to the information contributors provides a new level of communication between GPs and hospital consultants. This infrastructure could be used to target specific problems between primary and secondary care, such as demand management.

Efficient organization of knowledge is now one of medicine's biggest challenges; a challenge that also offers exciting opportunities. The results of the pilot provide evidence that WaX ActiveLibrary significantly improves GPs' access to relevant information sources, and by increasing appropriate patient management and referrals may also lead to an improvement in clinical outcomes.

References

Anderson, R.J. (1994) 'Why cryptosystems fail', *Communications of the ACM*, 37 (11), 32–40.

Audit Commission (1995) *For Your Information: A Study of Information Management and Systems in Acute Hospitals*, HMSO.

Berwick, D.M. (1996) 'A primer on leading the improvement of systems', *British Medical Journal*, 312, 619–22.

Connelly, D.P., B.H. Sielaff and K.E. Willard (1995) 'A clinician's workstation for improving laboratory use: integrated display of laboratory results', *American Journal of Clinical Pathology*, 104, 243–52.

Curley, S.P., D.P. Connelly and E.C. Rich (1990) 'Physicians' use of medical knowledge resources: preliminary framework and findings', *Medical Decision Making*, 10, 231–41.

Gorman, P.N. and M. Helfand (1995) 'Information seeking in primary care: how physicians choose clinical questions to pursue and which to leave unanswered', *Medical Decision Making*, 15, 113–9.

Haines, A. and R. Jones (1994) 'Implementing findings of research', *British Medical Journal*, 308, 1488–92.

Hanka, R. (1997) 'Information overload and the need for 'just-in-time' knowledge', in *Proceedings of the Asia-Pacific Medical Informatics Conference*, Hong Kong.

Heathfield, H.A., D. Pitty and R. Hanka (1998) 'Evaluating technology in healthcare: barriers and challenges', *British Medical Journal*, 316, 1959–61.

Hibble, A., D. Kanka, D. Pencheon *et al.* (1998) 'Guidelines in general practice: the new Tower of Babel?' *British Medical Journal*, 317, 862–863.

Nygren, E. and P. Henriksson (1992) 'Reading the medical record I: analysis of physicians' ways of reading the medical record', *Computer Methods and Programs in Biomedicine*, 39, 1–12.

O'Brien, C. (2000) 'Creating the books for the National Electronic Library for Health: expected barriers and useful lessons', *Health Libraries Review*, 17 (4), 209–214.

O'Brien, C. and P. Cambouropoulos (2000) 'Combating information overload: a six-month pilot evaluation of a knowledge management system in general practice', *British Journal of General Practice*, 50, 489–490.

Smith, R. (1996) 'What clinical information do doctors need?' *British Medical Journal*, 313, 1062–68.

Tang, P.C., J. Annevelink, D. Fafchamps *et al.* (1991) 'Physicians' workstations: integrated information management for clinicians', in *Proceedings of the Annual Symposium on Computer Applications in Medical Care*, New York.

Tierney, W.M., C.J. McDonald, D.K. Martin *et al.* (1987) 'Computerized display of past test results: effects on outpatient testing', *Annals of Internal Medicine*, 107, 569–74.

Tierney, W.M., C.J. McDonald, S.L. Hui *et al.* (1988) 'Computer predictions of abnormal test results: effects on outpatient testing', *Journal of the American Medical Association*, 259 (8), 1194–98.

Tierney, W.M., M.E. Miller and C.J. McDonald (1990) 'The effect on test ordering of informing physicians of the charges for outpatient diagnostic tests', *New England Journal of Medicine*, 322, 1499–1504.

Wyatt, J. (1991) 'Uses and sources of medical knowledge', *Lancet*, 338, 1368–72.

5 Knowledge management in the professions: a study of IT support in law firms

Petter Gottschalk

Introduction

A new perspective on knowledge in organizations is being created. Organizations are viewed as bodies of knowledge (Blaauw and Boersma, 1999; Davenport, Long and Beers, 1998; Nonaka, 1994, 1995), and KM is considered an increasingly important source of competitive advantage (Ginsburg and Kambil, 1999; Nahapiet and Ghoshal, 1998). Law firms represent an industry that seems very well suited for KM investigation (Lamb, 1999). Law firms are knowledge intensive, and the use of advanced technology may transform these organizations in the future (Terrett, 1998).

Little empirical research has been conducted on IT support for KM. Most published research develops recommendations for successful KM without an empirical basis (e.g. Davenport, Long and Beers, 1998; Fahey and Prusak, 1998). This study complements existing research by focusing explicitly on the use of IT to support KM in law firms, thereby adding to the body of empirical KM research (e.g. Alavi and Leidner, 1999; Ruggles, 1998).

To examine the use of IT to support KM in Norwegian law firms, a study was designed involving two phases of data collection and analysis. The first phase was an initial field study of the largest law firm in Norway. The second phase was a survey of Norwegian law firms on the subject of IT support for KM. This chapter reports on the research, discussing some key findings and implications for the use of KMS in the law profession.

Aspects of the research

This section explores some of the key topics explored by this study. In particular, it discusses knowledge, KM, IT and law firms – the essence of the research problem.

Knowledge

The special capabilities of organizations to create and transfer knowledge are being identified as a central element of organizational advantage (Nahapiet and Ghoshal, 1998). Knowledge embedded in the organization's business processes and the employee's skills provide the firm with unique capabilities to deliver customers with a product or service. Scholars and observers from disciplines as disparate as sociology, economics and management science agree that a transformation has occurred – knowledge is centre-stage (Davenport, Long and Beers, 1998).

Distinctions are often made between data, information, knowledge and wisdom. Knowledge is information combined with experience, context, interpretation and reflection (Davenport, Long and Beers, 1998). Knowledge is a renewable, re-usable and accumulating organizational asset that increases in value with employee experience and organizational life (Ginsburg and Kambil, 1999). Knowledge is intangible, boundless and dynamic, and if it is not used at a specific time in a specific place, it is of no value (Nonaka and Konno, 1998). According to Fahey and Prusak (1998), knowledge is what a knower knows; there is no knowledge without someone knowing it. According to Alavi and Leidner (1999), information becomes knowledge once it is processed in the mind of an individual. This knowledge then becomes information again once it is articulated or communicated to others in the form of text, computer output, spoken or written words, or other means.

Many authors are concerned with the distinction between explicit and tacit knowledge (e.g. Alavi and Leidner, 1999; Fahey and Prusak, 1998). Explicit knowledge can be expressed in words and numbers, and shared in the form of data, scientific formulae, specifications, manuals and the like. This kind of knowledge can be readily transmitted between individuals formally and systematically. Tacit knowledge is highly personal and hard to formalize, making it difficult to communicate or share with others. Subjective insights, intuitions and hunches fall into this category of knowledge. Tacit knowledge is deeply rooted in an individual's actions and experience, as well as in the ideals, values or emotions he or she embraces (Nonaka and Konno, 1998).

Knowledge management

KM is introduced to help companies create, share and use knowledge effectively (Davenport, Long and Beers, 1998). There is no single definition of KM, but in general the idea relates to unlocking and leveraging the knowledge of individuals so that this knowledge becomes available as an independent organizational resource. Much of the literature on KM is driven from an IS perspective and is based on the belief that KMS can be used to capture and stockpile workers' knowledge and make it accessible to others via a searchable application (Newell *et al.*, 1999).

Although potential benefits from KM are high, many scholars are concerned that this is just another fad (Swan, Scarbrough and Preston, 1999). Based on such warnings, it is important to keep realistic expectation levels when planning and implementing KM in organizations.

Information technology
The concept of coding and transmitting knowledge in organizations is not new: training and employee development programmes, organizational policies, routines, procedures, reports and manuals have served this function for many years. What is new and exciting in the KM area is the potential offered by modern IT (e.g. the Internet, intranets, browsers, data warehouses, data filters and software agents) to systematize, facilitate and expedite firm-wide KM (Alavi and Leidner, 1999). The critical role for IT lies in its ability to support communication, collaboration and the search for knowledge, and its ability to enable collaborative learning.

Many organizations have initiated a range of KM projects and programmes in which the primary focus has been on developing new applications of IT to support the digital capture, storage, retrieval and distribution of an organization's explicitly documented knowledge (Zack, 1999). There are several key groupings of knowledge IT: artificial intelligence systems – expert systems, neural networks, fuzzy logic and generic algorithms – capture and codify knowledge; group collaboration systems – groupware and intranets – share knowledge; office automation systems – word processing, desktop publishing, imaging, electronic calendars and desktop databases – distribute knowledge; and knowledge work systems – computer-aided design, virtual reality and investment workstations – create knowledge.

As examples of IT projects that support KM, Ruggles (1998) lists: creating an intranet, data warehousing, implementing decision-support tools, implementing groupware to support collaboration, creating networks of knowledge workers, creating knowledge repositories, mapping sources of internal expertise, establishing new knowledge roles, and launching new knowledge-based products and services.

An intranet may be classified as a KM application, since it is capable of distributing knowledge. While not every intranet project should be considered a KM effort, intranets are often used to support knowledge access and exchange within organizations (Ruggles, 1998). According to Newell *et al.* (1999), intranets are often implemented with KM as the primary focus. That is, intranet systems are seen as a tool for the more efficient sharing and creation of knowledge within organizations. Lamb (1999) studied intranets in international law firms in the US. She found that only 20 per cent of the law firms had intranets in 1998, but that this percentage was growing rapidly.

While having considerable potential, the availability of electronic knowledge exchange does not automatically induce a willingness to share information and build a new intellectual capital. Major changes in incentives and culture may be required to stimulate use of new electronic networks; motivated creativity is a fundamental influence in the creation of value through leveraging intellect (Nahapiet and Ghoshal, 1998).

Law firms

A law firm can be understood as a social community specializing in speed and efficiency in the creation and transfer of legal knowledge (Nahapiet and Ghoshal, 1998). Edwards and Mahling (1997) categorized the types of knowledge involved in the practice of law as administrative data, declarative knowledge, procedural knowledge and analytical knowledge. Administrative data includes all of the 'nuts and bolts' information about firm operations, such as hourly billing rates for lawyers, client details, staff payroll data and client invoice data. Declarative knowledge is that associated with the law, the legal principles contained in statutes, court opinions and other sources of primary legal authority. Law students spend most of their law-school careers acquiring this kind of knowledge. Procedural knowledge is that related to the mechanics of complying with the law's requirements in a particular situation: for example, what documents are necessary to transfer an asset from Company A to Company B, or what forms must be filed, and where, to create a new corporation. Declarative knowledge is sometimes labelled know-that and know-what, while procedural knowledge is labelled know-how (Nahapiet and Ghoshal, 1998). Analytical knowledge refers to the conclusions reached about the course of action a particular client should follow in a specific situation. Analytical knowledge results from analyzing declarative knowledge (i.e. substantive law principles) as it applies to a particular fact setting.

There are significant hurdles to be overcome in order to embed successful KM in the law-firm context, all of which may be categorized according to firm culture: individuality, time, success and lack of incentives (Terrett, 1998). Individuality is encouraged in most law firms; lawyers are not noted for their team-based approaches to legal work or for their willingness to share expertise. Time is money in a law firm; any time spent sharing knowledge and experience is time not spent billing. Success can be the enemy of innovation; many larger law firms have done very well without any recourse to KM, or even particularly innovative use of IT. Lack of incentive obscures the existence of a knowledge marketplace (Terrett, 1998).

In summary, treating law firms as a KM setting seems to make sense (Lamb, 1999). IT used to support KM may revolutionize law firms (Whitfield-Jones, 1999). Effective IT support for KM can serve as a competitive advantage and as a professional aid to law firms. The first phase of the work, a field study of the largest law firm in Norway, was used to identify issues and attitudes towards IT and KM in a law firm. This phase was used as a basis for developing the survey approach in the second phase, as explained below.

Initial field study

The largest law firm in Norway dates back to 1856, and has 150 employees, out of which 95 are lawyers (TKGL, 1999). The firm has offices in Oslo, Bergen, London and Brussels, and provides services relating to Norwegian and EU law, in all aspects of business and commerce to a wide variety of Norwegian and international clients. The field study was conducted in late 1998. Semi-structured interviews were conducted with fourteen employees: eight lawyers and six other staff. Respondents were asked questions about the role of IT at the organizational level and at the individual level. A questionnaire was also completed during the interview.

On a scale from 1 (little extent) to 6 (great extent), the respondents had a strong belief in the potential powers of IT: the statement 'IT will become a competitive tool' had a mean score of 5.2 and 'IT can improve effectiveness' scored 5.4. Further, respondents recognized the importance of KM (score 5.4). A relatively lower score for profitability than for effectiveness and competitiveness indicated that the value-added part-nerships in the firm were concerned with a strategy-based perspective on KM rather than an economics-based one. There was little recognition or acceptance of possible changes in the working environment, exemplified through the notions of paper-free offices (score 2.4) and the removal of traditional offices (score 1.4).

In conclusion, the initial field study confirmed a strong belief in KM in the law firm and a strong belief in IT as an enabler of KM. More speci-fically, analysis of the interviews identified three concepts of importance in the introduction of IT-enabled KM: law-firm culture, the importance of knowledge to the firm and the general level of IT use in the firm.

The research model

Based on the reviewed literature and the initial field study, a research model was developed. The research model is illustrated in figure 5.1. The dependent construct in the research model, use of IT to support KM, consists of five major categories of knowledge-focused activities: gener-ating knowledge, accessing knowledge, transferring knowledge, sharing knowledge and codifying knowledge (Ruggles, 1998).

There are three independent constructs in the model. First, law-firm culture consists of individuality, time, success and incentives (Terrett, 1998). Second, firm knowledge consists of administrative knowledge, declarative knowledge, procedural knowledge and analytical knowledge (Edwards and Mahling, 1997). Third, IT use by respondent, colleagues, chief executive and associates can be identified (Lamb, 1999; Yap and Bjørn-Andersen, 1998).

Three research hypotheses can be developed from the research model. First, a firm culture in which lawyers are stimulated to co-operate with each other, knowledge transfer between lawyers is rewarded, success is dependent on knowledge-sharing and time is allocated to knowledge-sharing will lead to greater IT use to generate, access, transfer, share and codify knowledge (Terrett, 1998). For example, major changes in incentives may be required to stimulate the use of new electronic networks (Nahapiet and Ghoshal, 1998). Dimensions of a co-operative culture include co-operation stimulation, knowledge-sharing incentives, a reliance that knowledge-sharing brings success, and knowledge-sharing time (Ring and Van de Ven, 1994). Co-operative culture can be defined as horizontal and vertical connections within the firm that share compatible

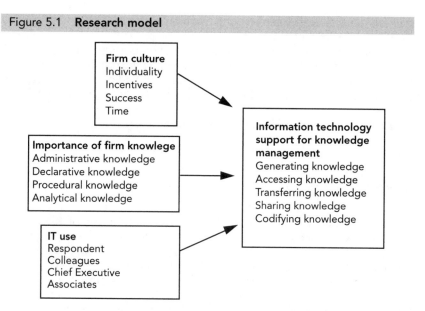

Figure 5.1 **Research model**

goals, strive for mutual benefits, and acknowledge a high level of mutual interdependence. Furthermore, joint efforts aim at results that each lawyer would find difficult to achieve acting alone (Aadne, Krogh and Roos, 1996). Hypothesis 1: the greater the extent of co-operative culture in a law firm, the greater the extent of IT usage to support KM.

Second, the importance of firm knowledge influences the extent of IT use for KM. It is suggested that a law firm with critical administrative, declarative, procedural and analytical knowledge will use IT to a larger extent to generate, access, transfer, share and codify knowledge (Terrett, 1998). Hypothesis 2: the greater the importance of knowledge to a law firm, the greater the IT use to support KM.

It is assumed that the survey respondent will be the IT-responsible partner in the law firm. A partner is an owner who is eligible for a share of annual profits; for example, in 1998, partners in the law firm Robins, Kaplan, Miller & Ciresi were entitled to more than $3 million (*Wall Street Journal Europe*, 1999). Dimensions of IT use include those of respondents, colleagues, chief executive and associates. If these users employ IT to a large extent, it is suggested that the degree of IT use for KM will also be large (Lamb, 1999). Although supporting KM can be a component of IT use, KM is a new application area for IT in the firm, thereby making IT support for KM and IT use two different constructs. Hypothesis 3: the greater the IT use in a law firm, the greater the IT use to support KM.

Research methodology

The objective of this study was to examine the use of IT to support KM in law firms. The initial field study and the reviewed literature was considered sufficient basis for conducting a survey. The sample comprised 256 law firms in Norway. The desired informants in this research were lawyers with special interest in or responsibility for IT. Many law firms have a senior lawyer referred to as the IT-responsible partner – an ideal candidate for this kind of research. Out of 256 questionnaires mailed, 73 were returned, providing a response rate of 28 per cent. Information was collected on the number of years the respondent had been in their current position and the number of lawyers in their firm, as listed in table 5.1.

Table 5.1   **Characteristics of respondents and organizations**

Characteristic	Mean	Standard deviation
Years in current position	10	6
Number of years in the firm	12	20

Respondents were asked to write their own definitions of KM. These responses were categorized according to the three perspectives suggested by Alavi and Leidner (1999). In terms of the information-based perspective, lawyers reported perceiving KM to be about characteristics of information, such as whether it is readily accessible, real-time and actionable information. In terms of the technology-based perspective, lawyers associated KM with various IS (including data warehousing, enterprise-wide systems, executive information systems, expert systems and intranets), as well as an assortment of tools (e.g. search engines, multimedia and decision-making tools). From the culture-based perspective, lawyers associated KM with learning (primarily from an organizational perspective), communication and intellectual property cultivation. A summary of responses, categorized by perspective, is given in table 5.2.

Table 5.2   **Definitions of KM**

Percentage	Definition
30	Culture-based perspective
19	Information-based perspective
10	Technology-based perspective
41	No response
100	Total

Research results

Four multiple-item scales were used to measure the constructs: one for the dependent variable and three for the independent variables (as listed in table 5.3). Each scale had an acceptable reliability, as measured by Cronbach's Alpha.

Hypothesis testing was carried out using multiple regression analysis. Table 5.4 lists the results of multiple regression analysis between the three independent variables and the dependent variable.

The full multiple regression between the three independent variables explains 34.7 per cent of the variation in IT use to support KM (i.e. the adjusted R-square is 0.347). The F-value of 13.22 is significant at the 1 per

Table 5.3   **Items for measurement of dependent and independent constructs**

Construct	Measurement of construct	Alpha
IT support for KM (Ruggles, 1998)	IT use for knowledge-generation IT use for knowledge access IT use for knowledge transfer IT use for knowledge-sharing IT use for knowledge-coding	0.92
Firm culture (Terrett, 1998)	Co-operation stimulation Knowledge-sharing incentives Knowledge-sharing success Knowledge-sharing time	0.87
Importance of firm knowledge (Edwards and Mahling, 1997)	Importance of administrative knowledge Importance of declarative knowledge Importance of procedural knowledge Importance of analytical knowledge	0.73
IT use (Lamb, 1999)	IT use by respondent IT use by colleagues IT use by chief executive IT use by associates	0.88

Table 5.4   **Multiple regression between use of IT and predictors**

Predictors	Beta	t-test
Firm culture	0.154	0.189
Firm knowledge	−0.18	−0.177
IT use	0.561	5.557*

* Indicates a significance level of 1 per cent

cent level, indicating that the null hypothesis is rejected; there is a significant relationship between the set of predictors – firm culture, firm knowledge and IT use – and the extent of IT use to support KM. The only significant predictor is IT, which implies that IT is used to a greater degree to support KM in law firms in Norway when IT is more generally used to a larger extent. Information on the degree of IT use in the various firms was obtained by questioning the extent of IT use among key users: respondents, colleagues, chief executive and associates.

To control statistically for organizational size, multiple regression was applied again, this time including the number of lawyers in each firm. The adjusted R-square decreased to 0.334, and the number of lawyers was not significant. Hence, no spurious relationships caused by this control variable were found.

Three research hypotheses were developed based on the research model. First, a firm culture in which lawyers were stimulated to co-operate with each other, knowledge transfer between lawyers was rewarded, success was dependent on knowledge sharing, and time is allocated to knowledge sharing will lead to a greater extent of IT use to generate, access, transfer, share and codify knowledge (Terrett, 1998). This hypothesis was not supported, which may be considered a surprising result. In contrast, Ruggles (1998) found culture the current biggest impediment to knowledge transfer. Practising lawyers argue that they just don't have time for knowledge sharing. However, one explanation for the lack of support for this hypothesis might be the direct link suggested between a knowledge-sharing culture and IT use for KM. An alternative formulation would be a path from culture to knowledge-sharing and then to IT use. This would lead to two hypotheses instead of one. Another explanation for the lack of support for the hypothesis might be firm size, although no spurious relationship was found.

Second, the importance of firm knowledge influences the extent of IT use for KM. It is suggested that a law firm with critical administrative, declarative, procedural and analytical knowledge will use IT to a larger extent to generate, access, transfer, share and codify knowledge (Terrett, 1998). This second hypothesis was not supported, which again may be considered a surprising result. However, one explanation for the lack of support for this hypothesis might be the direct link suggested between importance of knowledge and IT use for KM. An alternative formulation would be a path from knowledge importance to KM and then to IT use for KM. This would lead to two hypotheses instead of one. Another explanation for the lack of support for this hypothesis might be the self-evaluation that took place in this survey; respondents may have been biased towards the same importance of knowledge in different law firms.

Third, it is assumed that the respondent will be the IT-responsible partner in the law firm. Dimensions of IT use include that of the respondent, colleagues, chief executive and associates. If these agents use IT to a large extent, it is suggested that the degree of IT use for KM will be greater (Lamb, 1999). This hypothesis was supported. There are lessons to be learned from this research result. IT-supported KM will only take place if IT is generally used in the firm. Thus, a number of infrastructures are required in the firm: technical infrastructure needs to be in place, including a network, personal computers, databases and software; an application architecture has to be in place, linking the various software applications; and an information architecture is required, enabling the flow of information between various systems.

It may seem that support for the third hypothesis is obvious, since IT use for KM can be a component of general IT use. However, it is argued in this research that IT support for KM and general IT use may be treated as different constructs; IT support for KM is a new application area for IT. In other words, firms that use of IT extensively do not necessarily apply IT to KM. To test this assumed construct validity, factor analysis was performed with the nine items. All five IT support items loaded significantly on one factor, together with IT use items for respondent and colleagues. The remaining IT use items for chief executive and associates did not load significantly on the factor. Subsequently, this test did not reject discriminant validity for the two constructs, which may or may not be separate.

Discussion

It may be argued that the response sample contains many small firms. Although statistical control for organizational size did not provide new insights, a separate analysis of only large law firms was conducted. Out of 73 participating law firms, only 10 had more than 25 lawyers. Within this group, the adjusted R-square increased to 0.750, indicating that the research model explains more variation in IT support for KM. However, similar to the total sample, again only the third hypothesis was supported.

Law-firm size is of considerable interest to practitioners. Lawyers in large law firms suggested that there must be pronounced differences with small firms. In table 5.5, responses are categorized according to law-firm size: small, medium and large. Here, there appear to be only marginal differences. Nevertheless, one pattern that is perhaps easily recognized is in the use of IT to support KM, which grows with law-firm size.

Table 5.5 Responses for different law-firm sizes			
Construct	*Small** *(36)*	*Medium** *(27)*	*Large** *(10)*
IT support for KM (Ruggles, 1998)	3.3	3.7	4.1
Firm culture (Terrett, 1998)	5.0	5.0	5.3
Importance of firm knowledge (Edwards and Mahling, 1997)	4.5	4.2	4.7
IT use (Lamb, 1999)	4.5	4.3	4.9

* Small firms have fewer than five lawyers; large firms have more than 25.

During the survey in April 1999, and after mailing of the survey report in June 1999, many law firms contacted the author. They expressed both interest in the research and concern about certain concepts in the research. One such concept was the categorization of knowledge into administrative, declarative, procedural and analytical types, which was based on work by Edwards and Mahling (1997). Many respondents found this categorization hard to follow. Some translated declarative knowledge into knowledge about current laws. Some were unable to make a distinction between declarative and analytical knowledge. Both declarative and analytical knowledge have components of legally binding circumstances and interpretations. The procedural lawyer establishes working knowledge of the facts, and then searches for relevant laws that fit the facts. The business lawyer, however, first develops agreements and documents between the parties, which are then signed. He or she may later be called upon to solve disagreements by interpreting the original agreements and documents. In this situation, an inseparable mixture of declarative and analytical knowledge is applied. Consequently, one respondent expressed concern about lawyers' unclear perceptions of the constructs and terms used in the research.

Some lawyers commented on the results of hypothesis testing. One lawyer made the comment that the first hypothesis about firm culture was not supported because of other influencing factors: the lawyers' daily routines and the time and costs involved in training and administration of a knowledge support system. Similarly, responses suggested that the second hypothesis was not supported because no cases are alike; knowledge from one case can only serve as general knowledge for another case. Finally, comments indicated that the third hypothesis was supported because general IT use is a form of KM. This hypothesis was also supported because firms with low IT use have no practical ability to implement KM using advanced technologies.

Another comment was concerned with lip-service. One of the key obstacles to KM in law firms can be that firms pay lip-service to its importance, but then are not seen to value it. For example, they will tell fee-earners that time spent in generating and storing knowledge is important, but when it leads to a reduction in chargeable time billed, they will complain. It would be interesting to know whether any of the firms in the study had instituted reward mechanisms for KM contribution.

It would be desirable to discuss the findings of this study in light of other empirical studies. However, this field of research has only recently emerged, making the current availability of empirical studies limited. One relatively recent empirical study by *Management Review* (1999) lists obstacles to effective KM. In the study, 'keeping relevant technology up-to-date' was ranked as obstacle number seven; obstacle number one was 'getting people to seek best practices'. Hopefully, future research will produce more empirical studies of this nature.

Conclusions

The initial field study documents a strong belief in the potential benefits from KM, as suggested in the research literature. The current use of IT in law firms does not seem to be extensive, but combined with a KM perspective, law firms have substantial expectations.

The extent to which law firms in Norway use IT to support KM is significantly influenced by the degree of firms' general IT usage. Only those firms that are mainstream users of IT will begin to use it to support KM; law firms whose use of IT is limited will continue to avoid the technology.

Future research may concentrate on the dynamic processes going on within and outside the law firm: between lawyers and clients, between lawyers and other parties' lawyers, between lawyers and other parties, between lawyers and judges, between lawyers and assistants, and between lawyers in the same law firm. This will help to throw light on some of the complexities of information and knowledge processes in law firms.

In the practitioner literature, there has been a recent discussion regarding whether IT-supported KM will revolutionize or transform law firms. For example, Whitfield-Jones (1999: p.3) asks whether it will be 'business as usual or the end of life as we know it?' The answer is emphatic: 'business will continue much as usual' (p.10). This has also been underlined by the results of this study.

As a final point, although we have already mentioned that law firm size was not found to be a significant influence on IT-supported KM, the topic still continues to cause debate. Practitioners continue to question the validity of results based on mixed samples of 'law firms ranging from one to ninety-five lawyers'. Future research should look into this more carefully, and should take into account charging differences between large and small firms.

Acknowledgement

This chapter is reprinted with the permission of the *Journal of Information Technology*. The chapter first appeared as Gottschalk (2000).

References

Aadne, J.H., G. Krogh and J. Roos (1996) 'Representationism: the traditional approach to co-operative strategies', in *Managing Knowledge – Perspectives on Co-operation and Competition* (eds G. Krogh and J. Roos), Sage Publications.

Alavi, M. and D.E. Leidner (1999) 'Knowledge management systems: issues, challenges and benefits', *Communications of AIS*, 1 (7), 2–41.

Blaauw, G. and S.K.T. Boersma (1999) 'The control of crucial knowledge', in *Proceedings of the IRMA International Conference*, Hershey, PA.

Davenport, T.H., D.W.D. Long and M.C. Beers (1998) 'Successful knowledge management projects', *Sloan Management Review*, Winter, 43–57.

Edwards, D.L. and D.E. Mahling (1997) 'Toward knowledge management systems in the legal domain', in *Proceedings of the International Conference on Information and Knowledge Management*, Phoenix, AZ.

Fahey, L. and L. Prusak (1998) 'The eleven deadliest sins of knowledge management', *California Management Review*, 40 (3), 265–276.

Ginsburg, M. and A. Kambil (1999) 'Annotate: a Web-based knowledge management support system for document collections', in *Proceedings of the Hawaii International Conference on System Sciences*, Maui, Hawaii.

Gottschalk, P. (2000) 'Predictors of IT support for knowledge management in the professions: an empirical study of law firms in Norway', *Journal of Information Technology*, 15, 69–78.

Lamb, R. (1999) 'Using intranets: preliminary results from a socio-technical field study', in *Proceedings of the Hawaii International Conference on System Sciences*, Maui, Hawaii.

Management Review (1999) 'Survey on knowledge management', April, 20–26.

Nahapiet, J. and S. Ghoshal (1998) 'Social capital, intellectual capital and the organizational advantage', *Academy of Management Review*, 23 (2), 242–266.

Newell, S., J. Swan, R. Galliers *et al.* (1999) 'The intranet as a knowledge management tool? Creating new electronic fences', in *Proceedings of the IRMA International Conference*, Hershey, PA.

Nonaka, I. (1994) 'A dynamic theory of organizational knowledge creation', *Organization Science*, 5 (1), 14–37.

Nonaka, I. (1995) 'Managing innovation as an organizational knowledge creation process', in *Technology Management and Corporate Strategies: A Tri-Continental Perspective* (eds J. Allouche and G. Pogorel), Elsevier Science.

Nonaka, I. and N. Konno (1998) 'The concept of "ba": building a foundation for knowledge creation', *California Management Review*, 40 (3), 40–54.

Ring, P.S. and A.H. Van de Ven (1994) 'Developmental processes of co-operative interorganizational relationships', *Academy of Management Review*, 19 (1), 90–118.

Ruggles, R. (1998) 'The state of the notion: knowledge management in practice', *California Management Review*, 40 (3), 80–89.

Swan, J., H. Scarbrough and J. Preston (1999) 'Knowledge management: the next fad to forget people?' in *Proceedings of the European Conference on Information Systems*, Copenhagen.

Terrett, A. (1998) 'Knowledge management and the law firm', *Journal of Knowledge Management*, 2 (1), 67–76.

TKGL (1999) TKGL company information, Nettvik Online, http://nettvik.no.

Wall Street Journal Europe (1999) 'Lawyers ring up tidy profits as clients make deals', July 6, 4.

Whitfield-Jones, C. (1999) 'Business as usual or the end of life as we know it?', *Managing Partner*, May, 1–10.

Yap, A.Y. and N. Bjørn-Andersen (1998) 'Energizing the nexus of corporate knowledge: a portal towards the virtual organization', in *Proceedings of the International Conference on Information Systems*, Helsinki.

Zack, M.H. (1999) 'Developing a knowledge strategy' *California Management Review*, 41 (3), 125–145.

Part 2

Designing enterprise knowledge management systems architectures

6 A multi-layer architecture for knowledge management systems

Ulrich Frank

Introduction

KM aims at concepts and theories that help to generate, organize and leverage knowledge in social settings. This recommends focusing research in general on cognitive, social, cultural and organizational aspects, and in particular processes of 'organizational learning' (Easterby-Smith, 1997; Nicolini and Meznar, 1995; Tsang, 1997), organizational measures to promote the exchange of knowledge (see Nonaka and Konno, 1998), incentives for the acquisition, documentation and dissemination of knowledge, and the reconstruction of specific knowledge domains through 'ontologies' (Gruber, 1993). There is no doubt that, in addition to social and psychological aspects, IT – if applied in a sensitive way – can be a very effective driver of successful KM. The management of knowledge by specialized software improves availability, offers measures to adapt the mode of access to knowledge and its presentation to individual preferences and allows the deployment of specialized software that operates on digitized knowledge. For example, functions that can be performed by software include: retrieval, decision-support, simulation and teaching.

Despite the obvious relevance of IT for KM, there has been relatively little work on the application of software to this area. The term 'organizational memory' has been introduced for a category of IS that serves to represent knowledge that is subject to and the result of organizational learning. However, usually the descriptions of organizational memory systems remain on a vague level, or are essentially characterized as hypertext or hypermedia systems (see Euzenat, 1996). On the other hand, there are numerous systems that deal with the representation and dissemination of knowledge: to name a few, decision-support systems, management information systems, expert systems and groupware systems. Assuming that it makes sense to define a type of software that we could call a KMS, we have to face a number of questions:

- What is the difference between IS in general and KMS?
- What is the difference between KMS and specialized systems like organizational memory systems or knowledge-based systems?
- Are there any general requirements that a KMS should fulfil?
- Is it possible to provide a KMS with a generic body of knowledge that can be used in (almost) any company?

The answers that are developed in this chapter suggest that there are substantial similarities between KMS and conceptual enterprise models. Against this background, we will propose a multi-layer architecture of KMS as well as a generic content that can be applied and refined for a wide range of companies. Both content and architecture are inspired by a method for enterprise modelling that has been developed over a period of several years (Frank 1997, 1998). In the long run, it is not desirable to regard a KMS as an isolated system. Therefore, the architecture includes an interface to integrate KMS with existing IS.

Knowledge management systems and information systems

Any attempt to define the term knowledge faces a dilemma. On the one hand, knowledge – both as part of colloquial and scientific language – seems a self-evident term with no need for further explanation. Nevertheless, many different definitions exist. That makes it almost impossible to find a definition that is compatible with most existing notions of knowledge. On the other hand, knowledge represents a phenomenon that is very difficult to reflect upon. While we can speak about knowledge, any insight into knowledge can be regarded as knowledge itself. As with language, we can differentiate between knowledge and knowledge about knowledge (meta-knowledge). But although we can do that over many levels, in the end we cannot avoid a *regressum ad infinitum*. For these reasons, the development of a comprehensive definition of knowledge seems inevitably frustrating. Fortunately, such a definition is not necessary for our purpose. We mainly need a pragmatic image of knowledge capable of differentiating KMS from traditional IS.

At the same time, it is not satisfactory simply to refer to the colloquial meaning of knowledge. In this case, proposing KMS would mean the introduction of just another label that mystifies, and so seems impressive. However, because of the complexity of the term, we will not suggest yet another definition. Instead, we will focus on aspects of knowledge that are relevant for its management by machines and that are suited to the deduction of essential features of systems we could call KMS.

Knowledge and information: a preliminary and pragmatic differentiation

In philosophy, knowledge is essentially related to cognition, intellectual discovery, explanation and understanding. It is differentiated from belief, the emphasis being on the methods by which scientific knowledge is structured and evaluated (Habermas, 1985; Lakatos and Musgrave, 1970; Popper, 1962; Sneed, 1979). In sociology, the focus is on the social construction of knowledge, which includes the relationship of knowledge, language and power (Berger and Luckmann, 1967). While there is no clear difference from the term 'information', the analysis of information usually stresses other levels of abstraction. Within the engineering disciplines, information theory is focusing on mathematical descriptions of processing and transmitting information. The term 'information' is usually defined by the level of probability that certain events will take place (Shannon and Weaver, 1962). Semantic information theories (see Bar-Hillel, 1964), on the other hand, focus on the formal representation of meaning by symbols. In both cases, information is regarded as formal patterns only. Human perception and understanding are outside the scope of these theories.

While these philosophical considerations do not allow us directly to distinguish KMS from other types of IS, they provide some clues. Knowledge is related to describing, analyzing, understanding and eventually changing the world that surrounds us. Applied to the context of this chapter – corporate knowledge – we do not consider any real-world domain, but only businesses and their relevant surroundings. In addition to that, knowledge in this context is regarded as an organizational and not just an individual asset. That implies adequate measures to communicate and evaluate knowledge. In contrast to information that is usually stored in traditional IS, knowledge is hardly used within standardized procedures on the operational level. Instead, knowledge is required when it is used to understand, analyze and eventually change the organization and strategy of a corporation. Against this background, corporate knowledge – in contrast (not necessarily opposed) to information – can be characterized by the following features:

- Understanding and reflection. Knowledge implies perception and thinking, and so emphasizes, in business terms, reflection on organizing principles and competitive advantage. This is different from the information that is needed on an operational level, which for pragmatic reasons will usually not be the subject of further intellectual investigation. In other words, knowledge describes how we understand our surroundings. Therefore, knowledge is usually associated with a higher level of abstraction. It is expressed by propositions about classes or concepts, rather than by statements about single instances. IS typically contain representations of numerous instances. The conceptualization of instances of the same kind (through classes or types) happens usually outside the boundaries of the system to which the user has access.
- Communication and dissemination. Within an organization, communication is a prerequisite for the evolution and dissemination of knowledge, while knowledge in turn can be regarded as a medium

that fosters communication. It has to be taken into account that – at least in larger organizations – various terminologies or specialized languages are used to express knowledge. Language barriers often cause friction and misallocation of resources. Bridging these gaps requires special knowledge that we could call interface or translation knowledge.

- Subjects and results of organizational learning. In social settings, individual judgement of situations or concepts is often insufficient. Instead, it is necessary that many people agree on common interpretations. Hence, the content of a KMS should be regarded as the subject of, as well as a medium for, organizational learning.

Knowledge management systems: essential requirements

The features of knowledge that we have suggested, relevant for our purpose, are abstract in nature. To develop a more concrete notion of a KMS, we will first propose a number of requirements a KMS should fulfil. Against this background, the content of a KMS and its presentation is illustrated from a user perspective. In general, a KMS should serve everybody who is involved in processes of understanding, evaluating and (re-)organizing the business. Due to the nature of these tasks, the primary focus groups include consultants (internal and external), new employees who have to understand the company in general and their tasks in particular, executives, system analysts and customers and suppliers that participate in cross-organizational business processes. A KMS should provide these groups with relevant knowledge. At the same time it should support the documentation and exchange of knowledge. The following requirements reflect this purpose in more detail:

- Emphasis on conceptual level. Rather than providing data about a large amount of instances, a KMS should offer definitions of concepts needed for the description and analysis of a corporation. Examples of such concepts are: corporate strategy, organizational unit, business process, task and employee. Note that these concepts are usually not defined independently of one another. Instead, their semantics will usually include relationships between concepts.
- Re-use of existing knowledge. Although there is no unified terminology for the description of corporate knowledge, there are a number of elaborated and well-documented concepts available – provided, for instance, by textbooks of corresponding disciplines. This is also the case for the documentation of relevant causal relationships. A KMS should provide an adequate body of existing knowledge. This is for various reasons. The re-use of knowledge does not only contribute to the economics of a KMS; it should also improve the overall quality of its content. In addition to that, it should foster communication by referring to a body of knowledge many people are familiar with.
- Convenient and safe adaptation to individual needs. Sometimes the concepts provided by a KMS will not satisfy individual requirements. Therefore a KMS should allow modification of concepts. For instance, if the conceptualization of a task within a business process is not satisfactory in a particular case, there should be a way to change its semantics. However, in order to support the integrity of a system, it is not a good idea to allow for arbitrary modifications.

- Intuitive understanding. Often, the knowledge stored in a KMS represents a complex context. Nevertheless, in order to serve its purpose, the system should provide this knowledge in a comprehensive way. Users should be able to understand the contents of a KMS to the degree of their interest. For this purpose, a KMS should give users a chance to reconstruct concepts they do not understand by tracing these back to familiar concepts. An intuitive access to knowledge does not only depend on adequate semantics. The concepts as well as the artefacts (models) the user can design by applying them should also be rendered illustratively, so as to present material in a way that is familiar to a target group. We assume that graphical representations are often helpful in this respect, since they are used quite frequently within processes a KMS should support.
- Support of multiple perspectives. In order to support different users and different tasks, a KMS should provide various perspectives on the knowledge it stores. Managing complexity requires the offering of different levels of detail. For instance, sometimes it will be sufficient to get a description of a business process that is restricted to an outline of the temporal relationships between high-level tasks. In other cases it may be important to provide a comprehensive description of every task within the process, as well as of the required resources. The plethora of intellectual tasks to be performed in an organization is usually accompanied by a separation of concerns. Classes of problem are related to certain professional communities. In order to support these communities, a KMS should provide concepts that relate to corresponding specialized terminologies and abstractions.
- Integration of perspectives. While there is certainly a need for specialization, it is of crucial importance to foster communication between people with different professional backgrounds. Especially in those cases where there is a cultural chasm between different groups (like business people and IT professionals), a KMS should help to avoid redundant work and conflicts that block the effective use of resources. This purpose can be served by a conceptual integration of perspectives. Two perspectives are integrated by introducing a set of common concepts. In addition to this, providing comments or illustrations of concepts for non-experts can also narrow the gap between different communities. Note that the quest for integration is not restricted to different knowledge perspectives. Knowledge enriches information that is related to it, while information (focusing on the operational level) may contribute to a further illustration of knowledge. This suggests that a tight integration with an existing IS is an advantage.

The architecture

The requirements proposed still allow for a wide variety of systems. As with any other IT artefact, it would be presumptuous to claim one best solution. The following outline of a KMS is only a suggestion of how such a system could look. It is inspired by a method for enterprise modelling called MEMO ('Multi-perspective Enterprise MOdelling'; see

Frank, 1997). Enterprise models can be regarded as repositories of corporate knowledge. Usually, they emphasize intuitive representations for various user groups by featuring a number of different graphical representations. Therefore they can be regarded as a medium for organizational learning and the dissemination of relevant knowledge.

The different levels of abstraction that are suggested by MEMO correspond directly to the layers of the proposed architecture illustrated in figure 6.1. Therefore, we could also speak of a multi-perspective KMS. Notice that the interface layer is not an exclusive part of a KMS. Instead, it is shared with IS to allow for their integration.

Figure 6.1   Overview of the architecture

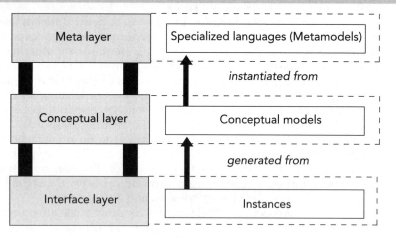

Conceptual background

Concepts rather than instances are the subject of KMS, and concepts are related to certain perspectives or abstractions, like processes or structures. Within these perspectives, knowledge about a company can be specified as a type of business process, a type of organizational structure, or a type of information structure. However, describing one of these types appropriately is no easy task. For instance, one has to take into account that a business process may be aggregated from many other processes, or that a process may refer to certain resources. It is also important to avoid inconsistent descriptions, like processes that may produce deadlock. An essential prerequisite for accomplishing this task is a specialized language that includes appropriate concepts as well as syntactic and semantic rules for the description of valid models. In order to foster consistent descriptions, a KMS would include a meta-level (or knowledge scheme) that provides specialized modelling languages used to define more concrete concepts. For example, the meta-level could provide a process modelling language to foster the consistent definition of business-process types. Hence, the meta-level provides generic, state-of-the-art knowledge, comparable to a proven specialized terminology. The conceptual level, on the other hand, represents knowledge that reflects the specific situation in a particular company. However, the conceptual level also allows the re-use of existing knowledge from external sources. This could be accomplished by the provision of a library of reference models for certain domains.

A multi-perspective KMS not only provides knowledge on different levels of abstractions and for different tasks, but allows navigation through an enterprise on different paths. Thereby, a user has the chance to enrich a preferred perspective with related ones. Also, it serves as a medium for focused discourses. Starting with the highest level, the different participants of a discourse could literally point to the subject they are interested in. On a more detailed level, the KMS allows the interconnection of concepts or instances that are part of different views. Notice that such an approach is different from those organizational memory systems that are implemented as hypermedia systems. A KMS includes more semantics, and ensures that relevant concepts are structured according to common standards (ensured by modelling languages and corresponding editors). Therefore it allows for more powerful machine operations, for instance, 'show all types of business processes', 'show the current corporate strategy' and 'calculate the bottlenecks within a particular business process type'. A user who has selected a particular view may either move to a higher level that provides meta-descriptions of the actual level or 'drill down' to a lower level. Figure 6.2 illustrates the different levels of abstraction provided by a KMS from a user's perspective.

Figure 6.2 **Levels of abstraction within a particular view, and their relationship to corresponding aspects of an IS**

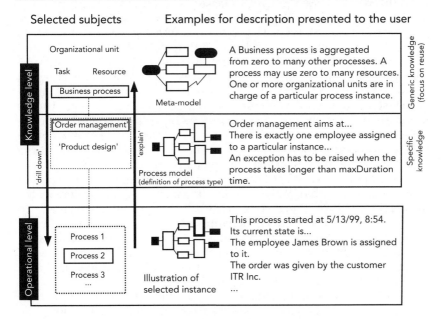

While a KMS clearly stresses these 'knowledge' levels, it is important to integrate it with the operational levels stressed by traditional IS. From the user's point of view, there is an obvious semantic relationship between the conceptual and the operational levels. The operational level manages instances of the concepts defined on the conceptual level. To give an example, on the conceptual level, one would describe the business process type 'order management' (see figure 6.2). Within a traditional IS, the user would either explicitly or implicitly deal with a particular process instance. In addition to that, creating and initializing instances could be done in order to provide a more illustrative representation or to prepare for simulation.

To construct a system that reflects the outlined idea, we suggest an architecture for KMS that is comprised of three layers that correspond directly to the described knowledge levels. Figure 6.1 gives an overview of the architecture that will be described in more detail later.

The meta-level layer
This layer, which we could also call the terminology or language layer, consists of special-purpose modelling editors. These editors provide a set of modelling languages, like a process-modelling language, a strategy-modelling language or an information-modelling language. Object models and additional constraints define the languages. The object model rendered in figure 6.3 illustrates an excerpt of this layer. It is specified in unified modelling language (UML). Classes of the object model represent the concepts of the modelling languages. For instance, the key concepts for modelling business processes are represented by the classes 'ProcessType', 'ProcessUse', 'ContextOfProcessUse', 'InputSpec', 'OutputSpec' and 'Event'. ProcessType is an abstract class that is specialized into two concrete classes: 'ComplexProcessType' and 'BasicProcessType' – with ComplexProcessType being composed of 'n' ('number of') ProcessType. The class ProcessUse serves to differentiate between many occurrences of the same ProcessType within an instance of ComplexProcessType. An instance of ComplexProcessType may be composed of many instances of ProcessUse, each of which is assigned exactly one instance of ProcessType. In case the decomposition hierarchy of an instance of ComplexProcessType contains more than one occurrence of a particular instance of ComplexProcessType, there is need to differentiate between the associated instance of ProcessUse. For example, a business process is composed of 'n' instances of the ProcessType 'Write User Documentation' which is aggregated from – among other things – instances of the ProcessType 'Create Figures'. The different occurrences of 'Create Figures' within 'Write User Documentation' can be differentiated by the instance of ProcessUse with which they are associated. To differentiate between identical instances of ProcessUse within different occurrences of 'Write User Documentation', each instance of ProcessUse would be assigned to exactly one instance of ContextOfProcessUse. An instance of ProcessType may require an instance of InputSpec, and may produce one or more instances of OutputSpec.

Business processes refer to an organization structure that can be specified by using classes such as 'OrganizationalUnit' and 'Position'. The conceptual description of IS requires adequate concepts to structure the information that is the subject of these systems. To support this task, the meta-level layer contains an editor for designing object models. It is based on concepts like 'Class', 'Service' and 'Attribute'. Other classes

Figure 6.3 Excerpt from the object model on the meta-level, with focus on the organizational perspective

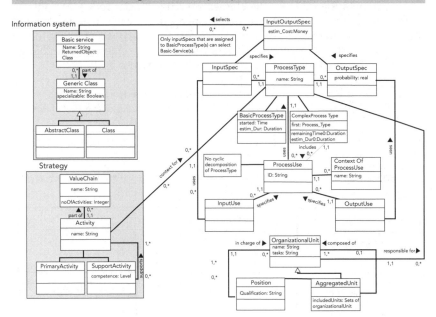

('ValueChain', 'Activity', and so on) on this level serve to model corporate strategies. They reconstruct, in part, the concepts offered by Porter's value-chain model (see Porter and Millar, 1985). The object model in figure 6.3 shows how the different languages are integrated: by connecting the corresponding object models through common classes. If there is need for more specialized languages, the corresponding language descriptions can be added via object models that are then integrated with the existing ones.

While every user of a KMS can access the meta-level, users should not modify it. The languages and terminologies provided by the meta-level layer are complex and valuable generic knowledge. It is not trivial to describe certain aspects of a company with concepts that support analysis and evaluation.

Conceptual level layer

This layer serves to create, edit and store domain-specific knowledge, which is captured in conceptual models. For this purpose, objects are instantiated from the classes that constitute the meta-level layer. The editors have to ensure that the models are compliant with the language definitions on the meta-level. While the conceptual models are rendered with specialized graphical notations, their semantics are defined within the objects that are instantiated from the meta-level classes. Note that these instances (like an instance of BasicProcessType) still describe types, not concrete instances. From a software engineering point of view, this is an important restriction, since it is not possible to derive concrete instances simply through instantiation. Usually, an instance cannot be instantiated from another instance. Figure 6.4 shows some of the instances needed to represent the business-process type rendered below. They are instantiated from the classes specified in figure 6.3. In contrast to the meta-level, the content of the conceptual level is usually created and manipulated by the users of a KMS. For this purpose, one would use the various editors to create objects of particular classes, and change their state by applying the functions provided by the editor.

Figure 6.4   Visualization of a process specification within an editor (below) and partial description of corresponding instances

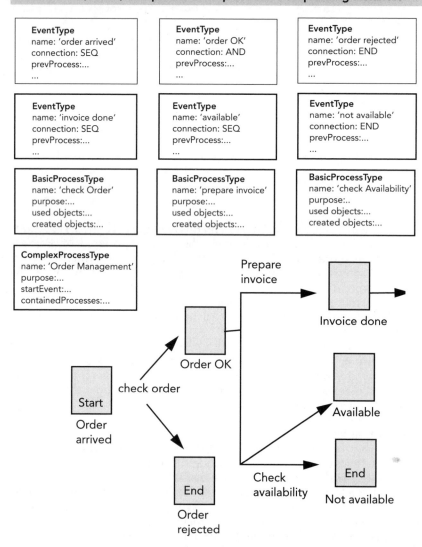

Re-use of knowledge on this level can be enhanced with a library of reference models (for business processes, information, corporate strategies and so on). For knowledge to be an organizational – and not only an individual – asset, it has to be represented in a structure that is well known throughout the company. Such a structure should not only include syntactic rules but also agreements on semantics. For instance, it is not satisfactory simply to define a standard graphic markup language (SGML) document type for a sales report. In addition, the meaning of the tags should be defined. In the best – but usually most expensive, if feasible at all – case, the meaning of concepts used to render knowledge is completely formalized. The KMS suggested in this report provides the user with formal concepts that they can use to describe certain perspectives on the enterprise. Nevertheless, it still allows use of natural language annotations where (semi-)formal descriptions would be feasible.

The interface-level layer

Usually, object-oriented languages distinguish between classes and objects. However, these two levels are not enough for our purpose. If a concept on the meta-level (like ComplexProcessType) is specified as a class, it can be instantiated into a particular object with the name 'order management'. However, it is not possible to create an instance from an instance, as would be necessary in order to represent a particular process. Within a traditional IS, no matter whether it includes an explicit or implicit notion of a business process, the user deals with a particular instance that starts at a specific time and has a specific state. Since the concepts of the interface-level layer cannot be created from the conceptual level through instantiation, we suggest generating representations that are appropriate to serve as interfaces with traditional IS. We also assume that such an IS is specified in an object-oriented way. Therefore, the interface level would consist of object models or class definitions from which particular IS could be instantiated. In addition to static object models, one would also need functional and dynamic descriptions – such as message flow diagrams, state charts or specific languages to describe workflows.

With respect to the protection of investment, it is a good idea to use standardized representations, like the UML (Booch, Jacobson and Rumbaugh, 1998), the object definition language (ODL) (Cattell, Barry and Bartels, 1997) for object-oriented database management systems, or the work process definition language (WPDL) as part of the Workflow Management Coalition (WfMC) standard (WfMC, 1996) for the specification of workflows. Figure 6.5 illustrates how concepts appropriate for the instance-level layer can be generated from corresponding concepts on the conceptual-level layer. Usually, generation is accompanied by the loss of semantics (certain aspects of the source have to be neglected; this is especially the case with the current version of the WPDL) as well as by adding further semantics (like the specification of user interfaces or information required by a compiler). Unfortunately, that compromises the promises of integration. It is not possible simply to generate a new version of the interface-level layer whenever the conceptual-level layer has changed. Therefore, generation recommends the application of restrictive policies for code or model management. In order to overcome this problem, it is necessary that the standardized languages used to specify schemata for IS provide richer semantic concepts.

Figure 6.5   Interfacing KMS and IS by generating (standardized) schema level representations for IS

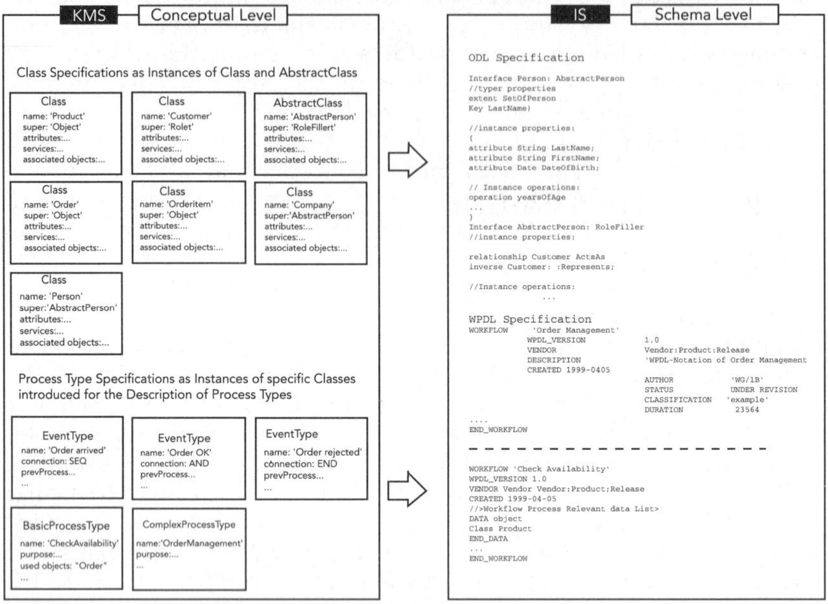

Usually, an IS will have been developed before a KMS. In this case, generating schema information is insufficient. In addition to that, the (hopefully) existing schema information of the IS has to be mapped to the generated schema (which will usually imply a further loss of semantics).

Knowledge management as a permanent process

While the focus of this chapter is on the design of KMS, one can hardly neglect questions concerning the use and evaluation of knowledge within these systems. In contrast to traditional enterprise models, the content of a KMS should be regarded as a permanent asset that is not created for a particular purpose (like the development of an IS). This means thinking about the organization of knowledge maintenance and evaluation. There are a number of criteria that have to be taken into account. It is not surprising that they resemble the evaluation and maintenance of software, because maintaining KMS means focusing on concepts.

Quality

Knowledge that is stored in a KMS should fulfil certain standards in quality terms. Of course, it should not be inaccurate. Often, however, the line between correct and incorrect is hard to draw. Knowledge reflects assumptions about actual or possible domains. These assumptions may be more or less adequate or even plain wrong. Applying such a sceptical view suggests that users of such a system should regard the concepts/ statements it represents as revisable – instead of taking them for granted as it is common practice with traditional IS.

Topicality
In order to be valid, knowledge has to be up-to-date. This requires the monitoring of relevant aspects of a company and its surroundings all the time. Whenever relevant changes are detected, they should be mapped to the system. Although this is a challenging task, we assume that changes in the domain of a KMS will happen less frequently than in traditional IS, since the focus is on concepts rather than on instances.

Internationality
With the globalization of markets and corporations, more and more users of a particular KMS will have different national and cultural backgrounds. In order to fulfil the requirement that a KMS should provide every user with comprehensive presentations of knowledge, it may be necessary to offer multi-lingual representations.

Maintenance
A part of the knowledge that resides in a KMS will become obsolete over time. In order to avoid confusion, it has to be removed. Unfortunately, it is not easy to establish a useful 'garbage collection'. Firstly, it will not always be clear when knowledge is sufficiently obsolete to be removed. Secondly, it can be appropriate in some cases not to remove knowledge but to create an outdated version of it – which requires the support of version management by the KMS. Besides removing or versioning knowledge, maintenance often requires the refining of existing knowledge as a result of new insights. Again, the problems are similar. It will not always be evident when and how existing knowledge has to be refined.

Any of the tasks associated with the criteria listed above imply that decisions have to be made. From an organizational point of view, this requires the clarification of a number of questions:

- Who is responsible for the detection of relevant maintenance events?
- Who is responsible for making the associated decisions?
- How should the corresponding processes of decision-making be organized?

Taking into account the complexity and extent of knowledge stored in a KMS, the answer to the first question has to be that every user has the responsibility of reporting maintenance events whenever they become aware of them. In order to ensure quality standards, specialists should co-ordinate the actual maintenance of a KMS. These specialists would have responsibilities similar to information managers or database administrators. Due to the fact that the specification and evaluation of knowledge depends on varying individual judgements, it is crucial that the person in charge of knowledge maintenance makes sure that representatives of different perspectives are involved when relevant decisions have to be made.

Conclusions

Based on a pragmatic notion of knowledge – which, nevertheless, is in line with some characteristics of knowledge stressed in philosophy – the concept of a multi-perspective KMS has been proposed. It is characterized by an object-oriented architecture as well as a generic body of knowledge. This is different to other systems that deal with corporate knowledge. Decision support systems are not associated with a specific architecture. Often, publications about decision support systems do not even touch this topic. Expert systems usually feature a specific architecture based on the separation of a declarative knowledge base and an inference engine. In most cases, they are not based on an object-oriented approach. Therefore the integration with an existing IS is often hard to accomplish. As distinct from decision support systems and expert systems, a multi-perspective KMS is not only directed at certain groups of users, like executives, but at a wide range of people with different skills and different needs for supporting knowledge.

In the long run, it is desirable to regard a KMS as an integral part of a corporate IS. Such integration promises a number of advantages. New users of an IS as well as new employees in general can move to the 'knowledge level' to get a deeper understanding of the corporation. Since a KMS offers different perspectives on an enterprise, inter-related through common concepts, it provides a medium for the fostering of discourses between people with different perspectives. In general, this helps to promote processes of organizational learning – in the sense that people are supported to understand positions of others with different professional backgrounds. In particular, a KMS can also contribute to overcoming the common barrier between businesspeople and IT professionals that Keen regards as 'the one factor that can block the effective use of computers and communications' (Keen, 1991).

References

Bar-Hillel, Y. (1964) *Language and Information: Selected Essays on their Theory and Application*, Addison-Wesley.

Berger, P.L. and T. Luckmann (1967) *The Social Construction of Reality: A Treatise in the Sociology of Knowledge*, Doubleday.

Booch, G., I. Jacobson and J. Rumbaugh (1998) *The Unified Modelling Language User Guide*, Addison-Wesley.

Cattell, R., D.K. Barry and D. Bartels (1997) *The Object Database Standard: ODMG 2.0*, Morgan Kaufmann.

Easterby-Smith, M. (1997) 'Disciplines of organizational learning: contributions and critiques', *Human Relations*, 50 (9), 1085–1114.

Euzenat, J. (1996) 'Corporate memory through co-operative creation of knowledge bases and hyperdocuments', in *Proceedings 10th Banff Workshop on Knowledge Acquisition for Knowledge-Based Systems*, SDRG Publications, 1–18.

Frank, U. (1997) 'Enriching object-oriented methods with domain specific knowledge: outline of a method for enterprise modelling', *Arbeitsberichte des Instituts für Wirtschaftsinformatik*, No. 4, University of Koblenz.

Frank, U. (1998) 'The MEMO object modelling language (MEMO-OML)', *Arbeitsberichte des Instituts für Wirtschaftsinformatik*, No. 10, University of Koblenz.

Gruber, T. (1993) 'Toward Principles for the Design of Ontologies used for Knowledge Sharing', Research Report KSL–93–04, Stanford University, Stanford, KY.

Habermas, J. (1985) *The Theory of Communicative Action Volume 1: Reason and the Rationalization of Society*, Beacon Press.

Keen, P.W. (1991) *Shaping the Future. Business Design through Information Technology*, Harvard Business School Press.

Lakatos, I. and A.E. Musgrave (1970) *Criticism and the Growth of Knowledge*, Cambridge University Press.

Nicolini, D. and M.B. Meznar (1995) 'The social construction of organizational learning: conceptual and practical issues in the field', *Human Relations*, 48 (7), 727–746.

Nonaka, I. and N. Konno (1998) 'The concept of "ba": building a foundation for knowledge creation', *California Management Review*, 40 (3), 40–54.

Popper, K.R. (1962) *Conjectures and Refutations: The Growth of Scientific Knowledge*, Basic Books.

Porter, M.E. and V.E. Millar (1985) 'How information gives you competitive advantage', *Harvard Business Review*, 63 (4), 149–160.

Shannon, C.E. and Weaver, W. (1962) *The Mathematical Theory of Communication*, University of Illinois Press.

Sneed, J.D. (1979) *The Logical Structure of Mathematical Physics*, Kluwer Academic Publishers.

Tsang, E.W. (1997) 'Organizational learning and the learning organization: a dichotomy between descriptive and prescriptive research', *Human Relations*, 50 (9), 73–90.

WfMC (1996) 'Interface 1: Process Definition Interchange', WfMC TC-1016, Version 1.0 Beta.

7 Managing knowledge in decentralized heterogeneous corporations

Ulrike Baumoel, Reinhard Jung and Robert Winter

Introduction

One of the major current business trends is the gaining of market power through merger and acquisition, and through the sale of those business units considered inefficient, or which no longer represent core competencies. The result of these restructuring activities is large, often multinational companies with many decentralized business units. The benefits are numerous, but there are some challenges that can lead to decisive inefficiencies if not properly addressed. A major problem is the integration as well as the separation of reporting systems, executive information systems, and – from an organizational point of view – decision processes. Due to time restrictions and business dynamics, it is neither efficient nor possible completely to integrate systems and processes of acquired business units. Therefore, a standardized IS architecture should be designed which enables decentralized units to make decisions based on decentralized as well as centralized information. Furthermore, such an architecture simplifies the separation of a business unit from the corporate body.

Once the problem of the IS architecture is understood and tackled, there is a new issue to be faced: the KM of the entire corporate body. Newly acquired business units must have access to corporate knowledge as well as being able to provide knowledge as soon as possible. In contrast to this, it is vital to keep valuable knowledge from those business units that are to be sold off. The emphasis, however, is in both cases on the word 'valuable'. In addition to a basic KM concept that supports the sharing and retention of knowledge in decentralized heterogeneous corporations, a framework of criteria for evaluating and selecting 'relevant' knowledge for each management level of the corporate network needs to be developed.

The managerial foundations of organizational decentralization and its consequences for information and knowledge supply are analyzed in the following section. In recent years, data warehousing emerged as a promising approach in the overcoming of many information supply problems. In the third section, the data-warehousing process is discussed from a managerial perspective. However, elaborate (and expensive) information modelling is needed to develop an appropriate data warehouse solution for a decentralized organization. For operational systems (e.g. enterprise resource planning systems), industry reference models support information and process-modelling tasks. Therefore, the role of reference models for informational and knowledge processes is discussed in the fourth section.

Based on the discussions in the second and fourth sections, the 'management middleware' approach to integrated management information and knowledge flows is conceptualized in the fifth section. A bi-directional variant of a data warehouse based on a reference schema of managerial information and knowledge could serve as an information pool that supports not only control and aggregation, but also planning and budgeting in a decentralized, homogeneous company. Of course, the management middleware concept is only outlined at this research stage. A summary of open research questions concludes the chapter.

Management holdings

Many monolithic large companies have recently been restructured according to the organizational principle of a 'management holding', or are currently under restructuring. Prominent examples in the German-speaking countries are DaimlerChrysler, Mannesmann, SAir Group (formerly Swissair), Novartis (formerly Sandoz and Ciba Geigy), Lufthansa, and in a 'pure', or perhaps radical, form, Hoechst. Once a conglomerate of many different companies under one roof, now one company, the management holding, is visible with no obvious connection whatsoever to its daughter companies. The business model of a management holding differs significantly from those of companies led by an operational management. The primary goal of a management holding is to meet the overall profitability and efficiency targets for the company. The major tasks of a management holding, therefore, are decisions regarding buying and selling business units and controlling the overall efficiency of the company. In contrast to the tasks of an operational holding, a management holding is concerned with strategic decisions rather than operational ones (Anthony, 1965).

Due to increasing globalization and a strong tendency to merge national companies into multinationals, the resulting entities tend to be geographically widely distributed. As a consequence, communication can only be efficient when it is done via networks and mostly electronically. Within a network of partnering companies, we expect most traditional businesses to emerge into either:

- the role of providers of (exclusive or shared) services/products
- the role of service/product integrators.

Service providers pursue economies of scale by 'producing' for a large number of service integrators, thereby utilizing some core competency or key technology. Service integrators create specific value-added solutions for small segments of end-consumers, maintain brands, and maintain customer relationships.

To exploit networking benefits, service integrators and service providers must be able to communicate and (if applicable) distribute services using a common infrastructure. Only the lower, more technical layers of such a 'business bus' – including transmission control protocol/Internet protocol (TCP/IP) networks, hypertext transfer protocol (HTTP) and extensible markup language (XML) – are available today. Research and standardization is still needed to specify the upper, business-oriented layers of the business bus (e.g. service-level agreements or product catalogues).

The business architecture of the information age (see figure 7.1) allows service providers and service integrators to collaborate using the business bus. If particular services or products are provided exclusively for one single 'customer' (i.e. service integrator), it may be useful to bypass the business bus and create individual communication or co-ordination standards. For end consumers, it is of course possible to integrate products or services individually by direct access to the business bus.

Figure 7.1   **Business architecture of the information age**

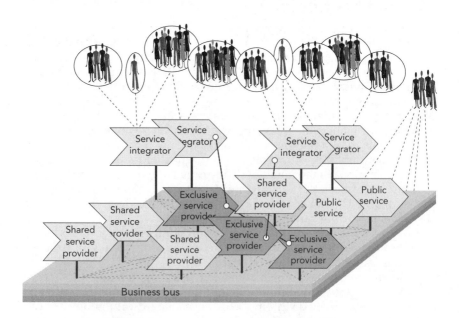

Such network-based business architectures of the information age are beginning to emerge in the financial services sector. For example, Quicken's 'insuremarket' (http://www.insuremarket.com) offers financial advice and insurance products from various companies. The website's structure is modelled after life events and consumer information needs instead of traditional insurance product lines.

However, one of the main problems of managing and controlling a heterogeneous company organized as described above is to create a flexible though standardized controlling system. When we look at the reporting system of such a company, it becomes obvious that a large number of different reports and performance indicators are created for the individual business units, which are useful for the management of these decentralized units, but are not suitable for managing the entire holding.

By various acquisitions and sell-offs, Mannesmann has emerged from being a leading producer of certain steel products to become a diversified company with many promising component businesses (e.g. telecommunications). Although its business unit 'engineering' could be controlled by the performance indicator 'order volume' (and others), this indicator is totally inappropriate for other business units or for the entire holding structure that comprises telecommunications, automotive and steel-tube businesses. A performance indicator that can be used for managing such a heterogeneous entity must allow for a high degree of generalization (e.g. capital employed or return on investment [ROI]). As a consequence, we need not only a very flexible reporting system on the level of the management holding, but also a range of highly standardized performance indicators that allow management to exercise control over the entire holding structure. Moreover, we have to define concisely what management information and performance indicators mean. Management information can either be detailed, non-aggregate data, aggregate data or a qualitative statement, which all serve as a basis for the decision-making process. Performance indicators constitute a subset of management information with some specific characteristics: they are always aggregate and their components can either be aggregate or non-aggregate. This differentiation is important because information is lost during the aggregation process. An IS, therefore, has to support the disaggregation of such information in order to enable analysis (e.g. of deviations), but also in order to enable the communication of performance indicator calculations from the top management level to lower organizational units (Reichmann, 1997).

According to the tasks mentioned above, the basic organization of the reporting system needs to be as follows:

- At top management (holding) level, we have the highest degree of generalization, and thus also need the highest level of standardization. This means that the performance indicators used on this level must be clearly and concisely defined for all the management levels below. A typical performance indicator on this level is, for example, profit. In order to be able to calculate corporate profit, all individual profits of business units must be calculated consistently. Otherwise, the aggregation of the individual figures would result in a meaningless value derived from heterogeneous sources (e.g. gross and net profits).

- At the business-unit management level, various performance indicators are needed in addition to the performance indicators created for the management holding. The performance indicators have to meet less strict requirements with regard to generalization and standardization. Here, we only need standards for the lower management levels, for the reasons mentioned above.
- At the lowest management level, the operational management, we do not need standards for company-wide management. The only standard needed is that appropriate to the individual operational unit itself.

However, it must be observed that all the lower management levels nevertheless have to obey the standardization rules of the management holding. Thus, an IS is needed that supports the information flow between the different and often geographically distributed levels (business units), provides a meta-model of performance indicator definitions, and enables an integration of the performance indicators from different levels into aggregate performance indicators.

The problems of KM in a decentralized heterogeneous corporation are mostly very similar to those of information management. First of all, we have to identify the relevant knowledge, and then we have to design a standardized architecture that combines a KM concept regarding aspects of both content and technology. Moreover, it must be integrated into the management middleware supporting the flow of managerial information. However, there are two major differences between KM and information management:

- There is no role profile whatsoever of a 'knowledge integrator'.
- Sharing knowledge is not mandatory in a corporation, whereas reporting is.

This leads to the questions, firstly, of how such a role must be defined, and secondly, of which incentives must be established to drive knowledge sharing. In addition to this, the role of a well established communication culture becomes even more important, because successfully and efficiently sharing knowledge absolutely depends on the way communication is handled throughout the corporation.

Today we observe the failure of many KM projects and although the reasons may be many, there are three main things that failed projects have in common. First, there is often an existing cultural communication barrier, arising from the fear of losing proprietary knowledge, and thus losing influence and status. Secondly, an organizational concept of creating, gathering, evaluating and sharing knowledge that corresponds to the requirements of the corporation is missing. And, last but not least, there is often insufficient communication of the benefits of KM and a lack of an attractive system of incentives.

The data-warehousing process

A lot of publications deal with data warehousing from a rather technical point of view (e.g. Bontempo and Zagelow, 1998). We consider data warehousing as an infinite process that aims at an efficient and effective information supply. Hence, in this chapter we take the business perspective in order to describe the characteristics and limitations of data warehousing.

Characteristics of data warehousing

In today's large companies, the operational IT environment is usually the result of one or more decades of changing development paradigms and a long line of technological innovations. Therefore, the IT environment is in most cases very heterogeneous. As far as data or information supply is concerned, we face a variety of proprietary data sources, ranging from flat files and hierarchical databases to relational or even object-oriented databases; some companies already have created 'legacy' data warehouses or data marts. On one hand, these heterogeneous data sources contain transactional data from daily operations, i.e. they are mission-critical. On the other hand, however, they are not appropriate to support management decision processes because they do not provide historical data, are implemented by unsuitable means (e.g. sequential files, highly normalized tables or detailed data) and, most importantly, lack data integration.

From a management perspective, two main reasons for the significance of data warehousing can be identified:

- Today's markets require immediate response to new trends as regards management and control. Hence, the time needed to provide management with actual, aggregate data and information becomes crucial if not mission-critical. Manual information supply by a hierarchy of specialized personnel is far too slow to meet this requirement.
- People responsible for the information supply spend huge amounts of time gathering detailed data from various sources for reports and decision-support. In large and decentralized companies these processes comprise a lot of identical steps, often gathering the same data. As a consequence, provided the semantics of the data elements are unambiguously defined, data integration into a single database (core data warehouse) leads to a more efficient information supply.

Figure 7.2 illustrates a data warehouse architecture that represents an abstract view on the various architectures of our research partners' data warehouses (see acknowledgements). Other authors (e.g. Bontempo and Zagelow, 1998; Kimball *et al.*, 1998) present quite similar architectures. The basis for data warehouse architecture is the operational IT environment and, especially, its data sources. The next layer deals with the 'ETL' processes – the extraction, transformation and loading of detailed data into the core data warehouse. In contrast to transactional databases, the core data warehouse comprises both actual and historical data in order to support all kinds of analysis. Since the data within this central component of the architecture is detailed and not aggregate, it is necessary to define specific views on the core data warehouse for the business units. If the views are materialized, i.e. if controlled redundancy is introduced, we call the set of views for one business unit a data mart. These views usually provide aggregate data and denormalized, or even multidimensional, data structures. The top layer of the architecture, called business intelligence, comprises end-user tools for *ad hoc* queries, on-line analytical processing (OLAP) and data mining. In order to enable the sharing of knowledge, there has to be a feedback from the business intelligence layer to the core data warehouse layer. We consider a central meta-data repository the most important component of the architecture. In particular, when knowledge is to be stored and deployed, it is crucial to describe every dataflow and data item within the architecture through meta-data.

Figure 7.2   **The data warehouse architecture**

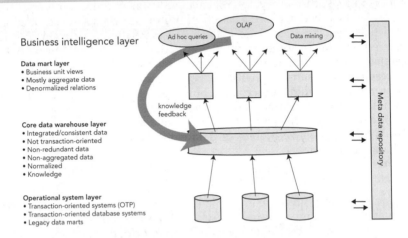

As regards the characteristics of the core data warehouse, it has to be mentioned that other approaches exist. Some authors favour:

- a core data warehouse that already contains aggregate data
- independent data marts (Gardner, 1998) (i.e. data integration takes place in independent, small-scale data warehouses).

We did not integrate these approaches into our architecture for the following reasons. Most of our partner companies are not able to anticipate all future requirements as regards the granularity of the data. Therefore, it is advisable to preserve the degrees of freedom for future data-mart projects by populating the core data warehouse with detailed data only (Kelly, 1997). Moreover, aggregate data on the core data warehouse level imposes restrictions on the drill-down depth of business-intelligence tools. The idea of independent data marts is also critical because independent data marts cannot efficiently serve top management information requirements, due to their lack of data integration, and their use may lead to complex integration problems in the long run (Chauduri and Dayal, 1997).

Limitations and potentials of data warehousing

The idea of an integrated data supply for management support is not new. Management information systems or executive information systems have been discussed extensively for decades. However, some good concepts could not be implemented until powerful database management systems and business-intelligence tools became available. Today, tools are available for every layer of the architecture, and for data transformations between the layers. Only where meta-data is concerned is there still a lot of technological work to be done. Almost every component of the data warehouse architecture 'produces' meta-data, as well as needing other components' meta-data (see figure 7.2). The challenge is to integrate not only data, but also meta-data in order to support all user groups of the data warehouse (developers, users, administrators and so on).

From our point of view, the most challenging tasks in the area of data warehousing are methodological ones. One of those tasks is the data integration as regards the conceptual schema, that is, the design of the core data warehouse. The data elements as they are used in the operational IT environment represent the business units' views on data. As soon as more than one business unit takes part in a discussion about 'their' definition of performance indicators or ratios (sometimes they even refuse to support the IT department), such as, for example, contribution to margins and revenues, the real challenge becomes obvious. The problem becomes more difficult if different divisions or daughter companies from completely different industries are involved. Data integration means the integration of similar data elements from different sources – and, therefore, definitions of different business units – into a common definition either:

- by agreeing on a suitable definition and modifying the affected operational systems
- by preserving individual definitions and integrating the data elements on a more abstract level.

It is obvious that the first alternative will face serious resistance because the operational systems are almost always mission-critical and cannot easily be modified. The second alternative means consensus on an abstract level, which is much easier to accomplish.

The idealistic and primary function of a data warehouse is to provide top management with appropriate information. This goal cannot be achieved in a short-term project. Instead of building an enterprise-wide data warehouse in a big-bang approach, most companies build up their warehouse over a longer period of time by implementing smaller increments, i.e. providing information supply to business units. Thus, it is much easier to accomplish project budget approval through, for example, short-term cost savings. However, this strategy leads to a warehouse that grows bottom-up. In order to be able to meet top-management requirements further on in the development process it is necessary to ensure a goal-driven design, i.e. a solution that is a combination of top-down and bottom-up.

Reference models

The basic idea of a reference model is to provide a generalized schema plus adaptation rules, so that specialized schemas can be derived consistently, without violating integrity constraints. Hence, the adaptation of reference models can be compared to configuration processes, thereby differing significantly from other information modelling paradigms, like component-based modelling (re-use of partial detailed schemas) or object oriented modelling (inheritance of abstract schema components).

In IS development, the utilization of reference models has been initially discussed for the data view of integrated systems (see Scheer and Hars, 1992). Subsequently, reference schemas proposed by software vendors are not only for data structures (e.g. SAP AG, 1994), but also for business processes (e.g. Curran, Keller and Ladd, 1997; van Es and Post, 1996). Recently, researchers have proposed reference models for electronic markets (see Lindemann and Schmid, 1998).

Various other approaches also claim to be based on reference models: for example, the Workflow Management Coalition created a workflow reference model (Workflow Management Coalition, 1996) and the International Standards Organization (ISO) defined the well-known Open Systems Interconnect (OSI) reference model (ISO 1983). Notwithstanding, while the former is quite abstract, so that adaptation to actual workflow schemas is not an easy task, the latter is more a regulation of protocol and service definitions than a template for actual systems development. If usable for systems developments, reference models should allow for the configuration of 'executable' schemas.

When grouping available reference models by process type, another problem becomes apparent: although reference schemas for transactional business processes – such as order entry, materials management or financials – are widely available, informational processes seem to have evaded this kind of standardization. As a consequence, executive information systems are usually implemented as individual software, while for transactional systems, standardized business packages are utilized whenever available and adaptable to specific needs.

This may be due to the fact that management processes are automatically interpreted as core competencies of any company, making standardization more harmful than helpful. If properly constructed, however, reference models do not restrict systems development to some pre-defined standard. Instead, the model integrates multiple perspectives that provide a framework for individual adaptation, thereby preserving some basic integrity constraints and basing systems development on a common terminological and architectural foundation.

For informational processes, the most important component of reference models is a complete data view, i.e. a data schema that implies all potential aggregations, thereby allowing consistent schema clustering and refinement operations to be applied (Winter, 1996). If only certain, validated aggregation rules have been used to derive aggregate schemas, schema refinements can also be formally validated. Since adaptations cannot validate overall integrity in such an environment, the predominant problem of disaggregation (as discussed in Ritzmann, 1979) is solved. Based on an abstract 'reference' schema and a set of adaptation rules, specialized schemas can be derived without having to guarantee consistency by special disaggregation procedures (Bitran and Hax, 1977).

As a consequence, management middleware should be based on an abstract schema derived from the detailed data view by selected, integrity-preserving aggregation procedures.

Management middleware

The management middleware is an adapted data warehouse architecture designed to enable an easy integration of additional companies into a management holding as regards the supply of management information.

This section describes both the technological and the business view on the management middleware concept. Furthermore, it presents some means that may help to implement the concept with respect to organizational integration.

The technological view

Today's data warehouse architectures are designed as read-only systems, i.e. the direction of the data and information flow is from operational systems to the core data warehouse and onwards to management or analytical systems (upstream). In order to serve as management middleware, the warehouse architecture has to be adapted. It is especially important that both the management holding and the daughter companies are able to push data from their individual data marts into the core data warehouse (downstream). Furthermore, the data warehouse must not only contain historical data but also forecasts and plans. In figure 7.3, an adapted data warehouse architecture serving as management middleware is depicted. The daughter company, for example, uses its actual data in order to calculate the actual ROI and the planned ROIs for subsequent periods and pushes the resulting values into the warehouse, later to be analyzed by the management holding. The management holding then communicates ROI targets for all its daughter companies by writing the values into the warehouse.

Figure 7.3   **A modified data warehouse architecture serving as a management middleware**

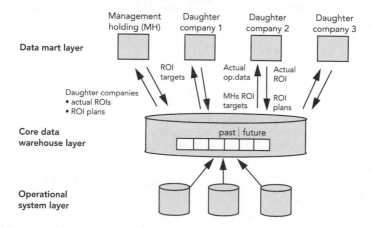

From the technological point of view, it is appropriate to realize Web applications based on an intranet for all front-end tools of management middleware in order to enable a seamless software introduction – especially in newly acquired companies.

The business view

The basic concept of management middleware is only feasible if data integration within the core data warehouse is achieved for management data. Therefore, we advocate the use of a hierarchy of reference models of performance indicators enabling a seamless integration of management information of a certain level into the reporting schema of the next level higher, because management information on each higher level needs to fulfil a higher degree of generalization.

In figure 7.4, a schematic hierarchy of reference models is depicted. These models, once available, enable data integration among heterogeneous companies, either through performance indicator consolidation within the same level or consolidation on the next level higher, i.e. through generalization. As a consequence, upstream dataflow will be possible. In order to facilitate downstream dataflow as well, either disaggregation mechanisms or agreements have to be established.

Figure 7.4   Schematic hierarchy of reference models

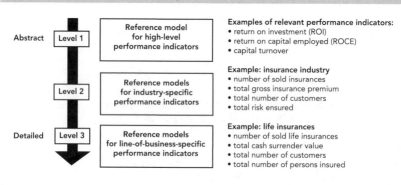

As far as time-series analyses are concerned, changing aggregation structures that usually come along with changing company structures impose some requirements on the way management information is generated and presented:

- Generation: comparability of, for example, area-related total turnover figures requires the application of either the former or the actual structure on the complete time-series.
- Presentation: the front-end tools should be able to indicate that the aggregation structure has been changed in the period of time under consideration, and show which structure was actually applied.

As far as the generation of aggregated figures is concerned, an obvious approach is to deploy related meta-data. Chamoni and Stock (1999) suggest the use of matrices to assign detailed data to aggregated figures. The cells contain periods of time in which the assignment is valid.

The model in figure 7.4 depicts a hierarchy of well-defined ratios. It has to be complemented with a suitable role model that enforces a consistent knowledge flow between the different levels. Within data warehousing, there is the concept of data stewardship; typically, there should be a person responsible for the semantics of every data element, i.e. the data steward should be able to provide a proper definition for each of the respective businesses. Data stewardship becomes even more important if knowledge is involved, because there is much more room for interpretation (and misinterpretation). At least one person should be named a data steward for each level of the hierarchy of reference models.

The systematic approach to the integration of KM into the information architecture, however, requires a model, which allows the assignment of relevant knowledge to each managerial and organizational level. Moreover, it ought to reflect the hierarchical structure of the reference model depicted in figure 7.4. The model we have chosen for integrating knowledge into the information management of a corporation is the business engineering map (BE-Map). Business engineering is based on the idea that innovations, especially IT innovations, have a decisive impact on business models and the partly radical change of business models. The BE-Map, which consists of four levels, as shown in figure 7.5, reflects this idea: IT innovations have an impact on decisions regarding the strategy and/or business model. The change of the business model requires engineering or re-engineering of processes, which leads to a demand for new or changed IS that support the processes. This chain of activity is accompanied by the cultural and political environment of the corporation, which has a major effect on the success of each step (Winter, 1999).

Figure 7.5   Business engineering map

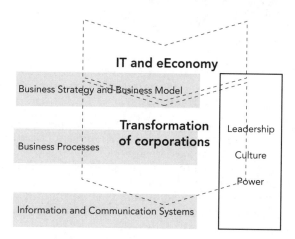

To integrate knowledge into this basic concept, we have to assign the relevant knowledge to each level (e.g. on the first level of strategy, the knowledge about adaptation processes as regards trends and changes in customer behaviour), thus creating a knowledge map (see Horn, 1989; Huff, 1990). The second, perhaps even more important, step is the analysis and structuring of the flow of knowledge between the different levels, primarily the communication activities or barriers. Only if it is possible to define clearly the knowledge flow and remove existing obstacles can effective and efficient KM be implemented, and moreover 'lived'.

The remaining question is how to depict the relevant knowledge objects. One way to do this is via knowledge scorecards (Eppler, 1999), which are based on concept of the balanced scorecard (Kaplan and Norton, 1996). Using knowledge scorecards, we can not only define relevant knowledge objects for each level of the BE-Map, but also a scorecard that integrates each level, including the knowledge flow, and thus allows an overview of KM and communication throughout the entire corporation. In figure 7.6, the exemplary integration of knowledge scorecards into the BE-Map is depicted.

Figure 7.6   **Exemplary integration of knowledge scorecards into the BE-Map**

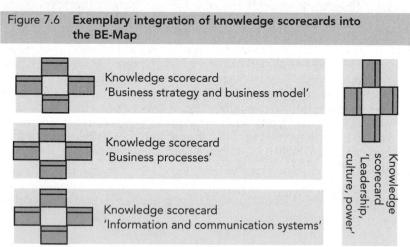

Knowledge scorecard
'Business strategy and business model'

Knowledge scorecard
'Business processes'

Knowledge scorecard
'Information and communication systems'

Knowledge scorecard 'Leadership, culture, power'

In the following, we exemplarily define a knowledge scorecard for the process level. This process-knowledge scorecard consists of the following knowledge objects and their indicators:

- Process competency: indicators include the number of process owners (ideally one), experiences with process design and the qualification of process owner(s) and process designers.
- Process performance: indicators include lead-time, quality of results and interfaces to other processes.
- Process development and adaptability: indicators include process-design time, implementation time and adaptation time (i.e. the 'visible' effect on the organization).
- Process documentation: indicators include completeness/granularity of documentation, actuality and availability (i.e. permanent availability via intranet versus paper documentation stored in an archive, which can be a sign of a communication barrier).

However, it should be observed that such knowledge scorecards must be defined according to the individual requirements of the corporation. This is of course also true for the integrated knowledge scorecard mentioned above. In the example in figure 7.7, a scorecard is defined for each level of the BE-Map. Additionally, a scorecard for the knowledge flow is defined that can be used for the analysis and management of the knowledge flow between each level.

Figure 7.7   Example of an integrated knowledge scorecard

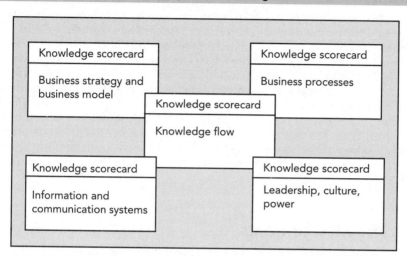

The above requires reflection upon the hierarchies of the reference models; thus defining knowledge scorecards for each organizational level can fulfill the standardization requirements. An example would be top-level knowledge scorecards for the management holding.

Organizational integration

Each merger or acquisition evokes resistance to a certain degree from employees. As a consequence, this resistance affects the integration process of the management systems as well as the IS. This means, for example, that people fear the loss of control over certain data and knowledge, and therefore their influence on the decision process. Thus, three steps are vital:

- The communication of the benefits of an integrated information architecture by 'road shows' and a thorough communication policy.
- The establishment of an incentive system to achieve both the pushing of data and knowledge into the system and the pulling of data and knowledge from the system.
- The definition of the role of 'knowledge integrator', dedicated to the integration of knowledge and responsible for the entire knowledge process of creating, gathering, evaluating and finally distributing relevant knowledge. Only if somebody or a team is clearly responsible for this can the process be driven, and thus successful. The role requires a very good communicator and someone highly qualified in the relevant field of knowledge. It can be compared to the role of a 'controller' in German-speaking Europe, who is responsible for the process of information supply and the integration of information according to specific managerial questions (see Reichmann, 1997).

Conclusion

The data-warehouse concept seems to offer some interesting opportunities for the management and control of heterogeneous companies, such as management holdings. The management middleware concept has been explained, and may be a suitable basis for this. In order to realize such a concept, it is necessary to enhance data-warehouse technology, especially as far as downstream dataflow is concerned. Moreover, a comprehensive hierarchy of reference models has to be elaborated for the management of both information and knowledge. Finally, additional research on the concept's impact on the organizational environment seems imperative. A validation of such a concept can only be done by implementing it into a 'real' corporation (which is the next step planned in the authors' ongoing research).

Acknowledgements

The Competence Center 'Data Warehousing Strategy' (CC DWS, details can be found at http://datawarehouse.iwi.unisg.ch) was founded at the University of St Gallen, Switzerland, in January 1999. The CC DWS is a joint, two-year research project of the Institute of Information Management and ten large German and Swiss companies from the insurance, logistics, telecommunications and consulting industries, and the Swiss Department of Defence. A basic version of this chapter appeared as Baumoel, Jung and Winter (2000).

References

Anthony, R.N. (1965) *Planning and Control Systems – a Framework for Analysis*, Harvard University Press.

Baumoel, U., R. Jung and R. Winter (2000) 'Adapting the data warehouse concept for the management of decentralized heterogeneous corporations', *Journal of Data Warehousing*, 5 (1), 35–43.

Bitran, G.R. and A.C. Hax (1977) 'On the design of hierarchical production planning systems', *Decision Sciences*, 8, 28–55.

Bontempo, C. and G. Zagelow (1998) 'The IBM data warehouse architecture', *Communications of the ACM*, 41 (9), 38–48.

Chamoni, P. and S. Stock (1999) 'Temporal structures in data warehousing', in *Proceedings of the First International Conference on Data Warehousing and Knowledge Discovery* (eds M. Mohania and A.M. Tjoa), 353–358.

Chauduri, S. and U. Dayal (1997) 'An overview of data warehousing and OLAP technology', *ACM SIGMOD Record*, 26 (1), 65–74.

Curran, T., G. Keller, and A. Ladd (1997) *SAP R/3 Business Blueprint: Understanding the Business Process Reference Model*, Prentice Hall.

Eppler, M. (1999) *Conceptual Management Tools*, NA Press.

Gardner, S.R. (1998) 'Building the data warehouse', *Communications of the ACM*, 41 (9), 52–60.

Horn, R. (1989) *Mapping Hypertext*, Lexington.

Huff, A. (1990) *Mapping Strategic Thought*, Wiley & Sons.

ISO (1983) 'Open Systems Interconnection – Basic Reference Model', IST7495, ISO.

Kaplan, R.S. and D.P. Norton (1996) *The Balanced Scorecard*, Harvard Business School Press.

Kelly, S. (1997) *Data Warehousing in Action*, Wiley & Sons.

Kimball, R., L. Reeves, M. Ross and W. Thornthwaite (1998) *The Data Warehouse Lifecycle Toolkit: Expert Methods for Designing, Developing and Deploying Data Warehouses*, Wiley & Sons.

Lindemann, M.A. and B. Schmid (1998) 'Elements of a reference model for electronic markets', in *Proceedings of the 31st Hawaii International Conference on Systems Science HICCS'98*, Vol. 4, 193–201.

Reichmann, T. (1997) *Controlling – Concepts of Management Control, Controllership and Ratios*, Springer.

Ritzmann, L.P. (1979) *Disaggregation – Problems in Manufacturing and Service Organizations*, Martinus Nijhoff.

SAP AG (1994) *SAP Information Model*, SAP Press.

Scheer, A.W. and A. Hars (1992) 'Extending data modelling to cover the whole enterprise', *Communications of the ACM*, 35, 320–328.

van Es, R.M. and H.A. Post (1996) *Dynamic Enterprise Modelling*, Kluwer.

Winter, R. (1996) 'Towards an integration of structured techniques for data modelling and function modelling in information systems development', in *Proceedings 4th European Conference on Information Systems*, Aix-en-Provence, 1003–1010.

— (1999) 'HSG Master of Business Engineering programme – qualifying high potentials for IS-enabled change', in *Proceedings of the 7th European Conference on Information Systems*, Copenhagen, 819–826.

Workflow Management Coalition (1996) *Workflow Management Coalition Terminology and Glossary*, TC-1011, WFMC.

8 Web-based knowledge management support for document collections

Mark Ginsburg and Ajit Kambil

Introduction

The primary focus of this chapter is KM support systems. These systems require new design principles because knowledge fundamentally differs from information and data in organizations. Knowledge is the experience and values of members of an organization combined with and shaped by the information contained in various systems and data provided to those members (Davenport and Prusak, 1998; Nonaka, 1994). It is intrinsic to organizational members, and focuses on the information recipient. In contrast, data refers to a set of discrete, objective facts about events recorded in an organization, and information provides members with contextual meaning for the data.

Knowledge can be tacit or explicit (Nonaka, 1994). Tacit knowledge refers to the beliefs and values that are hard to express but inferred from the behaviour of organizational members. Explicit knowledge is easily expressible, for example the formalization of an organizational routine or process through a flow diagram. Organizational and individual knowledge is created through a continuous dialogue between the tacit and explicit knowledge of individuals. Ideas are formed in the minds of individuals, but interaction between individuals typically plays a critical role in developing these ideas. Nonaka (1994) identifies four knowledge transformation processes: socialization (tacit to tacit), internalization (explicit to tacit), externalization (tacit to explicit), and combination (explicit to explicit).

While new knowledge comes from individuals, organizations play a critical role in articulating and amplifying that knowledge (Davenport and Prusak, 1998). This requires organizations to provide a working infrastructure, composed of a set of knowledge management support systems (KMSS), and meaningful policies for knowledge sharing. Such an infrastructure allows users to share information easily, with policies that provide incentives to members to participate in knowledge sharing and refinement activities. The information shared among members should reflect their values and beliefs about the information stored and exchanged to support KM.

As KMSS are embedded within an organizational system, they must also be designed to fit within the cultural values, authority structures and other design features of the organization. Thus, KM consists of both the implementation of IS and organizational systems with incentives, processes and tasks to generate collectively, refine and manage organizational knowledge. As IS increasingly support KM, we define systems supporting KM, KMSS, as a support tool in an overall organizational KMS.

The ideal knowledge network, as conceptualized by Nonaka, assumes efficient search and retrieval of an abstract knowledge base; however, he does not indicate design approaches that bring about this efficiency. This chapter introduces the Annotate system, to address the problem of designing an enhanced retrieval software tool for un- or semi-structured document archives. The Annotate system captures user histories in a typical search session and, through the annotation facility, leverages the collective intelligence of the search community (Ginsburg, 1998b).

The remainder of the chapter reviews critical issues for the design of KMSS, then moves onto KMSS challenges, both technical and organizational. The next section presents the Annotate system, a software tool to explore KM in the domain of Web-based document archive structure and retrieval. This is followed by a technical review of the two fundamental data structures underlying Annotate – the discussion and the session data – and an explanation of the organizational implications of this architecture. The penultimate section discusses an ongoing field experiment of the Annotate system with special emphasis on incentive considerations, and then the lessons learned from this project are covered in the conclusions.

Critical issues in the design of KMSS

Despite the widespread interest surrounding KM in general, there has been surprisingly little work on what might constitute an effective KMSS, and the trade-offs an organization might face in achieving its goals. For example, these systems often have some or all of the following components (O'Leary, 1998):

- Data or knowledge warehouse. As the organization ages and continues to store transaction data in the warehouse, the costs to ensure efficient retrieval from the data store may increase sharply.
- Knowledge search and discovery mechanisms. These are a particularly difficult problem in the case of multimedia: for example streaming audio and video.

- Knowledge representation via an ontology. This presents a significant trade-off. If an organization imposes an ontology on a series of document collections, there is the possibility of vocabulary conflict across business units. As Pejtersen (1998) notes, there is a significant cost associated with forming classification schemes that cover the organization's various work domains. For example, GrapeVine (a vendor product) uses a 'knowledge chart' to list topics of interest to end users. This chart is manually set up by domain experts beforehand, and in addition there is another setup cost: experts are designated for each topic by which documents in legacy databases such as Lotus Notes are sorted, and each is classified according to importance. Users set up profiles on the topic and importance dimension, and thereafter documents are broadcast to matched users via e-mail.
- Knowledge quality control. This is an important organizational goal. Quality covers, for example, the establishment of minimum levels of credibility for entries in a given knowledge base.
- Knowledge visualization techniques. This is a burgeoning field. For example, Phelps and Wilensky (1996) have been researching Java applets (programs written for and running on the Web browser) on the client side to improve the presentation of documents (separating them into text, scanned optical-character-recognition pages and other layers).

These components have to be integrated into a system that provides the required functionality and maps to organizational requirements. The integration is done through the human organization and processes that overlay a KMSS, and works best when the KMSS features fit well with the organization structure, processes and values.

Without effective retrieval, information islands in a federated organization do not diffuse well across intra-organizational boundaries. Hence, knowledge transfer is limited in any structure with sub-optimal retrieval facilities. For example, if an organization relies on Lotus Domino to search its Web document archives, only Notes databases will be consulted: other Web servers (Unix, NT or Macintosh) will not be included.

Challenges of designing a Web-based document KMSS

There are both technical and organizational factors that influence the design of a Web-based document KMSS. In this section, we review the key properties of documents in a Web development environment, and discuss key features of the organizational document-publishing process that we must keep in mind when designing the KMSS.

Documents as Web knowledge bases

In contrast to well-structured fielded databases, unstructured or semi-structured (template-based) documents represent an increasingly important part of organizational knowledge bases. Documents have the potential to be highly expressive, with embedded multimedia objects. While expressive and strong in presentational markup (rendering) they are often poor in semantic markup, making knowledge search and discovery difficult.

Table 8.1 Waterfall model of the intranet document life cycle

Step	Creation	Publication	Organization	Access	Destruction
1	• Document				
(1a)	• (Author meta-data)				
2		• Publication to selected server(s)			
(3)		• (Conversion to semantically richer, poorer or lateral file formats)			
4			• Placement in local server hierarchy		
(4a)			• (Inclusion into existing local ontology)		
(4b)			• (Update existing global ontology)		
(4c)			• (Build or update hyperlinks to and from new document)		
5				• Choose search strategy	
6				• Choose search terms	
7				• Navigate retrieval list	
8				• Read selected documents	
(8a)				• (Add annotation data and meta-data to document)	
(8b)				• (Provide search feedback)	
(9)					• (Stale documents deleted or overwritten)

Note: parenthetical items are optional features; underlined items are features of Annotate.

Table 8.1 shows a convenient 'waterfall model' to discuss enterprise document management (Ginsburg, 1999). Placing the Annotate system inside this framework, the five stages are: creation, publication, organization, access and destruction. Not all of these stages may be actually implemented in a given organization's intranet, most notably the destruction phase – many firms have no mechanism that systematically expires out-of-date documents. To discuss each of these stages in turn:

- Authors *create* a document locally and may, as stated previously, follow a template and create a well-structured document or create an *ad hoc*, ill-structured one. Presentational meta-data may be added, for example HTML tags or word-processing formatting tags. Other useful meta-data, such as author, keywords, title and so forth (see the 'Dublin Core' author meta-data standard) may also be added by the author.
- After the document acquires original content and meta-data, it is then *published* to one or more intranet servers. In the publication process, there may be conversion filters to change from one format to another (e.g. changing a Microsoft Word document to HTML, or changing Microsoft Powerpoint slides to graphics information file [GIF] images). The converters may introduce inefficiencies (Caillau, 1998) by increasing the net direct or indirect costs of document publication.
- After a document is published to the target server or servers, it must be integrated into an existing *organization*. First of all, a place in the local server's file system hierarchy must be selected. This selection may be up to the author's discretion, or controlled by publication software (i.e. a mapping between the author's subject area and an *a priori* file-system organization). Once the document is fitted into a certain hierarchical node, hyperlinks to and from the new document must be updated. Furthermore, it may be necessary to update the hub server's structure as well. Since the structure reflects the organization's view of the intranet 'reality' – a representation of reality from the perspective of the structure's creators – it is commonly referred to as an ontology. If an organization imposes an ontology on a series of document collections, there is the possibility of vocabulary conflict across business units.
- Documents that have been published and organized are subsequently eligible for *access*. This step is where the end user typically spends time searching for and then browsing documents.
- The final phase of the document lifecycle is, naturally enough, *destruction*. A failure to purge the archives systematically of stale documents contributes to an overall degradation in document quality. However, it is difficult to determine from a document's content its natural lifespan. Again, annotation facilities are useful here, to flag documents that have been supplanted by others, or which are simply no longer of interest.

The Web facilitates distributed document publishing by virtue of its open HTTP protocol (Baldwin and Clark, 1997). However, professional document work products typically incur a high cost of creation in time and effort. Another problem of documents in a Web environment is inadequate support of the HTTP protocol for shared editing. There is active research into a tighter integration of the Web with groupware systems. For example, Bentley, Horstmann and Trevor's (1997) BSCW system helps users manage projects and perform document workflow, much as Lotus Notes does. In addition, since the inception of the Web there has been interest in helping users to share documents. In a recounting of the origins of the Web, Robert Caillau (1998) relates in an interview that 'The first [CERN Web editor/browser] made no distinction between editing mode and browser mode. We lost all that along the way'. Later, Frivold, Lang and Fong (1994) modified the NCSA Mosaic client to support shared edits. Other early annotation facilities were described by Roscheisen, Mogensen and Winograd (1995); more recently, Salcedo and Decouchant (1997) delineated an architecture that enables workgroups to edit documents collaboratively at the sub-document (paragraph or sentence) level. The Annotate system does not make use of these advanced in-place edit or workflow features; rather, its lightweight annotation facility leaves the core document untouched. In general, though, annotations support Bush's (1945) notion that information seekers should be able to make use of 'associative trails' – the search might include a primary goal, but the searcher might also have a set of sub-ordinate goals that may be satisfied by the retrieval set. If sufficient numbers of users communicate their trails via interface changes in the search session, theoretically both workgroups and the organization in general could benefit. This contrasts with the approach taken in the Amalthaea system (Moukas and Maes, 1998), in which user information discovery and filtering agents are strictly compartmentalized and there is no inter-user co-ordination.

Document 'marketing' on the Web

Document repositories that span multiple intranet Web servers pose a marketing problem. With the advent of low-cost Web publishing, it is quite easy to place a document on a given intranet server. It is quite another matter altogether to let other business units know that a new document repository exists, or that interesting new documents exist on a server that another business unit may not consult very often.

The Web moves the firm to a peer-information model in which clients can easily access servers throughout the intranet. Intranets in federalist organizations (those with semi-autonomous business units) (Ross and Rockart, 1996) face practical difficulties. If each business unit maintains its own intranet server, a given business unit may become used to searching only its own server. One important question is how to increase the scope of the search so that functional overlaps between business units may be exploited. Note that the increased scope means that there is greater information throughput (and consequently greater potential for knowledge gain) in the aggregate.

Pre-coordination ontology versus post-coordination full-text search

Document indexing and search can be implemented through pre-coordination or post-coordination. In pre-coordination, the documents are associated with subject headers by a collection administrator. The subject headers follow a standard order, for example 'Mexico–Economy–Inflation'. Post-coordination is so named because the keywords are combined at search time; there is no subject term taxonomy specified *a priori*.

Pre-coordination implements a centralized ontology, but the effort to set up an ontology and classify documents is manually intensive. As a knowledge base grows, it becomes difficult and expensive to create ontologies and reconcile classifications to suit the interests of many different users. This problem is compounded as the interests of the knowledge or information-seekers increase and diverge. Any KMSS system that implements static ontologies for classification and selection of control vocabularies must face this issue.

If an organization decides to map documents in heterogeneous databases to knowledge structure, as described in the Andersen consulting case (O'Leary, 1998), the maps themselves are susceptible to political processes, often hiding controversial areas and thus limiting the total amount of information available (Davenport and Prusak, 1998).

Organizations usually resort to post-coordination or full-text search and impose no vocabulary control. In standard Web-based full-text search, we encounter problems such as homonymy, where words mean different things in different contexts, lowering precision and synonymy: search engines that lack a good thesaurus will artificially deflate the confidence scores of documents that contain synonyms to the keywords.

Organizational KMSS design challenges

In addition to technical challenges, organizations often lack adequate incentives for knowledge-sharing and management. These difficulties are often exacerbated in emerging federalist organizations, which are dynamic, team-based problem-solving structures with distributed authority. The first decision that business units make is the choice of specific groupware products, such as Notes (Domino) or intranet product suites (Ginsburg and Duliba, 1997); the broader issue is how to organize the documents accessed by the groupware product to facilitate knowledge transfer.

As a result, it is not surprising that most systems in the past have covered limited domains (see O'Leary, 1998). As document publishing is simplified, and intranets link individuals in organizations to rapidly expanding Web document bases, the previous problems in the design and maintenance of KMSS become more pronounced.

Annotate: a Web-based document KMSS

Typical web full-text search (WFTS) engines that provide post-coordination search have deficiencies, which translate into inadequate support for KM. For example, there is no way to share a resource discovery made during the course of an *ad hoc* search session for one's future use, or that of other users. There are also extremely limited data and meta-data clues to assist users as they traverse the system from the front-end (the query layer) to the intermediate layer, which is an array of hyperlinks to the core documents (the retrieval layer), to the bottom, the document layer. In a typical implementation, the user has no knowledge of others' prior searches or results at the query front-end, and has very few clues of what the most interesting documents might be at the retrieval layer.

To address some of these problems, we have developed Annotate, which provides a flexible KMSS to support federated document search and retrieval. Motivation for Annotate also comes from the computer-supported collaborative work (CSCW) field; Annotate is first and foremost a collaborative tool to help groups work together. As such, it stands rooted in the CSCW community. As some authors note, we need to move out of the laboratory when studying technologies that enable collaboration and into the field (Bentley, Horstmann and Trevor, 1997; Bowers, 1995). Thus we evaluate Annotate in a field experiment, realizing that work that appears to promise great gains may run into severe problems in their situations and use (Bowers, 1995).

Increasing the data and meta-data clues at each layer of the search navigation chain will aid search efficiency and the process of knowledge discovery, thereby realizing more of the knowledge potential of document archives, wherever they may be found in the corporate intranet. This is similar to the meta-data focus in recent electronic document management work. For example, in the document management system described by Balasubramanian and Bashian (1998), document meta-data (attributes bestowed by a legacy document management application) are captured and used by the Web search as an attribute-value search alternative mechanism to full-text search.

One of the driving factors behind the Annotate design is to enable Nonaka's KM processes of socialization, internalization, externalization and combination by:

- capturing individual and aggregate document appraisals (a means to aggregate individuals' externalization, or use of metaphor to express others' tacit knowledge)
- using individual appraisals of documents to augment document content (to support readers' internalization on an ongoing basis)
- using individual appraisals of documents to support a recommender system (which improves the efficiency of the search by filtering out unwanted documents, for example those from an untrusted domain)
- using individuals' free-text annotations to support combination or reshaping of information and data from one IS to another
- using the free-text annotations also to weakly support socialization or the transfer of tacit knowledge from one individual to another.

Annotate is predicated on the principle that the users and creators of knowledge best know the information relevant to their KM task, and that they can more effectively filter, discover and signal useful knowledge to their peers than an automatic system.

As annotations accrue in the system, so do the reasons the annotator had for making the note. Both the annotation text and its rationale (meta-data) are logically bound to the core documents, thus increasing the semantic content of the document repositories. Annotate implements a star structure (LaLiberte, 1998):

> for each document, there is only one level of annotations – annotations of annotations are not possible. Stars are simpler for users in some ways because one can read through all unread annotations in a sequence. Since new annotations are always appended to the end of the list, one knows that readers are seeing the same thing, and thus the conversational style of communication is well modelled.

The alternative, a tree structure in which annotations can be made to annotations, diminishes the distinction between the (lengthier) core document and the brief secondary annotation. We wish to make the annotation process simple, and limit the length of the annotation entity, while keeping attention on the core document, that was produced greater social cost. The tree structure works well where the core document is also a brief note, such as LaLiberte's HyperNews system (hosted at http://www.hypernews.org/) for Web-based threaded Usenet-style discussions. Note that the star structure does not preclude annotation post-processing to create more than one level of annotation. For example, one dynamic extension to Annotate is to scan annotations in batches for common hyperlinks or keywords, and create inter-annotation links at regular intervals.

A tour of the Annotate system

In a typical user session, the query interface, as shown in figure 8.1, resembles that of a standard WFTS engine, such as Alta Vista or Excite. The user enters a keyword or keywords to reach the retrieval interface, a set of hyperlinks to base documents. There is an enhancement to standard full-text search shown in this figure: the first is the ability to filter the result set by annotation domain, or to set a minimum aggregate quality rating. Here a cut-off point of 6.0 (out of 7.0) is shown as a quality filter, the search on only 'Fund Admin' group annotations.

Figure 8.1   **Annotate query interface with a social filter selected**

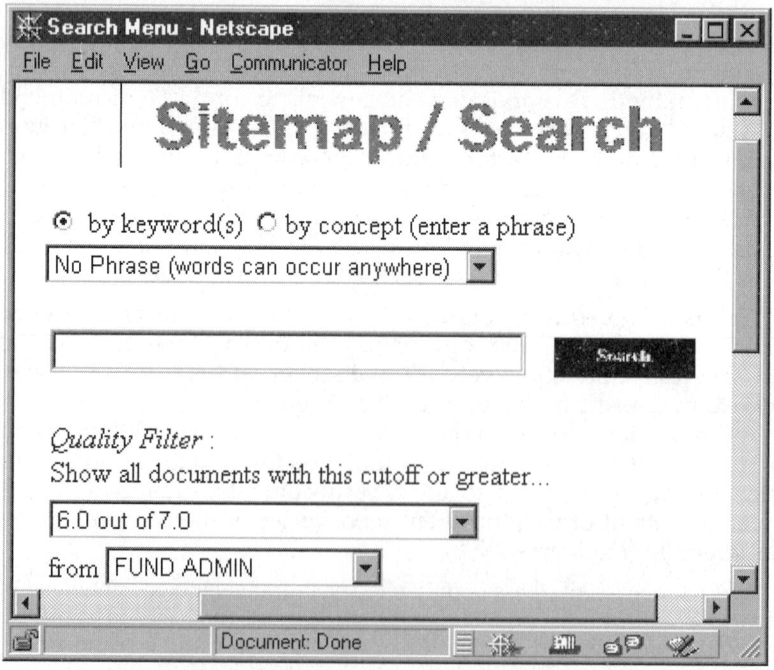

The result of the query is an array of hyperlinks – the retrieval interface. An excerpt of this screen is shown in figure 8.2. Figure 8.3 shows the icons and their meanings; the Likert scale (one to seven) is mapped to a spectrum of facial expressions similar to Koda and Maes (1996) in their interface agent usability study. Reading from left to right in the first row, the left-most four icons represent the most recent annotation for the document 'Interesting Servers on Related Subjects'. A user from 'D' (domain) of 'EQ' (Equities) assigns a 'Q' (quality) rating of three (out of seven) and an 'F' (factual accuracy) rating of six (out of seven). The reason for annotating is that the document was perceived to be out of date (the icon is a crossed-out clock). The next set of icons, 'D', 'Q', 'F' and 'G', represent the next-most-recent annotation. In this case, the 'FX' group (Foreign Exchange) assigns a 'Q' of six and an 'F' of seven, stating the reason: 'a more general lesson can be drawn' (the light-bulb icon).

Figure 8.2 Retrieval layer alterations in the Annotate system

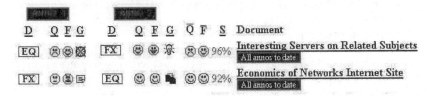

Aggregate statistics are presented about the document annotations to date: the aggregate quality rating and the aggregate factual-accuracy rating. On the right, we have the conventional Excite confidence score, 'S', followed by a hyperlink to the core document. The confidence score is colour-coded according to levels of annotation activity to provide an extra meta-data signal (blue is cold, green is medium and red is hot, where the exact cut-offs are an implementation decision).

Thus Annotate, with its timely modifications of the retrieval interface, contributes to the organization's memory store, which 'concerns itself with usually recent events and outcomes within an organizational context and for organizational purposes' (Ackerman, 1994). From the retrieval layer, users can also create a report on the most commonly used queries (i.e. keywords) to date, the most heavily annotated documents to date or the highest-rated documents to date along several dimensions, using the session data (see section on 'The session data-store', below).

The user selects a document hyperlink (see figure 8.2) to reach the document layer. The help in the system is a floating window (the annotation icon legend, as shown in figure 8.3). Figure 8.3 shows the complete range of possible icons that can be attached to the retrieval layer.

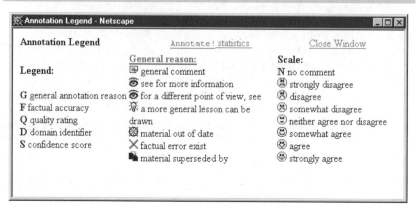

Figure 8.3 **The icon legend**

The form to create a new annotation is kept simple, in order to encourage participation in the system (i.e. lower the opportunity cost of annotating). Annotations grow the discussion data store and add value to the document recommender system. As users contribute annotations over time, filtering can become a powerful mechanism to limit spurious results.

To accomplish knowledge search and discovery mechanisms, documents and annotations are indexed using the Excite search engine. The user can search using keywords, and refine the search filtering on annotation variables. Knowledge quality control is a subjective process that is completely dependent on the user. Annotations can provide readers with rich data and opinions to aid belief development about the documents. Furthermore, readers who frequently contribute high-quality annotations become opinion leaders, and in a fully authenticated system gain a sort of 'brand name' recognition, causing their notes to gain readership.

To aid in knowledge visualization, the systems uses various small icons to denote appraisals and comments on the documents and convey them quickly to users.

Annotate system architecture

Two key data stores, discussion data and session data, underlie the Annotate system. In this section, we describe these data structures and show how they relate to the interface layers a user encounters in a search session.

The discussion data store

The discussion data store contains the appraisal ratings, the free text annotations of specific documents and the reason for annotating (e.g. if the document is out of date, a 'see' reference to another document, and so on). The discussion store is a hybrid of the originally published 'core' document with or without annotations. The annotation document type definition (DTD) is declared in XML.

Figure 8.5 presents the high-level view of the relationship between the discussion instances and the information retrieval interface layers (query, retrieval and document). The document layer is a receptacle to collect annotations. When an annotation event occurs, the discussion data store grows. This growth in turn may alter the look and feel of the retrieval layer, depending on simple trigger rules (refer to the section entitled 'A tour of the Annotate system' for a full description).

Annotations add value to existing data: a legacy HTML or ASCII document is now coupled with XML annotations, adding value to the existing document base by increasing its overall semantics. This conforms to Maurer's (1998) recommendation that meta-data be increased in legacy document stores to facilitate customized information access (Maurer, 1998).

The annotations help users to refine their search by filtering on the annotation categories, and enables collaborative (social) filtering, as discussed theoretically by Avery and Zeckhauser (1997). The annotations help users to socialize by allowing asynchronous collaboration, internalizing or combining knowledge through examination of user-defined annotations that guide to other sources, and supporting externalization by providing a mechanism for expressing annotations. Anonymous but authenticated annotations identifying the authors' workgroup can increase trust within an organizational setting.

Finally, discussion instances leverage the weaknesses of conventional full-text information retrieval. The Annotate system anticipates that the results of full-text queries lack precision and are often spurious in the context of the original query (Cooper and Prager, 2000). Annotations allow us to capture individuals' associative trails, and note interesting documents even if they did not match the original query; this has the potential to create new knowledge with subsequent system use. Figure 8.4 shows the composition of the new hybrid object (document plus multiple instances of annotation).

Figure 8.4   The document is now a hybrid object of data (original author work) and multiple instances of meta-data

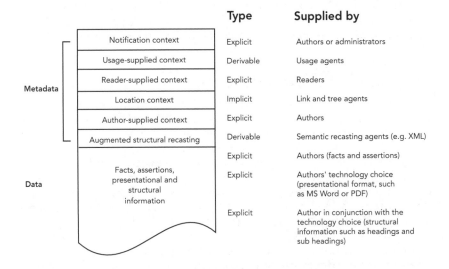

	Type	Supplied by
Notification context	Explicit	Authors or administrators
Usage-supplied context	Derivable	Usage agents
Reader-supplied context	Explicit	Readers
Location context	Implicit	Link and tree agents
Author-supplied context	Explicit	Authors
Augmented structural recasting	Derivable	Semantic recasting agents (e.g. XML)
	Explicit	Authors (facts and assertions)
Facts, assertions, presentational and structural information	Explicit	Authors' technology choice (presentational format, such as MS Word or PDF)
	Explicit	Author in conjunction with the technology choice (structural information such as headings and sub headings)

Metadata (covers the first six rows); Data (covers the facts, assertions, presentational and structural information rows)

Policies to manage the discussion instances

To realize the benefits of discussion data, organizations need to have supportive policies for KM. Three policy decisions include:

- The selection of incentives and rewards for adding annotations and, conversely, sanctions for non-participation. Without an explicit incentive scheme, Orlikowski (1992) demonstrated that Lotus Notes groupware was not well utilized at a management-consulting company because its workers had little incentive to share information. The trade-off to supplying annotation is the cost (time and effort) of constructing the notes versus the value of becoming an opinion leader and/or distinguishing oneself from one's peer group.
- The ability to specify the level of anonymity of the annotator: anonymous, semi-anonymous (only the workgroup identified) or non-anonymous. Prior research highlights the importance of anonymity but says little about group identification. For example, the social issues of anonymity and annotation have been explored in the group support system (GSS) setting by Connolly, Jessup and Valacich (1990), with the result that anonymous readers are more likely to offer critical remarks.
- The imposition of annotation controls. It is possible to limit the annotator population to designated experts in a given subject. For example, the Annotate system can be extended to form a scholarly peer-review system whereby domain experts annotate a draft manuscript.

The session-data store

The session-data store keeps track of user queries, keywords, retrieval lists and the timings of the users' navigation through the document base. We have written custom data analysis modules to perform more sophisticated tests of system usage, for example in-depth analyses of document readership demographics and the times spent at the query, retrieval and document-interface screens.

Using both session and discussion data, small interface agent software modules can be written to assist the user in the search, retrieval and document interfaces. Figure 8.5 shows an overview of these agent classes.

Evaluating the Annotate system

Annotate has been evaluated in a field trial at a federalist financial-services firm (Ginsburg, 1998a). System variables, such as user navigation timings, document-readership demographics and annotation statistics were collected, as well as qualitative data such as general user satisfaction measures and suitability of the system to the task at hand. In general, few readers (eight per week, with data collected weekly) chose to annotate in this setting. In each week's sample, there are between 5000 and 7000 intranet accesses and 60 Web searches. The Schelling diagrams shown in figures 8.6 and 8.7 depict this result graphically.

Figure 8.6 shows the simplest case in the absence of incentives to 'co-operate' (in this case, annotate). Going from the left (zero, or no co-operation) to the right (one, or full co-operation) we consider the marginal

Figure 8.5   **The search, retrieval and document interfaces**

These interfaces can all work in conjunction with interface agents to assist users and evaluators of the system

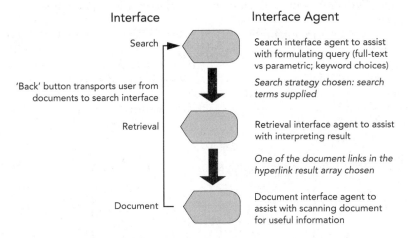

Interface

Interface Agent

Search

Search interface agent to assist with formulating query (full-text vs parametric; keyword choices)

'Back' button transports user from documents to search interface

Search strategy chosen: search terms supplied

Retrieval

Retrieval interface agent to assist with interpreting result

One of the document links in the hyperlink result array chosen

Document

Document interface agent to assist with scanning document for useful information

choice. The vertical distance from the horizontal axis measures 'V', the value to the individual (Margolis, 1991) in choosing free ridership ('FR'), where the user consumes but does not contribute, or co-operation ('C'). At all levels of co-operation at the margin the individual will choose free ridership, and the curve will unravel to 'Q', the point at which nobody co-operates. Clearly, incentive strategies are in order to try to flip sections of the 'FR' and 'C' curves at certain segments.

Figure 8.6   **A simple Schelling diagram**

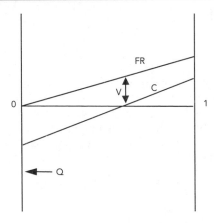

Figure 8.7 shows the hypothetical result of such incentive strategies; the 'FR' and 'C' curves have two crossover points. There exist two equilibria in figure 8.7. The inferior one, 'Q−', is reached when the co-operation level is shifted to the left of the tipping point, 't'. The superior equilibrium, 'Q+', is reached when one moves to the right of 't'.

The low levels of annotation activity in the field study (Ginsburg, 1998a) are consistent with an inferior equilibrium point of 'Q–'. Management has offered no explicit positive incentives to participate, and the promotional e-mail announcing the system merely solicited usage in general terms, which cannot be construed as a negative incentive (with risk to non-participants).

Still, some users may attach social value to the act of annotating. For example, a user might want to help his or her peers improve the quality of a work product and offer constructive feedback using the Annotate mechanism. Others may have private, self-interested reasons for annotating. Suppose an author wants to attract attention to his or her document. He or she might 'bootstrap' the system by adding some annotations to make the document appear 'busy' (changing the retrieval interface to add annotation icons).

Figure 8.7   **A more complex Schelling diagram with multiple equilibria**

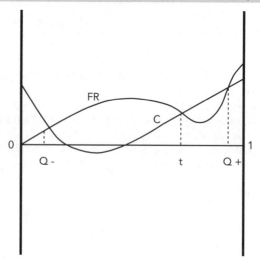

The social challenge, therefore, is how to move most effectively from 'Q–' to 'Q+'. Keeping in mind that the organization must be able to afford the incentives (the cost must be lower than the gain expected) one possibility is to recognize the most active secondary authors publicly in a broadcast e-mail. Another way to increase positive social perceptions of annotating is to broadcast the annotation event to the original author or authors, thus accelerating information throughput. Again, this extension must be carefully mapped to organizational policies and norms.

Conclusions

The Web and Internet technologies enable new ways of implementing KMSS. Annotate provides one mechanism to support KM in federated organizations, focusing on documents as repositories of relevant information for knowledge creation and use. Federated organizational forms are becoming more prevalent in a knowledge economy. The Web and intranets facilitate distributed document publishing necessitating effective storage, retrieval and KM mechanisms. KMSS should be designed to fit the organization form and enable organizations to implement policies for effective knowledge sharing.

Annotations improve the overall semantics of Web documents (ASCII or HTML) by formally declaring user values and beliefs about documents. Annotate in an intranet increases knowledge throughput by increasing the flow of relevant information across business units. Even when users pursue documents irrelevant to the original query, the possibility of capturing subjective reactions will help in this regard. Annotate begins to instantiate Nonaka's ideal of the 'knowledge network' through provision of recommendations and navigation assistance. Furthermore, by helping to increase the knowledge value of document repositories that span many business groups, Annotate is designed to increase the interoperability of federated document collections (Paepcke *et al.*, 1998).

Ultimately, such a system's effective use will be predicated on organizational policies and choices that users make to define their own ontology. As this tool is applied in organizational settings, current research examines incentives, authentication, anonymity and the impact of other policy choices on system use and effectiveness. Specifically, knowledge is being modelled as a 'collective organizational good', and different levels of authentication, anonymity and policy choices on system use and effectiveness are being examined. Tools such as Annotate enable the easy collection of data to study diffusion and sharing of know-how in organizations by electronic means.

Acknowledgement

The authors wish to thank Matthew Cordes for his technical assistance.

References

Ackerman, M. (1994) 'Answer Garden: A Tool for Growing Organizational Memory', Ph.D. thesis, Massachusetts Institute of Technology, MA.

Avery, C. and R. Zeckhauser (1997) 'Recommender systems for evaluating computer messages', *Communications of the ACM*, 40 (3), 88–89, March 1997.

Balasubramanian, V. and A. Bashian (1998) 'Document management and Web technologies: Alice marries the mad hatter', *Communications of the ACM*, 41 (7), 107–115.

Baldwin, C.Y. and K.B. Clark (1997) 'Managing in an age of modularity', *Harvard Business Review*, 77, 84–93.

Bentley, R., T. Horstmann and J. Trevor (1997) 'The World Wide Web as enabling technology for CSCW: the case of BSCW', *International Journal of CSCW*, 6 (23), 111–134.

Bowers, J. (1995) 'The work to make a network work: studying CSCW in action', in *Proceedings of the Conference on Computer Supported Co-operative Work*, 287–298.

Bush, V. (1945) 'As we may think', *Atlantic Monthly*, 176 (1), 101–108.

Caillau, R. (1998) *How it Really Happened*, Technical Report, CERN.

Connolly, T., L.M. Jessup and J.S. Valacich (1990) 'Effects of anonymity and evaluative tone on idea generation in computer mediated groups', *Management Science*, 36 (6), 689–703.

Cooper, J.W. and J.M. Prager (2000) 'Anti-serendipity: finding useless documents and similar documents', in *Proceedings of the 33rd Hawaii International Conference on System Sciences*, Maui, Hawaii.

Davenport, T.H. and L. Prusak (1998) *Working Knowledge: How Organizations Manage What They Know*, Harvard Business School Press.

Frivold, T.J., R.E. Lang and M.W. Fong (1994) 'Extending WWW for synchronous collaboration', in *Proceedings of the Second World Wide Web Conference*, NCSA, Chicago, IL.

Ginsburg, M. (1998a) 'Annotate: A Web-based Knowledge Management Support System for Document Collections', Ph.D. thesis, New York University, NY.

— (1998b) 'Annotate! A tool for collaborative information retrieval', in *Proceedings, WETICE98 Conference*, Palo Alto, CA.

— (1999) 'An agent framework for intranet document management', *Journal of Autonomous Agents and Multi-Agent Systems*, 2 (3), 271–286.

Ginsburg, M. and K. Duliba (1997) 'Enterprise level groupware choices: evaluating Lotus Notes and intranet-based solutions', *CSCW: The Journal of Collaborative Computing*, 6, 201–225.

Koda, T. and P. Maes (1996) 'Agents with faces: the effects of personification of agents', in *Proceedings of HCI'96*, London.

LaLiberte, D. (1998) 'WWW collaboration projects', UIUC Technical Report, http://www.hypernews.org/HyperNews/get/www/annotations.html.

Margolis, H. (1991) *Strategy and Choice*, MIT Press.

Maurer, H. (1998) 'Web-based knowledge management', *IEEE Computer*, 31, 122–123.

Moukas, A. and A. Maes (1998) 'Amalthaea: an evolving multi-agent information filtering and discovery system for the WWW', *Autonomous Agents and Multi-Agent Systems*, 1, 59–88.

Nonaka, I. (1994) 'A dynamic theory of organizational knowledge creation', *Organization Science*, 5 (1), 14–37.

O'Leary, D.E. (1998) 'Enterprise knowledge management', *IEEE Computer*, 31 (3), 54–61.

Orlikowski, W. (1992) 'Learning from Notes: organizational issues in groupware implementation', in *Proceedings of CSCW 1992*, London.

Paepcke, A., C.C.K. Chang, H. Garcia-Molina *et al.* (1998) 'Interoperability for digital libraries worldwide', *Communications of the ACM*, 41 (4), 33–43.

Pejtersen, A.M. (1998) 'Semantic information retrieval', *Communications of the ACM*, 41 (4), 90–92.

Phelps, T.E. and R. Wilensky (1996) 'Toward active, extensible, networked documents: multivalent architecture and applications', in *Proceedings of the First ACM International Conference on Digital Libraries*, Bethesda, 100–108.

Roscheisen, M., C. Mogensen and T. Winograd (1995) 'Interaction design for shared World-Wide Web annotations', in *CHI 95: Human Factors in Computing Systems*, New York, 328–329.

Ross, J.W. and J.F. Rockart (1996) 'Enabling new organizational forms: a changing perspective on infrastructure', in *Proceedings of the International Conference on Information Systems*, Cleveland, OH.

Salcedo, M.R. and D. Decouchant (1997) 'Structured co-operative authoring for the World Wide Web', *International Journal of CSCW*, 6 (23), 157–174.

9 Enterprise information infrastructures for active, context-sensitive knowledge delivery

Andreas Abecker, Ansgar Bernardi, Knut Hinkelmann and Michael Sintek

Introduction

Today's companies exist in a world in which markets are continuously shifting, technologies proliferating, competitors multiplying and products become obsolete overnight. In such highly dynamic environments managers increasingly recognize knowledge as one of the most decisive business factors with which to deal with the continuous change. KM is a strong trend in management science, and it must be appropriately supported by business IS and enterprise information infrastructures (see Nonaka and Takeuchi, 1995; Wiig, 1993). The KM hype is not fuelled by a single cause, but is driven by a number of current business phenomena – such as 'lean management' – that reduce middle management in many organizational structures. For decades, this level of employees was the most important stakeholder of know-how and experience about projects, customers and products. Indeed, such resources are important for tasks like information-gathering, filtering, interpretation and routing, in order to inform the decisions of upper management. Another trend is a shift from producing goods to providing knowledge-intensive services – particularly in developed countries of the North. This focuses interest on knowledge-intensive work processes and complex or 'wicked' problem solving (see Conklin and Weil, 1997; Davenport, Jarvenpaa and Beers, 1996).

These manifold business phenomena have created a general awareness of the importance of KM. However, it is not clear what specific contributions are expected from the IT and IS areas, or whether a comprehensive picture of IT support for KM exists. Instead, we find a wide variety of KM-related aims, including:

- better exploitation of documents already available but unsufficiently used
- formalization of business rules in workflows
- better usage of human skills and knowledge through computer-supported collaborative work (CSCW) techniques or enterprise yellow pages and competency databases
- explanation of experiences and know-how in best-practice databases or expert systems.

Many of these issues can be addressed with conventional document management, groupware, knowledge-based systems or information management tools. The focus here is the question of which new approaches and services are required or useful for comprehensive enterprise KM. Looking at the particularities of human knowledge and memory, and inspired by some industrial case studies (Kühn and Abecker, 1998), we propose that enterprise information infrastructures supporting KM (often called corporate memory, organizational memory [OM], or OMIS – see Stein and Zwass, 1995) should exhibit several distinguishing properties that make them an evolutionary step on from the existing generation of information management systems:

- Active support. In the rapidly changing business information world, users are often not aware that there is useful information available in the system. Even if they are, they do not necessarily know where and how to search for it (in an optimal way), or if they do know, searching costs time and effort. Thus, the OM should actively offer interesting knowledge.
- Integrative functions. Applications are characterized by a highly inter-woven handling of data, formal knowledge (e.g. workflow steps, formal decision rules and mathematical formulae), informal representations (e.g. memos, minutes of meetings, documentation, business letters, graphics and drawings) and knowledge embedded (or 'materialized') in artefacts or representations of work (e.g. a product design). Not only is the conjoint view and usage of all these representations important; even more so, the various inter-relationships among them are highly interesting. For example, a decision may be grounded on a dossier that employs some formal calculations, negotiated in a meeting and documented in the minutes, and lead to other decisions and effects on the final result of work. Furthermore, at the technical level, there is a huge amount of heterogeneity, especially since we typically need to build upon many legacy knowledge and information systems.
- Self-adaptiveness and self-organization. In a most ambitious scenario, the normal flow of work should not be disturbed by filling, structuring and searching the OM; rather, the system should accompany and observe the user doing their tasks and automatically gather and store interesting facts and information in an unobtrusive manner.

From these three points, this chapter mainly addresses active support by workflow-embedded, precise-content information retrieval from various, heterogeneous sources. The integration issues are partly solved in this approach, and have the potential to be solved to an even larger extent. Self-adaptiveness and self-organization are still far away, but some of the first ideas regarding these issues can be developed. In the following two sections, we will describe the basic functionality of our system prototype developed in the DFKI KnowMore (Knowledge Management for Learning Organizations) project, and elaborate on its realization principles and implementation issues. In the final section, some future work and questions to be resolved are discussed.

KnowMore knowledge services at a glance

KM support does not primarily address routine work, but tasks in which people generate or need very specific knowledge. Davenport, Jarvenpaa and Beers (1996) state that for knowledge work there are no predetermined tasks that, if executed, guarantee the desired outcome; further, they note that the inputs and outputs of knowledge work are less tangible and discrete than for routine work. Knowledge work, however, does not only occur in specific knowledge processes, but is also embedded in fairly structured business processes.

Let us examine an example. In an insurance company an important task within the structured process of accepting a new life insurance application is underwriting, that is deciding under which conditions the company should accept the application. While many of these decisions are routine, there are cases that require expert knowledge. The participant (i.e. the person responsible for the activity) has a lot of freedom over how to make his decision (e.g. he can ask the customer for additional information, search for similar cases in an IS, send the customer to a medical doctor for an examination, and so on). It would make no sense to specify the underwriting task in more detail, because there are a large variety of possible steps the underwriter can take. Instead, it is left to the expert to decide how to proceed.

To distinguish 'ordinary' activities from knowledge-work activities in a business process, we call the latter knowledge-intensive tasks (KITs). These KITs are the interesting activities for support by an OMIS. Instead of specifying in detail the single steps the expert has to do, an OMIS supports the participant with useful information that helps them in performing their work.

Business processes can be modelled using specific process modelling tools. A workflow management system can interpret these process definitions. It identifies activities that can be executed, assigns the activities to the responsible participant, starts associated application programs, and is responsible for the dataflow between activities. The KnowMore approach relies on an extended business-process model. In order to provide useful information actively, for each KIT a number of generic queries can be specified. At execution time, the generic queries are automatically instantiated and transferred to the OMIS that actively delivers – or offers – the answer to the user.

As a more detailed example, consider the business process for purchasing goods in an organization – in this case the authors' research institute. A purchasing process starts with an employee filling out a demand specification form, and primarily consists of a fairly deterministic sequence of relatively simple administrative steps, like checking the budget, writing the order or assigning an inventory number. This sequence can easily be modelled. Figure 9.1 gives an impression of the purchasing process represented with the ADONIS business process modelling tool (see Karagiannis, Junginger and Strobl, 1996; BOC GmbH, 1998).

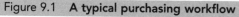

Figure 9.1 **A typical purchasing workflow**

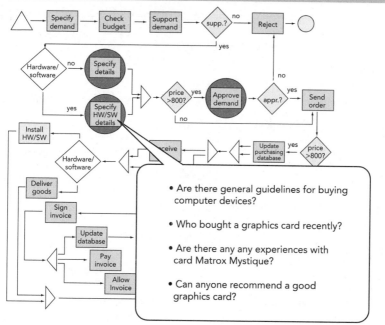

However, among these 'primitive' administrative aspects, there are a few working steps requiring expert knowledge and purchasing experience. Some of them are marked in the picture by a dark surrounding circle. We will focus here on the preparation of a detailed specification of the goods to be purchased (e.g. 'Which model from which producer delivered by which supplier?') based on the more-or-less concrete demand description of the employee who initiated the purchasing process (e.g. 'I need a high-end PC with a good graphics card'). If an inexperienced employee should accomplish such a detailed demand specification, questions similar to the ones shown in figure 9.1 could arise, and answering these would be a helpful service of an OMIS.

Figure 9.2 shows a screenshot of our experimental system prototype. On the left, in the background, we see an editor window used to create detailed demand specifications. The input mask accepts up to three items to be purchased and already contains the initial specification given by the end user, the requirement for a graphics card.

Now it has to be decided which card to buy (the 'product' slot in the input mask) and from which supplier (the 'supplier' slot). The KnowMore system supports this decision in the following way:

- When the activity is started, the system takes the generic query associated to the activity and finds out whether some element of the OMIS can already compute a decision suggestion (i.e., whether there

Figure 9.2   **The KnowMore system offers context-sensitive information supply**

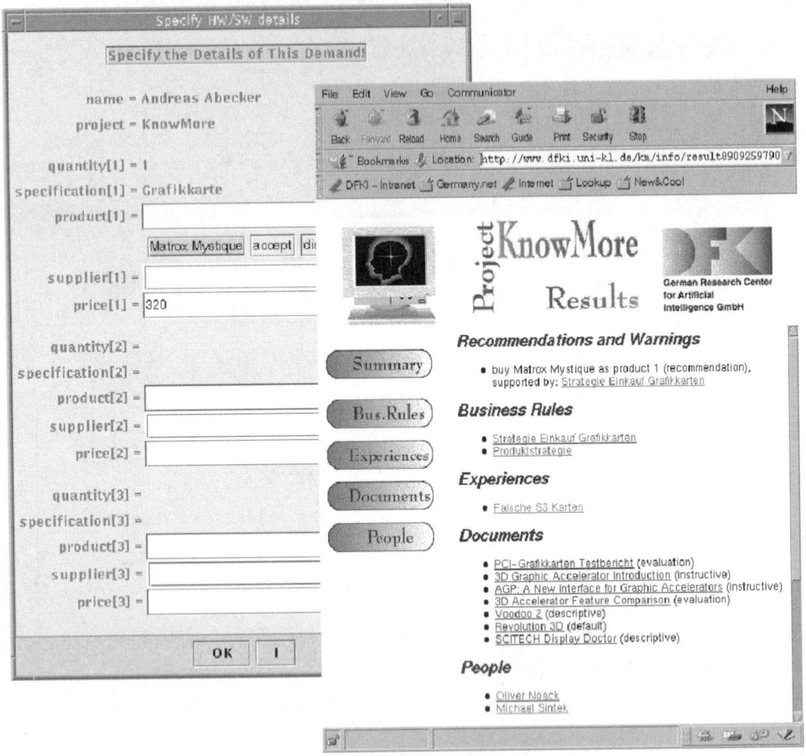

is some expert system or decision-support functionality available which can readily be evaluated). This suggested decision value is inserted in the user-input mask offering a proposed solution (in the example, the suggestion is to buy a Matrox Mystique card).

- Moreover, the system determines which decision variables it can offer some information about, and inserts information buttons, 'I', at the appropriate places in the input mask. If the user wants some supporting information on one of these decisions, pressing the 'I' button starts a query to the OMIS. This query may retrieve several classes of information with different relevance in the concrete situation. Examples of such information include: highly recommended company-internal business rules for purchasing in general or for specific product classes; technical information about possible buying alternatives; or pointers to knowledgeable colleagues known to be competent in such decisions from their entry in the personal-skill database, their training records or position in the company, or because they have recently made a similar purchase. These information sources are ordered according to their relevance, computed by the retrieval function, as well as to a pre-defined order based upon their information type, and are offered to the user as hyperlinks in the KnowMore information browser (on the right-hand side of figure 9.2).

The user can either accept or overwrite a suggested solution, and – in the case of a more detailed partial specification or a changed situation – again ask for KnowMore support via an 'I' button. The system recognizes the change in the state of affairs, and re-evaluates the query against the archive system.

Figure 9.3 shows the effect of taking into account the change in the process state: in the right-hand part of the picture, the user has selected the Matrox Mystique card, which considerably narrows down the search in the OMIS. Now, all documents that have no direct relationship to this specific card are eliminated. Only purchasing rules and specific information about the Matrox Mystique product remain. If we ask for information support concerning potential suppliers, the system yields only information about suppliers known to sell that product. In the previous process state (on the left-hand side of figure 9.3) all suppliers selling graphics cards in general are described.

Figure 9.3   Changes in the process status result in refined information support

To produce the functionality described, the KnowMore system makes the following technical provisions:

- Each KIT in a business-process model is equipped with a support specification describing the respective information needs as generic queries or query schemes to be instantiated at run-time, together with their appropriate preconditions and post-processing rules for the results. For this, we have to describe the appropriate representation means.

- There must be a component that recognizes when a knowledge-intensive task has been activated. The KnowMore system is extended by a workflow management system that has as input a workflow model derived from the business process model. As soon as a user starts a KIT, the workflow engine instantiates the generic query –

thus exploiting situation-specific knowledge and context parameters – and delivers it to the OMIS.

- In order to instantiate the query schemata at run-time, the business process models must be enriched by KIT variables. These variables describe the information flow between activities in the workflow, and are the communication channel between workflow and information retrieval agents (the 'product' slot in the above example is such a KIT variable). They are embedded into a domain ontology, meaning that it is specified that their values must be of a particular type, defined as an ontology concept. The ontology can contain concept-specific retrieval heuristics.
- For enabling precise-content retrieval from manifold heterogeneous sources in the OMIS, a uniform knowledge description must be provided. We propose logic-based modelling of structure and meta-data, information content and information context on the basis of formal ontologies.

Realization of the KnowMore system

Since a most innovative feature of our architecture is the workflow-triggered activation of information supply, which exploits workflow context for precise search, it is worth elaborating the question of how to achieve the workflow-retrieval coupling, i.e. how to model KIT support specifications.

Architecture

Figure 9.4 shows the basic architecture of the overall KnowMore system. It implements the OMIS architecture principles described in Abecker *et al.* (1998). Active support is achieved by declarative support specifications attached to the process definitions.

Figure 9.4   The three-layered OM architecture

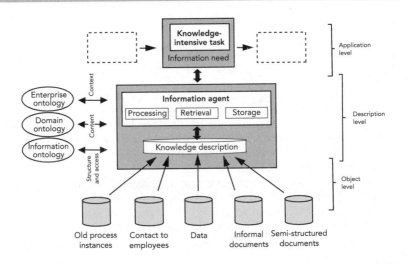

At the object level, the approach supports access to various hetero-geneous information sources. Important information can be found in structured databases, in informal or semi-structured documents. Human-resource databases can help in finding an expert to solve a difficult problem, or selecting people to form a project team.

Precise-content information retrieval (IR) and abstraction from tech-nical and semantic heterogeneity is achieved by homogeneous knowledge descriptions – declarative models of information sources and knowledge items. This offers the possibility of integrating already-available infor-mation sources into the OMIS. The knowledge descriptions are done on the basis of ontologies and meta-data, and can be used by the information agent as input for logic-based IR algorithms. More detail on the ontology and knowledge item descriptions can be found in Abecker *et al.* (1998) and Liao *et al.* (1999) respectively.

Knowledge use must be tightly integrated with the work of the people in the company. Technically, the application level corresponds to the execution of an application program, from which requirements for useful information are transferred to the information agent. The information agent then uses these requirement to find useful information sources and to assess the retrieved information for its relevance in the concrete situation.

The activities supported by the OMIS are knowledge-intensive tasks. In order to implement active support, a KIT must be extended by a description of the information needed.

Although this general architecture does not pose any restriction at the application level, in the following we assume that the applications are not isolated but part of a workflow (this is symbolized by the dashed boxes in figure 9.4). This gives the additional advantage that context information can be used to restrict retrieval results. The context information can be information generated in previous activities of the workflow, but it can also be workflow-relevant, such as data on the participant responsible for the activity.

Knowledge-intensive tasks

A process definition consists of a network of activities. By the definition of the Workflow Management Coalition, an activity is a description of a piece of work that forms a logical step within a process (WfMC, 1999). Depending on the granularity of the process model, tasks can be simple or complex. Finding a good granularity level, that is deciding what is the right division of work, is an important part of process modelling. If a piece of work can be performed by one person or by a single application program, it can be regarded as an activity. However, activities range from very simple, for example writing a number into a form, to quite complex, either because it is not possible to divide them any further or because of the rich variability of ways in which the activity can be performed.

A KIT is a complex activity, and concrete processing is left to the user. Although it may not be worthwhile or possible to divide the activity further, some support can be given by the provision of information on how to proceed, particularly in difficult situations. This can be achieved by specifying several (partial) information needs, each of which will result in some information that supports a particular aspect of the complete KIT.

As part of the project, we developed a KIT description schema that is shown in figure 9.5. It is used for more effective information search and presentation, and not for guiding and controlling KIT processing. The schema provides preconditions on the various information needs, and processing rules for their results. Both influence the way the information needs are interpreted and fulfilled during process execution.

Figure 9.5   Example of a KIT specification

```
Activity: Specify HW/SW Details

Participant: researcher or developer

Input variables: product_type, quantity, specification

Output variables: product, supplier, price

Information needs:

   {IN1:  precondition:   product_type isa Hardware
          parameters:     product_type, specification, price
          agent-spec:     information-agent-42
          contributes to: product_detail
          from:           Intranet

    IN2:  ...

    }

Postprocessing rules: ...
```

Technically, a KIT is a special case of an ordinary process activity extended by a support specification (containing information needs and processing rules) that may refer to the global and local process context (see figure 9.5). The support specification consists of five items:

- The precondition allows us to restrict the evaluation of information needs depending, for example, on the state of their parameters (e.g. only execute if some variables are already non-null, or skip this task if some parameter is already known) or on the state of the process (e.g. skip if time is critical).
- The parameters refer to process status and input/output variables of KITs; these specify in detail what the information agent has to search for. They carry the workflow context information from the workflow management system to the information agent.
- The agent-spec description of the relevant information is interpreted as a remote procedure call to a specific software agent. This agent is responsible for retrieving the relevant information. At run-time, the information agent is invoked and provided with the parameters.
- The 'contributes-to' field indicates the goal of the particular information need: it helps in finding values for the variables mentioned here. On the basis of this information, the interconnection between the different information needs can be deduced and evaluated by the information agent.

- Determining the information sources relevant to a particular information need is a central objective of the information agent. By computing 'info-source = function' (parameters, expected-output, callingActivity, processInstance), the information agent finds the knowledge source according to the goal and context information. If suitable information sources can be identified at process-definition time, for example the well-known databases of the enterprise, the 'from' slot can be used to specify them.

The post-processing rules govern a certain amount of post-processing of the retrieved information. Usually, the result of evaluating the information needs is presented to the user. In certain cases, however, it is possible to specify further operations (e.g. a formal knowledge item is used for direct computation by some algorithm). The result of an information need can also be used to trigger additional operations. To define such trigger conditions, we can formulate expressions about any variable accessible inside the KIT, or about meta-information provided by the information agent. Examples of meta-information are, for example, 'empty result' or 'count of produced information objects'. Possible post-processing actions comprise the calculation of values, the setting of variables or the activation of information needs.

Processing knowledge-intensive tasks

Concerning KIT processing, it must be stated that the central instance that works on the KIT is still the human workflow participant. This individual is responsible for solving the problem at hand. The work-list handler simply presents to the workflow participant an editor window with the KIT name and the input and output variables. The human user performs the task at hand by specifying the value of the output variables (in our current demonstrator system by completing the electronic form shown in figure 9.2). In parallel, the KIT representation is passed to the information agent (called knowledge agent in figure 9.6), which then evaluates the information needs and instantiates the parameters. It then presents the information needs as support offers to the user (e.g. 'I' buttons), using the name and the comment of the information needs (see figure 9.6). The user selects interesting offers. Subsequently, the information agent determines the relevant information sources, creates suitable queries from the information need and performs the information retrieval. The result is presented as supporting information to the user.

Any change in the variables that the user has to fill in must result in a re-evaluation of the information needs that depend on those variables. This again will be realized as a suggestion to the user: the previous results are marked as 'possibly outdated', but the activation of a new information retrieval is left to the user. As soon as the user completes the task and the filling of output variables, a message is passed to the work-list handler (as already indicated in the generic model by the Workflow Management Coalition). The knowledge agent automatically receives a 'close' signal for this particular KIT, closes the display windows under its responsibility, and exits.

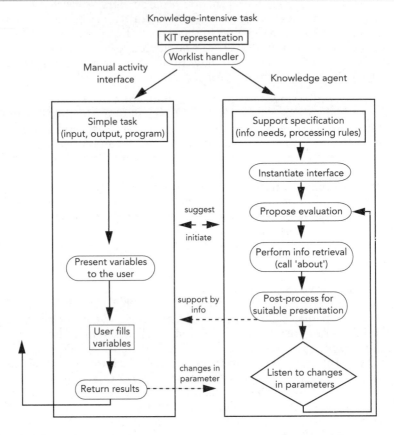

Figure 9.6   **KIT processing by worklist handler and information/knowledge agent**

Implementation

Figure 9.7 gives an overview of our current implementation. The KnowMore prototype is implemented in Java, which allows it to be used on all Java-enabled platforms. The KnowMore server holds all relevant data: the business-process model enriched by KIT variables and support specifications, along with the OM archive and the respective knowledge descriptions and the underlying ontologies.

Business-process models can be designed using the ADONIS tool, and are later parsed into the KnowMore representation formalism. One advantage of ADONIS is its meta-modelling capability, which makes customization easy. This is necessary in the KnowMore approach, because of the extended KIT specification (during development time, when the KIT specification formalism was not yet fixed, the KnowMore-specific extensions were modelled as a comment slot in the activity descriptions – an approach that can be used for any process modelling tool).

The core of all KnowMore knowledge representations is an object-centred knowledge representation formalism, the basic language constructs of which are mapped in turn onto conventional relational databases, which are coupled with Java via Java database connection (JDBC).

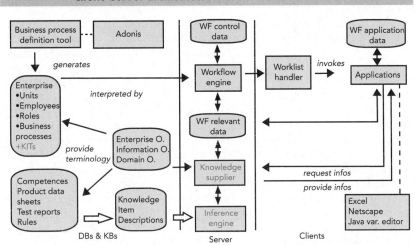

Figure 9.7   The KnowMore implementation is a Web-enabled client–server architecture

The KnowMore server hosts both the workflow engine and the knowledge-based retrieval machinery. Workflow enactment involves two parts: the server, implemented as a Java application, and client worklist handlers, implemented as Java applets that connect to the server via standard TCP/IP sockets. The architecture and communication protocols are designed in compliance with the Workflow Management Coalition standards. The rationale for standardization is that when the scenario is stable and proven, it may be possible to switch from our demonstration version of the KnowMore workflow engine to a commercial one.

Discussion

The work described here resulted in a usable prototype of an OM system that has been tested in several business-process scenarios; this text focused on the purchasing example. The OM system supports the user by actively providing context-specific relevant information. Regarding the three OM requirements given in the introduction section, the focus was on active, context-sensitive knowledge supply realized by workflow-triggered and embedded information retrieval. The knowledge description level, which has only been sketched here, addresses the integration issue by providing a homogeneous description of and access to the hetero-geneous information sources. The organization of the information sources relies on the various ontologies and the context available in the workflow instances. However, the work described here gives rise to some important research and development questions.

In order to improve the structuring of and access to the various infor-mation sources, a natural extension of the approach described here will consider individual user profiles to determine the relevance of information items. User modelling and its use in information retrieval is an important research topic. Indeed, it has already resulted in well-founded results (see Kobsa, 1993). Consequently, this topic has not been considered in any detail, although a broader view of an OM system must certainly integrate it.

The efficient handling of the various ontologies in the environment of an enterprise is crucial to a successful realization of our approach. There seem to be some knowledge structures applicable in a wider range of applications; for example, O'Leary (1998) identified quite similar repository organization principles used in most large international consulting companies. Nevertheless, building ontologies is costly, and it is not clear, in the general case, how stable they are, how detailed they should be and whether they will be accepted by employees for indexing their knowledge. The development of suitable support for building and maintaining ontologies in an enterprise is thus a research topic of utmost practical importance. It should be noted that in an enterprise the knowledge-acquisition process for building those ontologies has not necessarily to start completely from scratch. Organization structures of company libraries and documentation systems, indexing schemata of document management systems, or the structure and content of a company intranet can all be used as starting points for building the respective ontologies. Any support in this area can integrate approaches from several domains, among them:

- Identification of ontological structures from available information sources, using results from Machine Learning and Knowledge Acquisition from Texts (Staab *et al.*, 2000).
- Meta-models of business process modelling tools that correspond to enterprise ontologies (including BPMS [BOC GmbH, 1998] and the event-driven process chains of ARIS [Scheer, 2000]).
- Exploitation of existing formalized models in the enterprise as a starting point for ontology construction, for example database schema and database contents (see Sintek *et al.*, 2000).

In addition to the development of appropriate technical solutions, practical experiences must be gathered in order to develop suitable and comprehensive methodologies that enable the systematic realization of an OM approach in the enterprise. As the various modelling activities required for implementing a KnowMore-like system in a company will consume considerable resources, a comprehensive and reliable methodology seems indispensable in order to guarantee the achievement of the specified goals. The development of this methodology, however, remains an open research question tackled in various projects.

With respect to the KM processes identified by Probst, Raub and Romhardt (1999), we note that the approach described here focuses on the support of knowledge distribution and knowledge utilization. A natural future extension of the work covers the support of knowledge acquisition/ capture and knowledge development. To support know-ledge acquisition, the OM system should be able to capture and retain the actual context whenever an information item is stored. Thus, knowledge about the creation context of an information item is available when the relevance for a particular query is to be decided. The concepts necessary to this end are already present in the approach described here – more details can be found in Abecker, Bernardi and Sintek (2000) and Abecker *et al.* (2001).

A suitable support for knowledge generation can be offered if the OM stipulates and observes discussions in co-operating groups in their actual work situation. Centred around suitable representations of work, various contributions and discussion threads can be conserved in their context, and provide information about the history and the reasons for decisions taken during work. This, in turn, provides a solid basis for later discovery of new insights and best practices, which remains to be done by human experts. An example of this approach can be found in Sumner *et al.* (1998) and Mulholland *et al.* (2000).

In summary, this project presented an infrastructure for active knowledge supply, realized in the KnowMore prototype, which lays solid foundations for further developments towards an integrated OM technology.

Acknowledgement

The work described in this chapter was conducted as part of the KnowMore project – funded by the German Federal Ministry for Education and Research (Bundesministerium für Bildung und Forschung).

References

Abecker, A., A. Bernardi, K. Hinkelmann *et al.* (1998) 'Towards a technology for organizational memories', *IEEE Intelligent Systems*, 13 (3), 40–48.

Abecker, A., A. Bernardi and M. Sintek (2000) 'Proactive knowledge delivery for enterprise knowledge management', in *Learning Software Organizations – Methodology and Applications* (eds G. Ruhe and F. Bomarius), Springer.

Abecker, A., A. Bernardi, K. Hinkelmann *et al.* (2001) 'Context-aware, proactive delivery of task-specific knowledge: the KnowMore project', *Information Systems Frontiers*.

BOC GmbH (1998) 'The Business Process Management Toolkit – ADONIS', http://www.cso.net/boc/english/index.htm.

Conklin, E.J. and W. Weil (1997) 'Wicked Problems: Naming the Pain in Organizations', White Paper of Group Decision Support Systems, Inc., http://www.gdss.com/wicked.htm.

Davenport, T., S.L. Jarvenpaa and M.C. Beers (1996) 'Improving knowledge work processes', *Sloan Management Review*, 37 (4), 53–65.

Karagiannis, D., S. Junginger and R. Strobl (1996) 'Introduction to business process management systems concepts', in *Business Process Management* (eds B. Scholz-Reuter and E. Stickel), Springer-Verlag.

Kobsa, A. (1993) 'User Modelling: Recent Work, Prospects and Hazards' http://zeus.gmd.de/~kobsa/papers/1993-aui-kobsa.pdf.

Kühn, O. and A. Abecker (1998) 'Corporate memories for knowledge management in industrial practice: prospects and challenges', in *Information Technology for Knowledge Management* (eds U.M. Borghoff and R. Pareschi), Springer.

Liao, M., K. Hinkelmann, A. Abecker *et al.* (1999) 'A competence knowledge base system for the organizational memory', in *Proceedings of the 5th Biannual German Conference on Knowledge Based Systems*, Würzburg, Germany.

Mulholland, P., Z. Zdrahal, J. Domingue *et al.* (2000) 'Integrating working and learning: a document enrichment approach', *Behaviour and Information Technology*, 19 (3), 171–180.

Nonaka, I. and H. Takeuchi (1995) *The Knowledge-Creating Company*, Oxford University Press.

O'Leary, D. (1998) 'Using AI in knowledge management: knowledge bases and ontologies', *IEEE Intelligent Systems*, 13 (3), 30–33.

Probst, G., S. Raub and K. Romhardt (1999) *Managing Knowledge*, Wiley.

Scheer, A.W. (2000) *ARIS – Business Process Modelling*, Springer-Verlag.

Sintek, M., B. Tschaitschian, A. Abecker *et al.* (2000) 'Using ontologies for advanced information access', in *Proceedings of the Third International Conference and Exhibition on The Practical Application of Knowledge Management*, Manchester, UK.

Staab, S., A. Maedche, C. Nedellec *et al.* (2000) 'Workshop on ontology learning', in *Proceedings of the European Conference on Artificial Intelligence*, Berlin, Germany.

Stein, E.W. and V. Zwass (1995) 'Actualizing organizational memory with information technology', *Information Systems Research*, 6 (2), 85–117.

Sumner, T., J. Domingue, Z. Zdrahal *et al.* (1998) 'Enriching representations of work to support organizational learning', in *Proceedings of the European Conference on Artificial Intelligence*, Brighton, UK.

WfMC (1999) *Terminology and Glossary*, TC-1011, Workflow Management Coalition.

Wiig, K.M. (1993) *Knowledge Management: Foundations*, Schema Press.

10 Combining data from existing company sources: architecture and experiences

Jari Vanhanen, Casper Lassenius and Kristian Rautiainen

Introduction

One of the basic tasks of management is control. To exercise control over an organization in general, and new product development (NPD) or software development in particular, is a challenging task, demanding institutionalized management systems containing both planning and control activities. Planning is related to defining the organizational goals that should be achieved and how to achieve them. Control is about influencing the organization so as to achieve those goals. Successful control demands both status information gained (e.g. through measurement) and a way of influencing the organization. The LUCOS research project was focused on developing methods and tools for improving the controllability of NPD (Lassenius *et al.*, 1999; Lassenius and Rautiainen, 1999). This chapter focuses on measurement – specifically on the architecture and toolset built to support measurement definition and implementation. It is an example of a high-level KMS, using disparate data sources, and used by a wide variety of stakeholders.

The measurement system

Measurement requires data. In many organizations lots of data exists, but it resides in various applications, making it hard to combine and utilize the data. We have noticed that in the domain of NPD, the problem of dispersed data is no different. Useful data can be found in spreadsheets, project management software and version management systems, to name a few. Combining and presenting the data from the different applications allows observations and conclusions to be made that would otherwise be impossible based upon the data from a single application.

Large amounts of data allow numerous measures to be generated, which may actually be a serious disadvantage. In order for measures to be useful and meaningful to users, the users must be shown a minimum set of measures, customized according to their specific requirements. It is also crucial that the users understand the purpose of each measure they see, as well being able to interpret the measurement values correctly. This can be facilitated by deriving the measures from the goals of the organization and by documenting them properly.

Data warehousing systems

Data warehousing systems are typically intended to help business decision-making, based on combining large amounts of historical data from dispersed operational databases (Devlin, 1997). However, we think that an IS that borrows some of the ideas of data warehousing – such as combining data, presenting it to potential users and utilizing both historical and real-time data – is also useful in supporting NPD controllability improvement.

In general, the transparency of the NPD process is poor. The kind of IS stipulated above can improve the transparency of individual projects, as well as dependencies between projects, and help in summarizing data from individual projects to be used on process or strategic level management. Archiving and analyzing project data allows a company to learn from it for its future projects.

In the domain of product development, useful data is not necessarily explicitly collected in databases. It is not always even recognized that there may already be several data-collection systems in a project whose data can be utilized, especially if data from different sources were combined. Such data-collection systems include, for example, time-reporting systems, project-management applications, version-control systems and bug-reporting databases. Instead of simply querying the data from databases, it must often be extracted from application-specific files such as time-reporting spreadsheets or logs of a version-control system. In contrast to a typical data warehouse, the amount of data is moderate, but the real-time requirements are critical for daily project-management decisions, in addition to the observation of longer trends.

The design is an open architecture, the purpose of which is to serve as an IS for product-development organizations. It is intended for designing and documenting measures, collecting data for the measures and visualizing the measures. The measures are customized and presented in an understandable form for all stakeholders at all levels of an organization, including developers, testing personnel, project managers and corporate management. The implementation, based on this architecture, is a system that is simple to deploy and for which it is easy to write new modules for data transfer to the system or for data use from the system. The system is available for any authorized user with an intranet or Internet connection to the server, and it is scalable for large amounts of data and users.

The next section of this chapter presents the architecture and the implementation, including descriptions of all the constituent parts. In the last section, experiences on the use of the system in a small Finnish software company are reported.

Architecture

The architecture consists of the metrics server (MESS), external data gathering and replication modules (EDAMs) and applications that utilize the data. MESS stores collected data in its own database, performs user authentication and access control, caches database query results and provides services for manipulating meta-data. EDAMs are small programs that connect to an existing data source, perform optional data transformations (e.g. cleaning and reformatting), and then replicate the relevant data to MESS.

The LUCOS toolset (as shown in figure 10.1) consists of an implementation of the server, three finished EDAMs, and two applications, MeTo and ViCA. The measurement design tool (MeTo) is used to define measures, as well as to document their rationale and intended use. The visualization client (ViCA) shows graphical representations of measures. The client programs, that is EDAMs and applications, communicate with MESS over an intranet or the Internet using an HTTP-based protocol.

Figure 10.1 **The LUCOS toolset**

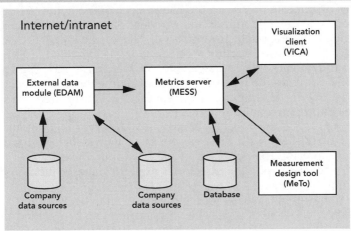

Metrics Server

The MESS is the central component in the framework providing the client programs with persistent storage facilities, user authorization, and data querying and manipulation. In addition, it can operate as a simple Web server. MESS is the only program that directly accesses the server database.

MESS stores and manipulates both the data replicated from the data sources and framework data entities, such as users, groups, schemas, views, charts, panels and measurement-system documentation. User and group information is required for authentication and for limiting access to any object in the database on a group level. Schemas describe the field names and data types of database tables in the server database. The replicated data is stored in these tables. Views are user-generated virtual table descriptions, typically used for simplifying complex queries. Charts and panels are generated and used by ViCA. Charts contain, for example, structured query language

(SQL) queries, data mappings and appearance of visualizations. Panels group related charts together. Measurement-system documentation contains all information created while designing measures in MeTo. In addition to entity-specific attributes, each framework data entity contains common meta-data: name, description, and read, write and administrative group name.

MESS allows client programs to create, read, update, and delete entities and manipulate their meta-data. Data can be dumped to user-created tables and SQL queries executed to read the data. As mentioned, MESS can also serve as a simple Web server, storing and returning any kind of file. The server also provides advanced logging facilities that can be utilized both for evaluating the use and performance of the system, and for improving its usability. MESS logs both internal housekeeping data, such as cache data, as well as providing an interface through which applications can write log entries.

All communication with MESS is done using the LUCOS tool protocol, which is based on HTTP 1.0 (Berners-Lee, Fielding and Frystyk, 1996). HTTP is a simple, lightweight and stateless protocol, working over TCP/IP communications. MESS processes incoming HTTP requests and returns a proper response to the client. Each HTTP request contains a method, a resource identifier and optional data (such as authorization credentials or meta-data information). The method ('GET', 'PUT', or 'DELETE') specifies the action to be taken on the identified resource, and optional data can alter the behaviour of the processing. The resource identifier specifies the type of resource using the top-level 'directory' of the identifier. For example, the request 'GET/user/fred HTTP/1.0' fetches information on user 'fred'.

In fact, MESS can be thought of as a Web server that implements a virtual file system with different types of named objects residing in different directories. Special directories ('/dump', '/sqlquery', '/meta', '/file') and files inside the directories exist for the execution of specific functions.

In some circumstances, source databases may be so huge that data replication to MESS is unfeasible. Replication can be avoided by connecting MESS to a database-management system capable of accessing remote, heterogeneous data servers – such as Sybase's Enterprise Data Studio (Anonymous, 1998). From the viewpoint of MESS, and subsequently the applications using MESS, the difference is noticed only in slower response times to SQL queries.

In one of the system industrial installations, response times for remote queries were unacceptably long, in the order of minutes. To alleviate the problem, a proactive caching of commonly used SQL queries was implemented. Since MESS relays SQL queries from clients to the server database, it can return the result from its cache, if available. MESS calculates query statistics, such as SQL query commonality, execution duration and execution time, as well as information on whether the query result changed between two consequent query executions. Based on this information, the server tries to maintain valid results for common queries in its cache by executing the queries using processor idle time. Note that since MESS does not know whether the data has been changed or not, but tries to guess whether the data is likely to have changed, based on earlier change patterns, the result returned by MESS can be outdated. In practice, it has been found that most types of data used have a fairly regular update frequency, making this approach feasible.

We chose to include a separate server instead of directly accessing a central database from client programs using open database connectivity (ODBC) – or some other protocol – for several reasons. MESS provides a high-level interface on top of SQL and ODBC for manipulating entities such as users, groups, application-specific entities and meta-data. Manipulating this information requires neither the writing of SQL queries nor knowledge of the database schema. The access-control mechanism is implemented in MESS, and provides read, write and administration rights to each entity and entity directory on a group basis.

HTTP is a very common protocol supported by several programming libraries. Therefore, it is easy to write communication code for client programs and they can be developed in most programming languages on a variety of platforms.

The proactive caching and the option not to replicate all data make the system more scalable for large installations.

External Data Modules

The EDAMs are typically company-specific programs that connect to some existing source of data (such as a database or log files), perform optional data transformation (e.g. cleaning and reformatting), and then replicate the relevant data to the server. Since an EDAM must connect to a company data source, the choice of architecture and programming tool or language is limited by the methods of access to the particular data source to which the EDAM should connect. Different EDAMs can be developed on different architectures with different programming tools as needed.

Typically an EDAM performs the following steps when executed. First it establishes a connection to MESS and authenticates itself to gain access to target tables on the server database. It checks if the required database tables are present in MESS and, if needed, creates the missing tables and gives them suitable access rights. After initialization, the EDAM connects to one or more data sources, fetches (or parses) the data and performs optional filtering, transformation or aggregation of the data. If possible, the EDAM only reads the new or changed data – thus minimizing the amount of data to dump to MESS. Finally, the source data that has been read and processed is dumped to the corresponding tables in MESS.

Usually, administrators of the system should write EDAMs to solve the organization's specific data transformation needs. However, a programming library and several EDAMs have been implemented to help minimize the initial effort in deploying the system. The LUCOS library is a C-language library providing high-level functions for communication with MESS. These functions include, for example, initializing and closing connections, creating and deleting tables and dumping data to a table. CSVTool is both a sample program for using the library and a useful generic EDAM that reads files containing data in CSV (comma-separated value) format and dumps it to a specified table in MESS. CSV is a format that many applications, including Microsoft Excel and Project, can generate.

Since many organizations use Microsoft Project and Excel for project-management purposes, the LUCOS toolset contains plug-in EDAMs for those products. The Excel metrics information exchange (EMIX) and project metrics information exchange (PMIX) plug-ins automate data transfer from these applications to MESS. They can be configured for each document separately to dump selected data in the document to specific tables in MESS. Thereafter, they can make the dump automatically whenever a user modifies and saves the document. For example, when a new spreadsheet template is created, the author marks in Excel all areas containing data to be transferred and specifies for each data area the table to which the data is to be dumped (figure 10.2). After this, any user may make a copy of the document template for personal use and EMIX will transfer the data automatically when saving or closing the document.

Figure 10.2 **EMIX**

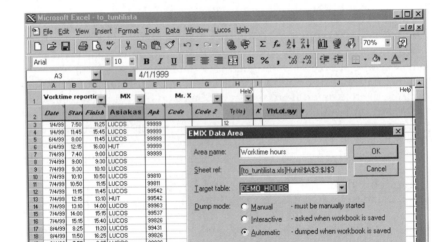

The mapping between columns of a data area and the target table fields is automatic if the header line of each area matches database table field names. Otherwise, the user must manually configure the mapping for each data area. A data area may be appended with constant-value columns. A constant is defined either as a reference to a worksheet cell or as a literal value. For example, the constants can be used to qualify time-reporting hours by a person without the need to have the username duplicated on each row in the worksheet.

The Measurement Design Tool

MeTo (as shown in figure 10.3) is used to define measures, as well as to document their rationale and intended use. MeTo is used by the designers of the measurement system, and is used every time new measures need to be added or existing ones changed.

Measurement is a crucial part of any management system, and there is a growing awareness that the traditional financial measurement systems need to be replaced by more sophisticated measurement systems (Eccles, 1991; Kaplan and Norton, 1992). This project has involved the implementation of measurement systems for software development and R&D organizations. Measurement is often not performed in these types of organizations, and measurement programs tend to be poorly received by development personnel (Kerssens-van Drongelen and Cook, 1997). Implementing successful measurement programs in such environments is therefore a particularly challenging problem.

Figure 10.3 **The measurement design tool (MeTo)**

Despite the problems, there are several available methods for designing such measurement systems, as well as several tips and 'tricks of the trade' that have been published in both practitioner and academic literature. MeTo is based on some fundamental principles for measurement-system design derived from several sources (e.g. Basili, Caldiera and Rombach, 1994; Grady, 1992; Grady and Caswell, 1987; Kerssens-van Drongelen and Cook, 1997; Meyer, 1994; Park, Goethert and Florac, 1996). Such principles include the following:

- Measures should be derived from explicitly stated organizational goals, in order to obtain a minimal set of relevant measures.
- Organizational goals often need to be broken down into sub-goals before becoming concrete enough to be measurable.
- Measurement goals that specify the purpose of measurement should be defined and linked to the organizational goals.
- Measures and goals are always linked to some organizational entity: the object of control.
- The link from objects via business goals and measurement goals to measures is important for the purpose of interpreting the measurement, and for motivation.
- A measurement system should be designed so as to be useful not only for management, but to all stakeholders, including the people being measured.

MeTo supports these principles by requiring the user to utilize the concepts of objects and business and measurement goals when defining the measurement system. Initially, MeTo was built to support the GQM approach (Basili, Caldiera and Rombach 1994), but based upon feedback from industrial pilot users, it was adapted to allow an organizational goal to be linked directly to a measure without using the measurement goal and question layers.

Measurement needs to be made part of the day-to-day management and self-management cultures of the organization. Goals and achievements should be made visible and understandable, and effectively and efficiently communicated to all stakeholders. To facilitate this, MeTo can export information related to the specified objects, goals and measures into a 'control plan'. The control plan is a HTML document directly linked to the visualizations in ViCA. This makes it possible for anyone to understand easily the rationale and use of the specified measures, since this information is only one mouse-click away. The measurement-system designer can also define the different kinds of visualizations that should be built in ViCA, thus also specifying the actual use of the measures.

The authors think that a tool like MeTo should be used for recording and maintaining the documentation related to the measurement system. The actual design of the measurement system is best performed in brainstorming sessions and workshops with different stakeholders, since this makes more knowledge available, and is important for ensuring commitment to the measurement system.

The Visualization Client Applet

ViCA shows graphical visualizations of sets of measures, collected into panels, and provides users with tailored panels, enabling them to see only the information that is relevant to them. Panels are either presented in separate windows or embedded in Web pages. Each panel may contain numerous charts, navigation buttons and images.

The charts are visualizations of data fetched from MESS. The contents of a chart can be scrolled, making it possible to put large amounts of data in a single chart. Charts can be created by the users themselves, or selected from a predefined set created by a system administrator. Collecting pre-defined charts to new panels and changing the visual attributes of charts (e.g. size, colour and labels) is simple. Typically, users can assemble new panels containing all the information they need themselves.

For an end user, using ViCA is as easy as Web browsing. However, implementing new charts from scratch requires good knowledge of SQL, ViCA and the contents of the MESS database. Data for the charts is fetched from MESS using SQL queries. The mapping of a query result to a chart is flexible and allows visualizing several data sets (e.g. information on several projects) in a single chart. Fourteen chart types – such as line, bar, area, pie and Gantt – are available for illustrative visualizations.

The difficulty in creating charts is eased by visualization libraries. These contain common domain-specific visualizations and data requirement definitions. Such libraries are added to ViCA as external components, depending on the needs of the users. A domain-specific library allows a user organization to know the minimum set of data required for practical visualizations and get the basic visualizations in use immediately. All the chart definitions in a library are built on an SQL-view interface. The installation of a library requires this interface to be mapped to the company's MESS database structure. Thereafter, a simple chart wizard can be used to create new charts based on the templates in the library.

Charts are typically grouped into proper panels providing information on, for example, a process or project, or some aspect of them, such as schedule follow-up. Panels may be linked together into hierarchies, making navigation possible. Navigation means that by clicking a button or a certain part of a chart, such as a task in a Gantt chart, a new panel opens, providing more detailed information on the clicked item.

The need to create several similar panels for the same purpose is minimized by parameterization of charts, that is allowing SQL queries to contain variables that get their values during navigation. Thus, for example, a general project panel may be constructed that shows information on a project that was selected for navigation in a project-portfolio panel.

Two sample panels are presented in figure 10.4. In the first panel, the Gantt chart shows all projects in a company. Clicking a bar in the chart opens a panel showing detailed data on the selected project. If another project had been chosen, a visually identical panel would have opened, but based on the second project's data.

ViCA is also used for some administrative tasks, such as the creation of new user accounts and groups, and the management of access rights of separate entities in the system. Implementing this functionality in a separate application would be a better solution, in order to reduce the size and complexity of ViCA. For research purposes, ViCA can be started

Figure 10.4 **Two ViCA panels and navigation from a chart to another panel**

with an option that makes it produce detailed log files on user actions, such as opening and saving panels and charts. This data can be used to calculate usage statistics at a detailed level.

ViCA is implemented as a Java applet, and works via a Web browser, thus allowing access to authorized users from a company intranet or from anywhere via the Internet. Use is not limited to any specific hardware or operating system – the only requirement is the availability of a Java-capable Web browser. This choice of technology has been made to allow access to the system regardless of the physical location of potential users, and without need for any software installation, except the Web browser.

Experiences

A prototype version of the LUCOS tool framework is in pilot use in the product-development departments of five high-technology companies. In two of the companies, the deployment has advanced to actual use of the system in several product-development projects. However, so far the use has largely been visualization of project progress with ViCA, without aggregating data on higher levels.

Deployment steps
Deploying the LUCOS toolset requires several steps, both technical and non-technical. The most important, most difficult and a non-technical

step is the definition of the measures that will be visualized using ViCA. As discussed earlier, there are several methods available for measurement definition. When the measures have been defined, they can be documented using MeTo. Following measurement definition, data collection procedures and systems have to be defined and deployed. Usually, the existing reporting systems in a company do not provide all the required data for the desired measures. Therefore, the reporting systems must be enhanced, or new systems brought into use.

The deployment of the LUCOS tool framework can begin when the required reporting systems are in use. First, the database schema for the data to be stored in MESS must be designed, and an EDAM for each data source configured or implemented. If some of the provided EDAMs can be used, the configuration takes only a few hours for each data source. Otherwise, the EDAMs must be programmed, requiring a couple of days of work for each EDAM.

Finally, the charts, panels and navigation structures must be built in ViCA, and the correctness of the data in the charts must be verified. Chart creation and validation is the responsibility of a dedicated ViCA system administrator – other users will only watch the visualizations. The effort required in creating a chart depends on the complexity of the chart, the SQL knowledge of the user, and whether some provided visualization library contains the desired chart or not. Therefore, creating a chart may take anything from a few minutes to several hours. When the charts are ready, any user can construct a personal panel in minutes, or immediately examine a predefined panel.

Naturally, there is a continuous cycle in the development of measures and visualizations. Whenever new goals and measures are defined, new visualizations should be created for them in ViCA.

A deployment case

Our system has been in production use for some time in one of our pilot companies: a small software house developing IT systems for wholesalers. The system is used for monitoring the status of both software projects and the customer-support process. This section reports on the experiences from one of the software projects. The goal of the project was to modernize a legacy software system consisting of about one million lines of code. Due to the size and the uncertainties involved, the project was divided into incremental releases, each with a duration of about nine months. The project staff consisted of a project manager and seven designers and testers. Our system was used for monitoring project progress during two of these releases. The installation, as used in the case project, is shown in figure 10.5.

In the case project, project planning was done with Microsoft Project. The project manager planned the project at a very low granularity; each task had a maximum duration of three days, and was typically assigned to a single person. Whenever updated, the project plan was dumped to MESS using the PMIX plug-in. All project personnel used pre-formatted Excel templates for time reporting, which was done daily at half-hour granularity. Each row in the Excel sheet contained a task ID that either linked the task to the project plan or indicated unplanned work. The data from the project plan and the timesheets were combined in MESS.

Figure 10.5 **The LUCOS toolset installation**

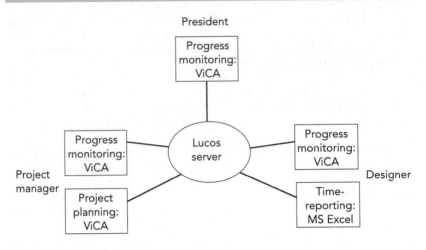

Figure 10.6 **A project control panel in ViCA**

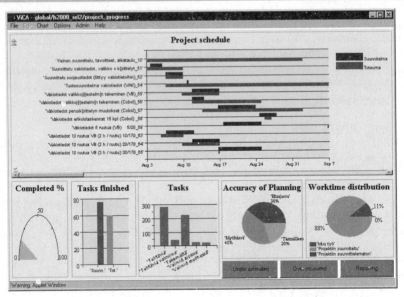

Several visualizations were built for use in the project. Figure 10.6 shows the main project panel, and figure 10.7 the set of panels to which it is possible to navigate from the main panel.

The main project panel consists of a Gantt chart showing planned versus actual details at a task level, as well as visualizations of earned value, accuracy of planning and work-time distribution. By clicking a bar in the Gantt chart, a new panel opens, showing the daily effort put into the task by each employee and their daily estimation for effort required to finish the task. The company also utilized data from version

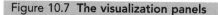

Figure 10.7 **The visualization panels**

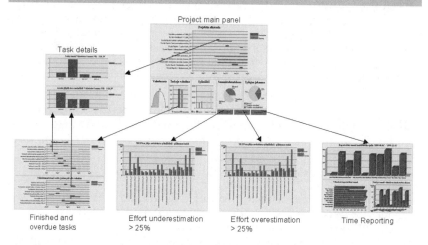

control system log files. The stability of design documents is observed by visualizing change rates.

The usage and effect of the usage of the system was analyzed through interviews with both project personnel and management, as well as by the use of log files generated by ViCA. An analysis of the usage logs shows that company management used the system to visualize project progress on average three times per week, whereas the project manager and project personnel used it much less, averaging once per week (per individual). The main reason for the relatively low usage by project personnel was, according to the interviews, that those individuals already knew what was going on in the project, as they all were co-located and the project was quite small. Another reason was that they did not think the panels were useful. Indeed, from discussions, they would have preferred panels containing information that concerned them directly – tailored individual panels. This is possible with the technology, but these have yet to be developed.

Company management, which did not participate in the day-to-day workings of the project, instead relied on ViCA to get up-to-date information on the project's progress. The Vice President in charge of product development felt that having such a system made it possible to understand what was going on in development for the first time in the company's history. At one point in time, the system really proved its worth, as the following quote from the Vice President reveals:

> in the second release of the case project, the measures had showed that the project was lagging behind schedule for a couple of weeks. In the weekly progress report, this could also be seen in the 'hard' project management information included: completed and unfinished tasks. The verbal comments by both the developers and the project manager mentioned only 'slight delays' that would easily be corrected.

When the steering group had its meeting and assessed the situation based upon the verbal report by the project manager as well as the visualizations of the project status provided by ViCA, there was a big discrepancy. The project manager indicated that the project was only marginally late, the measures indicated a delay of about three weeks. The project manager's opinion was that the measures must be wrong. He immediately investigated, and found out that the project was indeed three weeks late. In accordance with the project-control principles agreed upon, the steering group decided that about 30 per cent of the content planned for the release had to be taken out, and gave the project manager two days to replan the project in order to meet the schedule realistically.

We acknowledge that this does not prove the value of visualizations *per se*, but we believe that the fact that the Vice President could easily check the data by himself and draw his own conclusions made a difference. During discussions with management, the visualizations were constantly referred to.

The logs also give some indication of the effort needed for chart and panel development. The time used for developing the charts varied from one to forty minutes, with a mean of five minutes. According to the person who developed the charts, the effort depended on the complexity of the SQL query, and on the possibility of re-using previous queries. Building one panel (which also typically includes time for chart editing) took between one minute and eleven hours, with an average of ten minutes. As expected, the time needed depended on whether new charts had to be developed or existing ones used. All in all, the development of the charts and panels used in the case project took 46 hours on the system, spread over several calendar months.

On the whole, all people involved in using the system felt that having up-to-date visual feedback on project status was valuable. The developers and the project manager stressed the need for panels tailored to their specific needs. Management was satisfied, and decided to extend the usage of the system to other projects and company processes. The system administrator felt the system was useful, but complained about the complexity and error-proneness of defining SQL queries for the charts. He also stressed the fact that in practice most measure and visualization development is iterative – this made it difficult to get input from the organization before building some example visualizations.

Lessons learned

The case taught several valuable lessons about introducing such a system in a small organization. First of all, it is most important to get both management and personnel committed to measurement and visualizations. This demands considerable effort and good communication at all levels in the organization. Secondly, deploying the system is a quite long process, even in a small organization. Thirdly, the system could work usefully in a small-scale setting without requiring extensive overhead.

Both technical and non-technical issues slowed down the deployment of the system. Initially, we thought that companies themselves would write EDAMs to transfer data from their systems. In practice, however, this proved difficult. The companies involved lacked the necessary skills to do this, or did not want to invest their own resources. Consequently, the authors created EDAMs that would allow connection to the most commonly used data-collection systems in the companies.

The non-technical issues proved even harder than the technical ones. Non-technical problems pertain mostly to the difficulty in defining good measures. Defining measures based on the strategic goals of the company requires commitment and effort. Most measures were in practice first prototyped and then iteratively improved. Verifying the correctness of the SQL queries is important, since even an advanced user can easily make errors.

Conclusions

This chapter has presented an architecture for combining and utilizing data from different sources, and a toolset based on this architecture that can be used in defining and implementing a measurement system. The architecture allows EDAMs and client applications to be added, written on almost any platform and with most programming tools. However, providing users with 'plug-and-play' configurable EDAMs is essential in decreasing the effort required in deployment. Other advantages of the architecture are its flexible access control and the hidden database interface – except for SQL queries from clients.

Part of the study involved a deployment case, which showed that the system can be brought into use with relatively little effort, and can be useful. Through deployment experience, it was learned that it is important to tailor the information display to different stakeholders. Each individual is likely to have specific knowledge needs. The authors propose that the system's usefulness is greater in larger, more complex projects.

References

Anonymous (1998) *Sybase Enterprise Data Studio Feature Guide*, Sybase Inc.

Basili, V.R., G. Caldiera and H.D. Rombach (1994) 'The goal question metric approach', in *Encyclopedia of Software Engineering*, Wiley.

Berners-Lee, T., R. Fielding and H. Frystyk (1996), *Hypertext Transfer Protocol – HTTP 1.0*. MIT/LCS, MIT Press.

Devlin, B. (1997) *Data Warehouse: From Architecture to Implementation*, Addison-Wesley.

Eccles, R.G. (1991) 'The performance measurement manifesto', *Harvard Business Review*, 69, 131–137.

Grady, R.B. (1992) *Practical Software Metrics for Project Management and Process Improvement*, Prentice Hall.

Grady, R.B. and D.L. Caswell (1987) *Software Metrics: Establishing a Company-Wide Program*, Prentice Hall.

Kaplan, R.S., and D.P. Norton (1992) 'The balanced scorecard – measures that drive performance', *Harvard Business Review*, 70 (1), 71–79.

Kerssens-van Drongelen, I.C. and A. Cook (1997) 'Design principles for the development of measurement systems for research and development processes', *R&D Management*, 27 (4), 345–357.

Lassenius, C., M. Nissinen, K. Rautiainen *et al.* (1999) 'The interactive goal panel: a methodology for aligning R&D activities with corporate strategy', in *Proceedings of the IEEE Conference on Engineering Management*, San Juan, Puerto Rico.

Lassenius, C. and K. Rautiainen (1999) 'An incremental approach for improving the controllability of product development', in *Proceedings of the 6th International Product Development Management Conference,* Cambridge, UK.

Meyer, C. (1994) 'How the right measures help teams excel', *Harvard Business Review,* 72 (3), 95–103.

Park, R.E., W.B. Goethert and W.A. Florac (1996) *Goal-Driven Software Measurement – A Guidebook,* CMU/SEI-96-HB-002, Software Engineering Institute.

Part 3

Implementing knowledge management solutions

11 Knowledge management: the human factor

Jacky Swan, Maxine Robertson and Sue Newell

Introduction

KM is being lauded as an important new approach to the problems of competitiveness and innovation currently confronting organizations. The theoretical argument for the development of KM rests on a presumed paradigm shift in the business environment, in which knowledge is increasingly central to organizational performance (Drucker, 1993). The practical case for KM is also convincing many academics and practitioners that to avoid costly problems associated with 'reinventing the wheel', organizations need to find ways of learning across projects distanced by time and space.

The next section begins by defining KM and outlines the case for research in KM. The chapter continues with an examination of the salient literature on KM. Through this, the major findings from a recent review of the now burgeoning literature on KM are presented (Scarbrough, Swan and Preston, 1999). This reveals that much of the literature on KM is driven by a 'hard' IS view, which promotes the belief that IT-based tools (for example intranets and groupware) can be used to capture and stockpile workers' knowledge and make it accessible to others via a KM application, so that it can be used in other related projects (Cole-Gomolski, 1997). It is claimed, then, that IT-based tools can facilitate the exploration of knowledge – that is the pursuit and identification of new options, through knowledge creation and construction. They can also facilitate the exploitation of knowledge through the use and development of things that are already known within the organization but currently under-exploited, through capture and distribution (Levinthal and March,

1993; Fletcher, 1997). Importantly, this review reveals a major gap in the literature in its treatment of people. By contrasting the KM literature with that on organizational learning (OL), it can be seen that the management of people and behavioural issues identified as critical in the latter (such as culture, leadership, motivation and rewards) are rarely addressed in any depth in articles about KM. Indeed, the lack of concern with people in the KM literature is oddly reminiscent of earlier problems with business process re-engineering (BPR), referred to by some as 'the fad that forgot people' (Davenport, 1996).

The fourth section of the chapter addresses the implications of this lack of concern with people management in KM. A survey is presented of KM practice in a broad sample of UK firms, predominantly in the manufacturing sector. This demonstrates that the major predictors of problems with respect to organizational possession of the knowledge needed to develop new projects are concerned with people's behaviour and reward and appraisal systems, and not IT-based tools.

The fifth section of this chapter examines why there is a continued emphasis on IT in KM initiatives, and the limits of this. Here the authors argue that IT-driven KM initiatives place greater emphasis on exploitation than on exploration, and yet exploration is arguably more central to innovative capacity and competitiveness. Moreover, these initiatives place more emphasis on the supply of information than on the demand, application and utilization of information for processes of knowledge creation. Taken together, this means that the success of such IT-based KM tools in facilitating processes of innovation and promoting knowledge creation is likely to be limited. This chapter thus aims to encourage a more critical view of the impact of IT-based tools on knowledge creation and knowledge sharing (e.g. Clark and Staunton, 1989; Earl, 1996; Grant, 1996). Finally, the chapter ends with a summary and some conclusions.

Defining KM – the case for research

The growing emphasis on 'knowledge assets' (rather than labour or capital), 'knowledge work' and 'knowledge workers' as the primary source of productivity in contemporary society suggest that the current interest in KM will endure, even though the label may change (Drucker, 1993). This is not to say that knowledge was ever insignificant in industrial development. However, what is distinctive about the current period is a shift in patterns of knowledge production such that knowledge now acts upon itself in an accelerating spiral of innovation and change (Castells, 1996).

The intellectual argument for research in KM is accompanied by a more practical one. This is that KM addresses the very tangible problems associated with the redesign of work organizations. Indeed KM could be seen as an antidote to earlier initiatives such as BPR that, despite claims of 'faddishness', left very real consequences, and some problems, in their wake (Mumford, 1994). In organizational terms, flatter structures, decentralization, networked organizational forms, process management and increasing use of information communication technologies accompany the new 'era'. However, as businesses are stretched across time and space, and restructured around virtual teams and networks, opportunities for the sharing of knowledge and learning induced by physical proximity and specialism are lost. As Prusak (1997) notes, 'If the water cooler was a font of useful knowledge in the traditional firm, what constitutes a virtual one?'

Practitioners are increasingly recognizing KM initiatives that address these concerns as important. For example, a survey of 100 leading companies in the UK revealed that only 2 per cent considered KM as a fad that would soon be forgotten, and 43 per cent of respondents considered their organization to have a KM initiative in place (KPMG, 1998). KM, then, is worthy of investigation both as a new managerial discourse and as an enduring managerial practice.

There is no single definition of KM, but in general the idea relates to unlocking and leveraging the knowledge of individuals so that this knowledge becomes available as an organizational resource. In this way, the organization dependent on knowledge for its competitive advantage is deemed less susceptible to individuals 'walking out of the door' with this key asset (Marshall, 1997). The purpose of this chapter is not to privilege one narrow set of definitions, because we recognize that both knowledge and KM are best understood as complex multi-layered and multi-faceted concepts (Blackler, 1995). Here, then, the term KM is scoped out broadly as any process or practice of creating, acquiring, capturing, sharing and using knowledge, wherever it resides, to enhance learning and performance in organizations (Prusak, 1997; Quintas, Lefrere and Jones, 1997).

KM is part of a much wider debate about the shifting demands of the business environment and the sources of competitiveness in advanced economies. This debate has raised a number of questions about ways of organizing, the management of people and the role of technology. The review outlined in the next section considers the extent to which these questions have so far been addressed in the KM literature.

Knowledge management in the literature

This section summarizes a review of the KM literature. The review covered the concept of the 'learning organization' alongside KM because both of these management ideologies are centrally concerned with enhancing organizational performance through improved opportunities for learning and developing knowledge. This contrast was informative in terms of understanding the core themes and discourse of KM, and key drivers of this discourse. Details of the review process can be found elsewhere (see Scarbrough, Swan and Preston, 1999; Swan, Scarbrough and Preston 1999). The review covered mainstream journal articles from January 1993 to August 1998. These articles were located via searchable databases of social science and management journals (in particular Proquest Direct [PQD] and BIDS ISI). The review was limited, then, by those journals listed (mostly those in English). That said, PQD alone is quite comprehensive (1562 different journals), and the findings from this review were supported by a broader examination of a wide range of additional sources (e.g. websites, news, book listings).

The PQD search yielded 334 references to KM and 439 references to the learning organization over the period 1993 to 1998, whilst a similar search of BIDS yielded a total of 68 KM and 92 learning-organization references. Further searches carried out using combinations of core terms allowed a classification of numbers of articles by dominant subject areas. This search was accompanied by a qualitative analysis of the content of the abstracts of all articles covered by the review. This provided a reasonably thorough coverage of the core themes and issues in the KM and learning organization literatures (Crossan and Guatto, 1996).

The analysis allowed the development of management ideologies (in this case KM and the learning organization) and their associated 'buzz-words' to be tracked over time. Figure 11.1 indicates rapid emergence in the discourse of KM, with more references to KM in the first six months of 1998 than cumulatively in the previous five years. This contrasts with a rise and fall in references to the learning organization – a profile that mirrors the normal distribution observed across a number of other managerial practices (Abrahamson, 1996). Abrahamson notes that these diffusion patterns reflect the prevalence of fashion cycles in management literature.

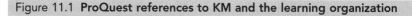

Figure 11.1 **ProQuest references to KM and the learning organization**

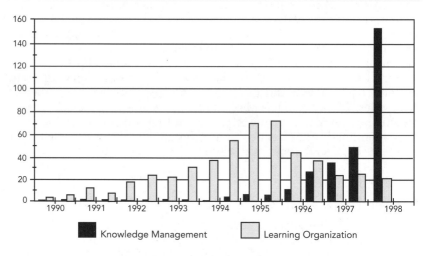

It might be tempting to conclude here that KM is driven by the same philosophy as the learning organization, but has merely replaced it as the latest management buzzword. However, an analysis of the major themes discussed in the literatures on KM and the learning organization highlight significant differences. The findings are summarized in tables 11.1, 11.2 and 11.3. The separation in table 11.1 between IS and IT reflects an attempt to distinguish broader information management and strategy (IS) from 'harder' information software and tools (IT). As seen, IT articles were the most prevalent of all KM articles. Articles on intellectual capital also focused mainly on development and exploitation of knowledge 'assets' (often via IT-based tools), with relatively little attention to people management. Tables 11.1 to 11.3 suggest that the shift in emphasis from learning organization to KM shown in figure 11.1 has been linked both to a sharp decrease in attention to people management, training and development themes, and to an equally sharp increase in attention on IS and IT. For example, nearly 70 per cent of KM articles in 1998 focused on IS or IT.

Table 11.1 Comparison of core issues in the the learning organization and KM in PQD articles, 1993–8

No. of hits (%)	'Learning organization' and...	No. of hits (%)	'KM' and...
98 (29)	'training'	58 (26)	'information technology'
65 (19)	'organizational development'	48 (22)	'intellectual capital'
		40 (18)	'information system'
48 (15)	'HR' or 'HRM', 'human resource'/'personnel management'	26 (12)	'training'
		17 (8)	'HR' or 'HRM', 'human resource'/'personnel management'
25 (8)	'management development'		
18 (5)	'employment'	8 (3)	'career'
16 (5)	'people management'	7 (3)	'people management'
14 (4)	'information technology'	4 (2)	'organizational development'
11 (3)	'career'		
10 (3)	'information system'	4 (2)	'rewards or appraisal'
7 (3)	'diversity'	2 (1)	'human resource information systems'
7 (3)	'rewards or appraisal'		
5 (2)	'intellectual capital'	2 (1)	'management development'
3 (1)	'human resource information systems'	5 (2)	all other combinations
6 (2)	all other combinations		

Note that percentages are subject to rounding errors, hence total is greater than 100

Table 11.2 1993 Learning organization thematic categories

	Count	Percentage
Management: general prescriptions and cases	17	39
Training and development	7	16
Quality and TQM	6	14
Leadership	4	9
Human resource	3	7
IS/IT	2	5
Societal context	2	5

Table 11.3 1998 KM thematic categories

	Count	Percentage
IT	73	40
IS	51	28
Strategic management	35	19
Human resource	9	5
Consultancies	8	4
Others: libraries, academic, accounting, marketing	8	4

It is also feasible that KM is not distinctive from, but merely a subset of, a broader literature on the learning organization with a closer emphasis on IT. However, an analysis of the types of journals that published articles on KM and the learning organization suggests that these concepts have been developed among distinct professional communities. The development of KM has been concentrated within the IT and computer science community, so that almost 48 per cent of articles written about KM were found in computing journals. In contrast, people or human resource management (HRM) and organization science theorists have been the dominant groups concerned with the learning organization. More than half (51 per cent) of all of the articles published on the learning organization were found in HRM, organizational theory and general management journals. Only 0.5 per cent of organizational learning articles were published in computing journals.

It is highly unlikely that these different professional communities read or author each other's journals and magazines. Therefore, this analysis suggests that KM is a divergence from, and not a development or a subset of, the learning organization, a concept developed mostly within the domain of people management. In particular, the concept has focused on the creation of a learning culture and the development of trust and commitment engendered through appropriate people management practices. In contrast, the fact that the concept of KM has been developed mainly within the IT community has led to a much heavier emphasis on IT, IS and organizational accrual of intellectual capital.

This analysis also indicates an emerging gap in articles on KM in terms of the treatment of issues concerning people management. Despite observations that 'the most dramatic improvements in KM capability in the next ten years will be human and managerial' (Davenport, 1995), most articles continue to focus on developing and implementing KM databases, tools (e.g. decision-support tools) and techniques. The reasons for this emphasis in KM on IT-based tools will be fully examined in the discussion. Next, its implications for KM practice within firms is considered. There are two main possibilities here: one is that the literature is merely a reflection of the centrality of IT-based tools in driving successful KM; another is that people-management issues do pose real problems for KM, but that these have been neglected in existing research. The latter would suggest that KM, like its predecessor, BPR, may be in danger of becoming the next 'fad that forgot people' (Davenport, 1996), a re-labelling of information management, rather than a genuinely innovative attempt to create opportunities for the creation, development and use of knowledge in organizations.

The human factor: a survey of KM practice

This section outlines the findings from a pilot survey of KM practice in UK firms. The survey aimed to assess the extent to which IT and/or people-management issues pose problems for KM practice in terms of learning across projects. The focus here is not on whether firms use the label 'KM' – all firms are likely to be engaged to some degree in problems of managing knowledge (Coombes and Hull, 1998). Rather, the survey examines the actual practices firms use to encourage learning across projects. When approached to conduct a much larger survey of UK members of the Institute of Operations Management (IOM), the authors had the opportunity to include questions about KM practice. Given constraints on sample selection and questionnaire size, this survey must be considered a pilot. Nonetheless, the paucity of systematic research on actual KM practice (in a literature dominated by anecdotal examples) means that a more systematic, albeit exploratory survey is timely.

The questionnaire

Questions on KM practice were developed drawing from earlier research on knowledge communication and KM practice, in particular Scarbrough (1996) and Coombes and Hull (1998). In order to get a handle on actual KM practice, using a language that would be interpretable by respondents, the survey focused at the level of projects, specifically addressing practices related to learning from one project to another. Further details on the design of the questionnaire, the methodology used, and the analysis are presented elsewhere (Swan and Robertson, 1999). The main purpose here is simply to demonstrate that people-management issues do indeed pose critical constraints on knowledge-sharing across projects. This reinforces the importance of attending to these issues as core rather than peripheral in research and literature on KM.

Specifically, the questions chosen referred to:

- The use of recorded information from past projects; the benchmarking of recorded information across projects; encouragement for archiving, or the recording of learning or knowledge from projects; the use of various IT-based tools and communication media for knowledge sharing (including e-mail, Internet/intranet, groupware/Lotus Notes and hard copy); the difficulty of use of such systems for capturing learning across projects.
- The involvement of people in projects based on records of relevant expertise; the reluctance or otherwise of people to share knowledge; difficulties arising from changes in people across projects.
- The reward systems used to reinforce knowledge sharing; the decision structures (from centralized through to networked); the type of manu-facturing process in which relevant (from unit through to large batch/repetitive); available time for capturing learning across projects.
- The extent to which learning across projects occurred through either formal or informal (i.e. personal contact) channels, and the use of informal contacts to involve people in projects.
- The extent to which lack of knowledge and information was seen as a critical constraint on developing projects. This question was treated as the critical dependent variable in the analysis below.
- Whether the concept of 'knowledge management' was recognized as an important issue in respondents' firms. This gives further indication as to the extent to which the KM discourse was being used in practice.

The response sample

The questionnaire was mailed as part of a larger survey to the entire IOM membership (of approximately 4000). This resulted in 617 usable responses. The characteristics of the sample should be noted when evaluating the findings. The majority of respondents worked in manufacturing industry (67 per cent) across a wide range of sectors in areas related to operations management. The remainder worked in consultancy (12 per cent), software supply (8 per cent), education (4 per cent), services (4 per cent) and a scattering of other sectors (5 per cent). A significant number (43 per cent) worked in senior management or director positions, with most of the remainder in middle or junior management (26 per cent and 8 per cent respectively) or technical specialist (13 per cent) positions. Approximately 75 per cent classed their companies as multinational and 58 per cent were owned by a larger corporation. In terms of size, 30 per cent worked in companies with more than 1000 employees and 33 per cent in companies with 300–1000. A total of 89 per cent of respondents had access to e-mail at their place of work, and 72 per cent had access to the Internet at work.

Analysis

The initial analysis confirmed the importance of KM practice. The discourse of KM had diffused quite widely, with around half the sample recognizing it as quite important, important or very important. Lack of knowledge and information was also seen by the majority as a constraint on developing projects – with only 14 per cent indicating this was 'rarely' or 'never' a constraint. This suggests that the problems associated with knowledge sharing across projects are pervasive.

The majority of firms (95 per cent) relied on some form of recorded hard-copy information for knowledge-sharing across the firm. IT-based tools were also used quite widely for this purpose, with 83 per cent using e-mail, 61 per cent using intranets and 42 per cent using some form of groupware (including Lotus Notes). In terms of the problems of capturing learning across projects, however, difficulty in using these systems appeared to play a relatively minor role. Only 17 per cent reported this as a problem as compared to: lack of time (70 per cent); reluctance to share information (31 per cent); and people changing across projects (24 per cent). This suggests that for these firms problems in knowledge sharing were predominantly and critically concerned with people management issues.

Table 11.4 summarizes the response frequencies to the questions about KM practice. This suggests that in general, learning from past projects is often recorded or archived (77.4 per cent do this at least 'sometimes') or benchmarked (78.6 per cent do this at least 'sometimes'). Further, this recorded information does tend to be used in developing new projects (91.4 per cent do this at least 'sometimes'). Learning across projects occurs via both formal (e.g. recorded information, e-mail or Lotus Notes) and informal (e.g. personal contact) channels, although significantly more often via informal than formal channels (t=12.19, p<0.001, 2-tailed). People tend to be selected for projects equally often on the basis of informal personal contact as on the basis of formal records of their expertise. However, in many cases knowledge sharing is not really rewarded by the company's reward and appraisal systems. Over half (58.5 per cent) of respondents indicated that knowledge sharing was rewarded either 'not at all' or 'not very much'. The responses to questions shown in table 11.4 were also correlated with the critical question on knowledge sharing: 'to what extent is lack of knowledge and information a constraint on developing projects?' Where the correlation was significant ($p<0.01$, 2-tailed), this is indicated in table 11.4 with a double-asterisk. All relationships were in expected directions; the more the particular practice was used, the less problem there was with a lack of knowledge-sharing.

Table 11.4   Response frequencies and relationship to critical variable of KM practices

Question	1	2	3	4	5
Use recorded information from past projects? (r=0.04)	19.8	32.6	39.0	6.5	2.1
Benchmark information from past projects? (r=0.04)	15.0	29.2	34.4	17.0	4.3
Encouraged to archive/record learning from projects?** (r=0.17)	28.9	30.4	18.1	14.4	8.2
Involve people based on recorded relevant expertise? (r=0.03)	19.5	36.9	33.1	7.3	3.1
Reward/appraisal encourages knowledge-sharing?** (r=0.21)	6.9	19.4	15.1	31.5	27.0
Learning across projects occurs via formal channels?** (r=0.13)	16.8	37.5	19.3	20.2	6.2
Learning across projects occurs via informal channels?** (r=0.19)	29.8	44.0	15.1	10.6	0.5
Involve people in projects based on informal contact? (r=0.07)	18.8	37.2	35.3	7.5	1.2

Note: numbers shown indicate percentages of respondents answering on a 1–5 scale. On this scale, 1 is the highest score ('always/a great deal'), 5 the lowest ('never/not at all').

To test these relationships further, stepwise regression analysis was conducted to assess which, if any, of the KM practices addressed in the survey independently predicted the critical variable, 'lack of knowledge-sharing'. The questions in table 11.4 were entered into the regression, together with the questions concerning the use of KM tools, the difficulties in capturing learning, company structure and manufacturing type, company size, and job position of the respondent. This analysis revealed only two significant predictors of lack of knowledge-sharing: first, people being reluctant to share (multiple $R=.26$, $F=24.18$, $p<.001$); second, the extent to which knowledge sharing was rewarded by the companies' reward and appraisal systems (increasing multiple R to 0.32; $F=18.25$, $p<.001$). Both of these barriers to knowledge sharing are associated with people rather than systems. Notably, the use (or lack of) of IT-based communication tools did not independently predict lack of knowledge-sharing.

Discussion

This chapter has argued that the literature on KM has been dominated by an emphasis on IT-based tools. Notwithstanding, the survey found that these issues – specifically the willingness of people to share knowledge and the ways in which their companies reward knowledge-sharing – are crucially related to constraints on project development through lack of knowledge-sharing. This implies that people-management issues do need close attention if KM is to be effective. The introduction of formal IT-based tools for KM may also have important implications for the management of people and social relationships, including their willingness to share knowledge. These implications warrant much closer research attention if KM is to avoid the same fate as BPR, and thus become another fad that forgot people. The reasons behind the emphasis on IT-based tools and its implications need to be understood if KM is to develop, both as a managerial practice and a discourse.

Reasons for the emphasis on tools-based KM

Much of the KM literature is practice- rather than theory-driven, with many articles appearing in practitioner-oriented computer-science journals and magazines. The emphasis on IT-based tools in KM can be understood, then, in terms of the need to diffuse KM concepts to the widest possible number of practitioners. This places heavy demands on the codification and commodification of KM concepts. To become more widely accessible, portable and marketable, ideas on KM practice need to be abstracted from their local contexts. At the same time, there need to be incentives for intermediaries (e.g. consultants or suppliers of KM tools) and firms to engage in the diffusion and adoption of these ideas. 'Black-boxing' KM as a technological 'fix' for what are often complex, intangible and intractable problems of managing knowledge addresses both these needs (Scarbrough, 1995).

Commodification of new ideas through 'black-boxing' strategies is an important element of the diffusion of innovations or fashions (Abrahamson, 1996). It is probably not coincidental that the surge of interest in KM has mirrored the earlier widespread diffusion of the BPR fad. The reasoning is as follows: BPR's emphasis on de-layering and process-based organizations has eliminated important forms of organizational knowledge embodied in middle-management groups and embedded within functional or professional disciplines. Eventually, the value of what has been lost has been recognized, and a new fashion cycle, this time centred on KM, has been initiated. Many of the same groups (and some of the same individuals) who promoted BPR – IT or IS specialists, consultants and management 'gurus' (e.g. Davenport and Prusak, 1998) – are now driving the debates and discourses of KM. In evidence, KM now features as a core component of the services and internal organization of major consultancies, several of which feature frequently as case examples in the literature (e.g. Hildebrand, 1994). However, labels aside, it is widely argued that KM is more than just a fad, and the problems it seeks to address will endure (Ruggles, 1998). This is supported to a degree in the survey reported in the previous section; managers recognized the difficulties of managing knowledge in projects, even though they did not necessarily use the label KM.

It is also clear that behind the KM discourse there lays a 'resource-based' view of the firm, in which intellectual capital assumes greater importance than financial capital (Roos and von Krogh, 1996). The emphasis is on identifying and capturing the 'knowledge assets' of the firm so that they can be both fully exploited and fully protected. The language of knowledge as a resource and something to be exploited pervades the KM literature. The logical quest, then, has been for tools that leverage knowledge and put it to use: 'The idea behind KM is to stockpile workers' knowledge and make it accessible to others via a searchable application' (Cole-Gomolski, 1997). KM is often equated to mining for data. Indeed, mining, digging and drilling metaphors are frequently used (Leonard-Barton, 1995). People do feature, but only in as much as they are fundamental to the intellectual resource. The dominant discourse of KM to date (i.e. to capture, codify and exploit the knowledge of employees by developing better tools and methods) is not fundamentally about managing and developing people. It is also demonstrably different to that of the learning organization, which does emphasize people; to harness the learning capability of the firm and individuals necessitates the management of complex issues, including values culture, people commitment and leadership.

It does not seem too speculative, given the numerous KM articles in the IT and IS literature, to suggest that this community provides an important professional sponsor for the diffusion of KM. Again, this has implications for the shaping of KM concepts. For example, the emphasis on codification in KM probably reflects the dominance of the IT and IS lens, which has specific advantages. By focusing on specific tool-based projects, the practical implications and outcomes are relatively easy to see, at least in terms of systems improvement. The emphasis on codification of knowledge through tools has also meant that the responsibility for KM has conveniently fallen to IS and IT experts who are well equipped to develop IT strategy and to offer education and training in the application of the tools. The chief knowledge officer (CKO) role, for example, is often filled by personnel with IT backgrounds. Maglitta (1995) cites examples of KM projects in General Motors, Fidelity Inc., Hewlett Packard and a number of other leading firms. In each case, 'IS plays a key leadership or support role. IS's systemic thinking, technology know-how, and experience of working with many departments can be the perfect background for KM' (Maglitta, 1995). It makes good sense for IT or IS professionals to colonize KM, as this can serve to increase their involvement in core strategic issues within their own organizations and enhance the status of their community more generally. The IS colonization of KM is perhaps another explanation of the marginalization of people-management concerns. That is not to say that these are not seen as important, but rather the discourse and practices surrounding KM serve a different set of priorities. Equally, HRM specialists (who have been central to discourse on the learning organization) have not really taken onboard the issues or ownership of KM (Johnson, 1998). This is despite KM's emphasis on intellectual capital and its obvious relevance to HRM.

The review presented here suggests that KM has not really drawn from the lessons of past failures, for example in BPR, to acknowledge human and behavioural issues. Nor has it taken many hints from the large pre-existing literature on the learning organization. The disconnection between the practices of people management and KM may, in part, be explained by the different languages and discourses of the different professional communities (IS/IT or HR) that promote these practices. The problem is that there appears to have been very little cross-learning between these communities, or between the literatures with which they engage.

Implications of tools-based approaches to KM

IT-based KM solutions promise a way of redressing the balance of power between autonomous knowledge workers and the knowledge base of the firm; by codifying individuals' tacit knowledge, intangible knowledge assets can no longer 'walk out of the door'. However, they also represent a potentially damaging approach to KM: first, they over-emphasize the exploitation of existing knowledge and de-emphasize exploration; second, they offer a limited understanding of tacit knowledge; third, they de-emphasize social relationships and networks in shaping processes of knowledge creation.

Firstly, in terms of the 'exploitation' of knowledge, the idea is that by using KM systems a reinvention syndrome can be avoided; instead of people in projects starting afresh each time, IT-based KM systems enable them to learn from past projects and experiences. KM is based on the premise that this learning can be codified, stored and made available to others at different times and in different places. However, the codification and objectification of knowledge from past experience into formal systems (even if possible) may generate its own pathology in terms of innovation and learning. This is because fluid, organic, informal and locally situated practices that are seen as essential in creative processes of innovation may become rigidified by the system (Scarbrough, 1996). Further, the direction of new projects may be dictated by information from past ones stored in systems (which, after all, are there to be used). The paradox, then, is that whilst KM tools may increase the effectiveness with which existing knowledge is exploited, they may simultaneously reduce opportunities for knowledge exploration and lower the knowledge-creating potential of the organization.

The limits of tools-based approaches to KM also emerge from their treatment of tacit knowledge. Polanyi (1966) was among the first to distinguish between tacit and explicit knowledge. Explicit knowledge is that which is easily expressed in formal, systematic language. Tacit knowledge is rooted in action and involvement in a particular context (Nonaka, 1994). This type of knowledge cannot be easily articulated or transferred, because it is context-specific. The objective of tools-based approaches to KM is to store explicit knowledge in a form that can be easily accessed by others for whom it might be useful. However, this approach to KM is limited because, arguably, it is tacit knowledge that will typically be of more value (Grant, 1996; Hall and Parker, 1993). Moreover, some tacit knowledge is probably impossible to codify; for example, intuitions and hunches, which are a form of tacit knowledge (Nonaka, 1998), are not readily codified, since by definition they occur 'immediately and without reasoning' and cannot be expressed. Of course, some tacit knowledge can be codified, as Tsoukas (1996) points out: 'tacit knowledge can indeed be linguistically expressed if we focus our attention on it'. However, even if codified, tacit knowledge cannot be understood or used without the 'knowing subject' (Popper, 1972); 'the realization of its [tacit knowledge] potential requires the close involvement and co-operation of the knowing subject' (Lam, 1998). That is, it can be transferred only by example or observation, demanding practical experience in the relevant context.

When considering tacit knowledge, a more fundamental question is why this knowledge has not been codified in the past in IT systems. There appear to be a number of explanations for this, each providing a fundamental challenge to the likely success of a tools-based approach to KM. Some valuable tacit knowledge in a firm may not lend itself to capture because it is: difficult to explain; ambiguous or uncertain; seen to be unimportant; highly changeable; contextually specific; politically sensitive; or seen as too valuable to the people concerned for them to want to share it. Therefore, forcing tacit knowledge into codified forms may result in knowledge which is: useless (if it is too difficult to explain); difficult to verify (if it is ambiguous or uncertain); trivial (if it is unimportant); redundant (if it is continuously changing); irrelevant (if it is too context-dependent); politically naïve or disruptive (if it is too politically sensitive); or, inaccurate (if it is too valuable to the people concerned). Tools-based approaches to KM typically fail to consider the multi-faceted characteristics of knowledge, especially tacit knowledge, and KMS cannot adequately address the problems associated with the codification of tacit knowledge.

The limits of tools-based approaches to KM are perhaps even more apparent when we turn to the wider literature on organizational knowledge creation (e.g. Blackler, 1995; Nonaka, 1994). This literature highlights the social embeddedness of knowledge – the importance of relationships, of shared understandings and of attitudes and behaviour to knowledge formation and sharing within organizations. Accepting the view of knowledge as socially constructed through processes of interaction means that issues of managing power and social relationships come to the fore. KM tools such as intranets, for example, may be used to protect the expert power base of particular social groups and restrict knowledge sharing:

> An intranet is a powerful tool that, when used correctly, can enhance communication and collaboration, streamline procedures, and provide just-in-time information to a globally dispersed workforce. Misused, however, an intranet can intensify mistrust, increase misinformation, and exacerbate turf wars [Cohen, 1998].

In their theory of what it takes to become a knowledge-creating company, Nonaka and Takeuchi (1995) note the central importance of generating commitment to knowledge sharing. Even if perfect systems existed, people need to be willing to make them work.

A core assumption in much of the literature is that technology enables effective KM. One problem is that this perspective essentially views knowledge as a static stock (Nonaka, 1998). IT-based KM tools are presented as unproblematic, and the social exchange and political aspects of the ways they are devised and used are sometimes even ignored (Liff, 1997). Moreover, this privileges an information-processing view of knowledge as cognitive abilities (inputs) that can be identified and processed using technology (e.g. which codifies and distributes) to produce certain outputs. In contrast, understanding knowledge as embedded in, and constructed from, a social relationship highlights a need to unpack the 'black box' of human interactions in KM (Silverman, 1970).

Conclusions

By identifying the problems associated with IT-tools-based approaches to KM, this chapter hopes not to dismiss them, but to stimulate alternative theorizing about their use and impact within organizations. IT-based KM tools clearly have a role in the new 'knowledge era'. In particular, they may facilitate the efficient exploitation of knowledge and reduce the amount of reinvention that occurs. However, even here it must be recognized that not all knowledge that is 'known' within an organization is readily codified and transferred; nor is all knowledge that is supplied readily found and applied. Seeing knowledge as socially constructed, negotiated and interpreted leads to the possibility that technology may disable as well as enable KM.

Our analysis of the literature and the diffusion process for KM suggests that the label applied to BPR, the 'fad that forgot people', is in danger of applying equally to KM. Recently, critics (including IS specialists) have argued that there has been far too much reliance on IT-systems ideas for KM: 'successful KM requires a skilful blend of people, business processes and IT' (Dash, 1998). This recognizes that KM is related to individual cognitive skills, along with organizational and institutional characteristics such as employment systems, career development patterns and organization design (Hedlund, 1994) and sector-specific labour markets and communities of practice (Lam, 1998; Spender, 1992). However, few KM articles discuss these issues in anything other than very broad terms. Yet the survey outlined here suggests that these are the bedrock of KM. As clearly demonstrated with earlier initiatives, such as BPR, unless issues of commitment, trust, culture and leadership are addressed, employees will not be willing to engage. The findings presented in this chapter imply a central, not peripheral, role for people-management issues in KM. As Hibbard and Carrillo (1998) note: 'Getting people to share their knowledge requires not only new processes but also a new covenant between employer and employees'. Perhaps those engaged in KM could take onboard their own messages and prevent more 'reinvention of the wheel' – learning from the failures and successes of earlier management ideologies such as BPR and the learning organization.

References

Abrahamson, A. (1996) 'Management fashion', *Academy of Management Review*, 21, 254–285.

Blackler, F. (1995) 'Knowledge, knowledge work and organizations: an overview and interpretation', *Organization Studies*, 16 (6), 16–36.

Castells, M. (1996) *The Rise of the Network Society*, Blackwell.

Clark, P. and Staunton, N. (1989) *Innovation in Technology and Organization*, Routledge.

Cohen, S. (1998) 'Knowledge management's killer applications', *Training and Development*, 52 (1), 50–53.

Cole-Gomolski, B. (1997) 'Users loathe to share their know-how', *Computerworld*, 31 (46).

Coombes, R. and R. Hull (1998) 'Knowledge Management in R&D Laboratories', ESRC Report, Swindon, UK.

Crossan, M. and Guatto, T. (1996) 'Organizational learning research profile', *Journal of Organizational Change Management*, 9 (1), 107–112.

Dash, J. (1998) 'Turning technology into TechKnowledgey', *Software Magazine*, 18 (3), 64–73.

Davenport, T.H. (1995) 'Think Tank', *CIO*, 9 (6), 30–32.

— (1996) 'Why reengineering failed: the fad that forgot people', *Fast Company*, 1, 70–74.

Davenport, T.H. and L. Prusak (1998) *Working Knowledge*, Harvard Business School Press.

Drucker, P. (1993) *Post-Capitalist Society*, Butterworth-Heinemann.

Earl, M.J. (1996) *Information Management: The Organizational Dimension*, Oxford University Press.

Fletcher, L. (1997) 'Information retrieval for intranets: the case of knowledge management', *Document World*, 2, 32–34.

Grant, R. (1996) 'Toward a knowledge based theory of the firm', *Strategic Management Journal*, 17, 109–122.

Hall, D.T. and V.A. Parker (1993) 'The role of workplace flexibility in managing diversity', *Organizational Dynamics*, 22 (1), 5–18.

Hedlund, G. (1994) 'A model of knowledge management and the N-form corporation', *Strategic Management Journal*, 15, 73–90.

Hibbard, J. and K.M. Carillo (1998) 'Knowledge revolution', *Informationweek*, 663 (5), 49–54.

Hildebrand, C. (1994) 'The greater good', *CIO*, 8 (4), 32–39.

Johnson, M. (1998) 'HR looks in the mirror', *HR Focus*, 75 (7), 304.

KMPG (1998) 'Knowledge Management', KPMG Research Report.

Lam, A. (1998) 'Tacit knowledge, organizational learning and innovation: a societal perspective', Presentation to the British Academy of Management, Nottingham.

Leonard-Barton, D. (1995) *Wellsprings of Knowledge*, Harvard Business School Press.

Levinthal, D. and J. March (1993) 'The myopia of learning', *Strategic Management Journal*, 14, 95–112.

Liff, S. (1997) 'Constructing HR information systems', *Human Resource Management Journal*, 7 (2), 18–30.

Maglitta, J. (1995) 'Smarten up!' *Computerworld*, 29 (23), 84–86.

Marshall, L. (1997) 'Facilitating knowledge management and knowledge sharing: new opportunities for information professionals', *Online*, 21 (5), 92–98.

Mumford, E. (1994) 'New treatments or old remedies: is business process reengineering really socio-technical design?' *Journal of Strategic Information Systems*, 3, 313–326.

Nonaka, I. (1994) 'A dynamic theory of organizational knowledge creation', *Organization Science*, 5, 14–37.

— (1998) 'The concept of "ba": building a foundation for knowledge creation', *California Management Review*, 40 (3), 40–54.

Nonaka, I. and H. Takeuchi (1995) *The Knowledge Creating Company*, Oxford University Press.

Polanyi, M. (1966) *Personal Knowledge: Towards a Post-Critical Philosophy*, Harper Torchbooks.

Popper, K. (1972) *Objective Knowledge: An Evolutionary Approach*, Clarendon Press.

Prusak, L. (1997) *Knowledge in Organizations*, Butterworth-Heinemann.

Quintas, P., P. Lefrere and G. Jones (1997) 'Knowledge management: a strategic agenda', *Long Range Planning*, 30 (3), 385–391.

Roos, J. and G. von Krogh (1996) 'The epistemological challenge: managing knowledge and intellectual capital', *European Management Journal*, 14 (4), 333–338.

Ruggles, R. (1998) 'The state of the notion: knowledge management in practice', *California Management Review*, 40 (3), 80–89.

Scarbrough, H. (1995) 'Blackboxes, hostages and prisoners', *Organization Studies*, 16 (6), 991–1020.

— (1996) *The Management of Expertise*, Macmillan.

Scarbrough, H., J. Swan and J. Preston (1999) 'Knowledge Management and the Learning Organization', Report, IPD.

Silverman, D. (1970) *The Theory of Organizations*, Heinemann.

Spender, J. (1992) 'Knowledge management: putting your technology strategy on track', in *Management of Technology III*, Institute of Industrial Engineers.

Swan, J. and M. Robertson (1999) 'Prevent reinventing the wheel: putting the people into knowledge management', in *Proceedings of Information Systems Research in Scandinavia*, Finland.

Swan, J., H. Scarbrough and J. Preston (1999) 'Knowledge management – the next fad to forget people?' in *Proceedings of the European Conference on Information Systems*, Copenhagen.

Tsoukas, H. (1996) 'The firm as a distributed knowledge system: a constructionist approach', *Strategic Management Journal*, 17, 11–25.

12 Fundamentals of implementing data warehousing in organizations

Pat Finnegan and David Sammon

Introduction

In a dynamic and uncertain business environment, with increasingly intense competition and vibrant globalization, there is a growing demand by enterprises for both internal and external information. This demand has led to organizational changes in strategy, structure and performance, while also placing pressures on IS within organizations (Finnegan, Murphy and O'Riordan, 1999). The demand to analyze business information quickly has led to the emergence of data warehousing. Data warehousing overcomes the problems associated with traditional approaches to accessing large amounts of information in heterogeneous, autonomous distributed systems, as it builds a 'logically centralized data repository to fulfil the requirements of such demands' (Taha, Helal and Ahmed, 1997).

Data warehousing is a relatively new (Gray and Watson, 1998) and immature field (Barquin, 1996) that is informational, analysis and decision-support-oriented, rather than oriented towards transaction processing (Babcock, 1995). The strategic use of information enabled by data-warehousing technology promises to solve, or at least improve upon, the negative effects of many of the challenges facing organizations (Gupta, 1997; Love, 1996). These warehousing technologies, if positioned and properly implemented, can reduce business complexity, help organizations discover ways to leverage information for new sources of competitive advantage and to realize business opportunities, and provide a high level of 'information readiness', enabling quick and decisive response under conditions of uncertainty (Love, 1996; Park, 1997).

Implementing data warehousing

Data warehousing systems have to be 'custom-built' and 'organization-specific' to represent the unique architecture and specific set of requirements of an organization (Ladaga, 1995; Myers, 1995), as well as its political and financial constraints (Eckerson, 1995). Nevertheless, every organization that initiates a data-warehousing project encounters its own unique collection of issues around a common set of factors. These include the business climate in which the organization exists, project sponsorship and organization issues, the information intensity of the organization, the technological sophistication of the organization, the age and quality of the operational systems, the quality of the data, and the existing decision-support environment (DWN METIS, 1997).

The argument that an enterprise should assess its readiness for data-warehousing implementation prior to project initiation is identified in light of the high number of project failures that are attributable to technical, organizational, cultural, non-technical, economic, political and socio-technical factors (Kelly, 1997; Wells and Thomann, 1995). Although the causal factors associated with such failure are not directly concerned with the initial stages of the project, they can lead to failure at some stage of the warehousing implementation. If the causes of likely future problems can be identified in advance, then they can be addressed, or at least signposted and worked around, thus improving the data-warehousing project's chances of success prior to implementation (Boon, 1996).

Trade research to date has focused on the identification of corporate readiness for the implementation of data warehousing (Boon, 1996; Wells and Thomann, 1995) and an organization's suitability for data warehousing (Park, 1997). A dearth of academic research in the area of enterprise readiness for successful implementation is evident, particularly in the lack of methodological 'scholarly rigour' (Barquin, 1996) being applied to the existing models (Boon, 1996; Wells and Thomann, 1995). The use of a corporate-readiness model in a data-warehousing project implementation is incorporated into the 'preparatory stage' of an implementation methodology (e.g. DWN METIS, 1997). As a result, the organization cannot assess its readiness until the project has been initiated. Furthermore, these models are complex and not suited to use within the organization.

There are numerous similarities in data-warehousing projects (Boon, 1996; DWN METIS, 1997), and there is a common set of critical factors that have been identified for data-warehousing initiatives (Gray and Watson, 1998; Kelly, 1997; NCR, 1996; Singh, 1998). If the criticality of these factors can be pre-specified, then organizations would be able to determine the suitability of their organization for data warehousing, and identify those areas requiring attention prior to the initiation of the project. We have called these factors organizational prerequisites, and define them as 'necessary elements existing within the organization, which are examinable by the implementing organization, prior to undertaking the data-warehousing project'. If an organization can identify those areas requiring the greatest focus, prior to initiation, the organizational-prerequisites model can be used internally by the implementing organization. To achieve this, it is proposed that we should be able to identify how and why certain factors are critical to a data-warehousing project implementation, generalize these factors through the use of a structured-format model, and in effect signpost their incidence within organizations. From this, a set of organizational prerequisites for the successful implementation of a data-warehousing project can be generated.

Data-gathering

The objective of this study is to identify organizational prerequisites for the implementation of a data-warehousing project. To satisfy the research objective, research questions were formulated to determine how and why certain factors affect data-warehousing implementation. Specifically, these factors relate to technology and systems, data, skills, project-management and organizational issues.

Due to the exploratory nature of the study, a multiple-case-study research design was chosen. The rationale used was that mature users of data-warehousing technology would have the implementation experience necessary to explain the factors that they considered critical to the success of a project. The comparison of these factors across different organizations would lead to the foundation of an organizational prerequisites model. The case-study approach is considered appropriate, as it allows the researchers to probe the relationship between project variables and implementation in more depth than other research methods, such as surveys and experiments. The four organizations studied were purposely chosen to provide a breadth of implementation experience. They differed in nature of business, organizational structure, project scope, methodology employed, and in their strategic uses of the warehousing system. However, these organizations represent a minority of industrial sectors, an issue that must be addressed by further studies. Nevertheless, the researchers believe that the collective implementation experience of these companies is sufficient grounds for the proposed model.

The primary data-collection methods used for the study were semi-structured interviews and document analysis. Each organization was pre-selected on the basis of their implementation experience and their willingness to co-operate. Having received an overview of the project implementation, the researchers, in conjunction with a contact person, identified the key decision-makers in each organization. These decision-makers were interviewed over a four-month period during mid-1998. Each interview was semi-structured, to facilitate an examination of the company's experience in relation to the factors identified, as well as a consideration of other aspects of the company's data-warehousing initiatives. The data was analyzed using decision-tree analysis and meta-matrices. This approach facilitated both an exploration of the key issues within each company and an analysis of these issues across companies.

Data warehousing in the companies studied

Bank of Ireland is a nationwide financial institution with a significant number of subsidiary companies. Bank of Ireland had emerging information demands that prompted them to commission a study in

1991 to review and assess the organization's ability to deliver future MIS to the organization. Within the existing MIS systems architecture, there was considerable duplication of information, which resulted in a considerable amount of time being spent, by both the IT and business functions, on reconciling the outputs (reports) from the various systems. Furthermore, the systems were poorly documented, which led to the systems being highly people-dependent; there was a total reliance on the knowledge of people around the systems.

In 1992, an architecture was implemented to reposition the provision of financial and management information for retail branch and international banking. The information warehouse was designed to provide decision-makers with 'single-system image' access to data residing in many disparate operational and legacy systems. The Bank of Ireland initiated the project with a primary emphasis on decision-support and reporting systems in an attempt to achieve a required level of group customer exposure within the organization.

In 1996, there was a business requirement from group credit control (GCC) that necessitated a review of the whole credit area within Bank of Ireland in terms of strategic and operational systems. Within Bank of Ireland, the data was sourced from 24 business units, and loaded to a multi-dimensional database using Commander and System W software. However, the existing System W application, implemented in 1990, only provided access to data at an area level. However, the type of functionality required, due to the organizational hierarchy of the organization, needed to allow access to data at a region, district, branch, sub-office and account level. Therefore, in representing the five levels below the area level, the data-warehousing project leaders pointed out that data at the region, district, branch, sub-office and account level was 'completely ignored' in the existing system. As a result, Bank of Ireland required the implementation of a solution to break data down and examine the products, market sectors, credit rates and quality of the loan book right across those dimensions.

OilCo International (a pseudonym) is a major multinational group with over 1700 companies operating under various ownership arrangements. The management information and data services department is part of OilCo Services International, whose geographical scope is worldwide and business relates to IT services and solutions.

OilCo International initiated the implementation of a global distributed warehousing project with the objectives of providing consistent management information, better global customer exposure, more informed marketing decisions, and the ability to monitor the accounting procedures of various trading countries (to facilitate the ability to 'drill-down' through globally standardized 'distribution cost-allocation' data).

OilCo International had its first operational data warehouse up and running in 1989. However, this warehousing initiative lacked 'flexibility in design' to cope with the increasing rate of change of business requirements. Therefore, as a result of the lessons learned from the first initiative, OilCo International is restructuring the provision of global management information through the implementation of a global distributed-warehousing architecture, known as GENIE (GENeric Information warehousE). The GENIE architecture was developed, and is implemented, within OilCo International to address the challenge of sustainability, maintaining the integrity of the data at a sustainable cost. The organization is now approximately halfway through the process of rolling out the global distributed data-warehousing project.

This global strategy for data warehousing exists across multiple companies within OilCo International, resulting in no one company having an individual data warehouse. Project implementations are undertaken in the various businesses of OilCo International, and the project consists of two connected components:

- a common piece of technology based on a proprietary design that the organization developed
- common data models relating to business rules embedded within the technical platform.

Rover Group was the largest automobile manufacturer and exporter in the UK in 1998, having merged with BMW Group to create autonomous business units to exploit new opportunities. In May 2000, Rover Group was sold to the Phoenix Consortium, while Land Rover was sold to Ford. Furthermore, the organization is undergoing a programme of structural renewal within its major business units. Within Rover Group, the standardization of communications and data systems has led to improved conditions for close and efficient co-operation in product development. Group-wide efforts to improve business processes and the deployment of new information technologies has strengthened the group's competitive position within the market; the group now delivers to 120 markets worldwide.

Between 1991 and 1995, around 15–20 teradata data marts (databases measured in thousands of gigabytes) were implemented at Rover Group. These data marts related to: dealer information; Society of Motor Manufacturers and Traders; sales statistics; vehicle distribution information; order information; parts logistics activity; and financial-analysis reporting databases. However, it was later identified that the MIS environment was implemented in an essentially 'uncontrolled and unmanaged' manner. As a result, an enterprise data warehouse (EDW) initiative was introduced in 1995.

The EDW initiative was undertaken to make consistent corporate-management information more accessible to the entire organization (as opposed to individual business units). The ideal of the EDW initiative was to address the technical issues – overlapping databases, duplication of effort, fragmented data, data inconsistency, accessibility, inflexibility and re-keying – evident in the teradata data-mart initiative, while at the same time improving business performance by loading data that Rover Group needed into the warehouse.

The first EDW pilot project commenced in 1996, loading supplier data into the data warehouse. The EDW initiative encapsulated all of the teradata data marts that existed within Rover, while further building areas of data for the business where coverage did not exist (e.g. data coverage of suppliers, inbound logistics and core vehicle information). By providing links between the existing data marts and the EDW, the business can get additional information to complement that already existing in the data mart environment. The architectural environment that now exists within Rover Group is a combination of a central EDW with dependent data marts.

BankCo Group (a pseudonym) is the UK's premier business bank. It is one of the most innovative personal banks, a major provider of wealth-management products to personal and corporate customers, a key provider of card products and services, and is a leading participant in the world of electronic commerce. As a result of enormous change in financial-services markets, it has made significant progress in repositioning its business and improving its overall strategic focus. It is a unified organization, structured into 14 separate business units; units form a cohesive set of businesses that either take products and skills from, or provide introductions and business opportunities to, the group.

Initially, the business requirement for the client customer database (CCD) warehousing initiative was driven by competitive pressure in the market. BankCo Group's competitors were very aggressive in their marketing to customers. Competitors had targeted information about their customers; BankCo Group, therefore, required all credit-card transaction data to be loaded onto the warehouse to enable similar analysis and target marketing. Due to the competitive pressures in the market, there was a short timescale imposed by the business for implementing the data-warehousing project.

Like the CCD, the customer marketing database (CMD) warehousing initiative was driven by competitive pressure in the market. Therefore, there was no formal appraisal technique undertaken for the initiative. The CMD warehousing initiative had identifiable problems in implementation, in which the decision-making process of the business-focused direction of the project implementation collapsed. This was due to the fact that low-level funding for the CMD initiative was unavailable, and there was a politicized organizational concern in relation to the issue of data sensitivity within the project. Consequently, this led to a technically focused decision: IT management took onboard the CMD initiative and implemented the warehousing project on a minimal budget. Therefore, within BankCo Group, the CMD warehousing initiative is considered a failure.

Table 12.1 illustrates the experience of these organizations in relation to the factors considered important for data-warehousing initiatives. These factors are classified under the headings of systems, data, skills, organizational and project management.

An analysis of table 12.1 reveals a diversity of experience in relation to data warehousing. However, it is clear that the view of each company is influenced by the degree to which each factor affects the success of a project. For example, OilCo initially recognized the importance of systems factors, but had little difficulty in the area in practice. Indeed, they had more difficulty with factors in which they had not invested so much up-front effort, such as data, skills and organizational issues. This pattern is also reflected (in other factors) in the other three companies.

Table 12.1   Data warehousing experience in the organizations studied

Factors and categories	Initially considered critical but now not deemed critical	Initially considered critical and still deemed critical	Initially not considered critical but now deemed critical
Systems factors			
Hardware platforms	B	C, D	A
Applications (software)	B	C, D	A
Operating systems (processing)	B	C, D	A
Data extract tools	B	A, C	D
Data factors			
Source data (availability and quality)			A, B, C, D
Data standards	A, B	C, D	
Data models			A, B, C, D
Data management			A, B, C, D
Skills factors			
Users technical knowledge	A		B, C, D
Users business knowledge	A	C, D	B
Education and training	A	B, D	C
Experience of similar projects	A	B, D	C
Organizational factors			
Business factors			A, B, C, D
Information systems factors			A, B, C, D
Commitment to project			A, B, C, D
Project support			A, B, C, D
Data ownership	A, D		B, C
Project management factors			
Project drivers/enablers		A, B, C, D	
Funding of project		B, C	A, D
Project management experience		A, B, D	C
Perceived goals, benefits or expectations			A, B, C, D

Key
A   Bank of Ireland
B   OilCo International (pseudonym)
C   Rover Group
D   BankCo (pseudonym)

Organizational prerequisites for data warehousing implementation

From the experiences of the companies studied, we have extracted a set of organizational prerequisites. Rather than giving an account of the experience of all companies in relation to each prerequisite, we have chosen to illustrate prerequisites with salient data from one or two companies, in an effort to explain the underlying concepts.

A 'business-driven' data warehousing initiative

The study shows that the chances of successful implementation are higher when the data-warehousing project is planned, committed to and managed as a business investment, rather than a technology one. All of the organizations studied initially implemented a warehousing initiative that was 'IT-driven'. They subsequently identified that commitment, funding and management 'buy-in' were difficult to achieve and maintain. As a result of these experiences, further warehousing initiatives were 'business-driven'.

The first iteration of Bank of Ireland's information warehouse implementation, primarily relating to retail branch banking, was an IT-driven initiative. However, the second and third iterations, relating to international banking, area credit departments, the lending centre and group credit control, were business-driven, the business taking hold and leading implementation. The data-warehousing project leaders pointed out that since the project was business-driven there has been no problem with commitment.

The Global Practice Manager of OilCo International stated that 'the key factor that makes this work is that the warehouse design and scope is directly related to the business strategy'. The business strategy was broken into a set of critical success factors (CSFs) which were, in turn, used to generate a set of key performance indicators (KPIs). According to the Global Practice Manager:

> these KPIs are the most high priority items for the business, and should be in the form of what is called a Balanced Scorecard, incorporating some financial, customer and employee measures. The data warehousing initiative should be based on this set of Key Performance Indicators.

Executive sponsorship and commitment

Since many of the benefits of DW are unlikely to be foreseeable, projects need a champion at the senior-management level. This is especially true when the warehouse is to be implemented at an enterprise-wide level; the key goal of the warehouse is to build on a number of different data areas so that the critical issues across many topics can be investigated. All of the organizations studied had a problem with commitment to the project at some stage in implementation.

Within BankCo, for the CCD initiative, the Group IT Project Director states that 'there was a lot of support within card services. The head of card services had appointed an aggressive project manager for the duration of the project, who was determined to see the warehousing project initiative through on time'. He believes that 'the key factor in getting the system through was a good support network', but pointed out that 'the CCD initiative did experience problems interacting with the parent bank, due to the fact that the parent bank have their own set of priorities, which differed from that of the CCD initiative'. To overcome similar problems, both data-warehousing project leaders at Bank of Ireland believe that a data-warehousing project should have three areas of commitment: senior management, IT and business.

Funding commitment (budgeted and unexpected) based on realistically managed expectations

Funding for large projects such as data warehousing is difficult to attain, due largely to the fact that traditional cost justification is difficult. The lack of a strong business case with measurable benefits significantly reduces the chances of successfully funding a project. In many instances, the business case may have to be made on the basis of competitive necessities. Although it is difficult to achieve, projects need flexibility in justifying funds, and commitment to a stream of funding that may not at the time of implementation appear justified, based on traditional measures. In addition, many of the benefits from a data-warehousing initiative are unquantifiable. Consequently, expectations need to be realistically set and managed.

The Information Architecture Manager of Rover Group pointed out that:

> a data warehouse itself provides zero benefit. It is what the business does with the data in the warehouse that provides the benefits. The data warehousing initiative itself is pure and simply a cost. It is only the business action around the data warehouse that can justify it.

The data-warehousing project leaders of Bank of Ireland believe that an organization should set expectations from the start of the project, and manage the expectations by explaining what it is that the organization will have at the end of the initiative. The Information Architecture Manager of Rover Group stated that 'although benefits and expectations are unquantifiable, there is a quantifiable plan within the organization to measure the benefits and expectations realized from the initiation of the data warehousing project'.

The Group Finance Project Director of BankCo pointed out that 'benefits are seldom quantifiable, due to the size and scale (complexity) of the data warehousing project. However, benefits can be delivered even though they are unquantifiable'. The Group IT Project Director stated that 'it is very difficult to track the benefits of a warehousing project, and within the environment of the Group it is up to the business units to manage the expectations'. Consequently, business-unit justification and project funding, which reflects the organizational structure, was used for the initiation of the data warehouse. The Group IT Project Director pointed out that for the client customer database warehousing initiative 'funding was handled within card services, with justifications based on competitive threats'. The business case was founded on customer retention. The Group Finance Project Director stated that within BankCo 'the financial appraisal process is an afterthought, with the initial concerns relating to achieving the required level of "buy-in", "commitment", and "executive sponsorship" for the project to be undertaken'.

Project team with access to cross-functional project management and implementation experience

The scale and complexity of a data-warehousing project implementation is something that most organizations are neither familiar with nor prepared for. A warehousing project, which is representative of all business units, is in fact several different project initiatives. Therefore, an organization needs to have strong project-management and implementation skills. In each of the organizations studied, there were several business units represented in the implementation of the data-warehousing initiative, and the requirements of each of these units had to be represented. A typical case was Rover.

There are five manufacturing business units represented in the enterprise data warehouse initiative within Rover Group. The Information Architecture Manager points out that:

> One warehousing system, which is supposed to be the same in all five business units, is in fact five different systems. This means that the organization has five different projects to implement in terms of defining the data, identifying the source of the data, and loading the data to the warehouse.

Although the project management is different from that required in traditional systems development, he believes that there is a 'need for very strong "traditional" project management skills'. He states that 'the organization is still learning in relation to data warehousing project implementations, due to the fact that no two projects are identical. Furthermore, no two business sponsors or project teams are identical'. He adds that 'if Rover had not undertaken the teradata data mart initiative, the organization would have probably started off repeating the "teradata type processes" in the EDW initiative, without understanding what was actually required'.

Attention to source-data quality

The complexity of the data and the number of source-data quality problems generally only become evident once the data is loaded onto a warehouse. The issue of data quality should therefore not be underestimated by organizations.

The source data in all four organizations was dispersed across many different systems and stored on a variety of platforms. Consequently, each organization experienced problems with data quality. Inconsistencies in the data related to field naming, data currency, data duplication, data fragmentation, and the inflexibility of the data. An example outlined by the Global Practice Manager of OilCo International identified the existence of a source system containing 100,000 customer-related entries when only 20,000 customers existed. He concluded, 'traditional data-entry methods undertaken by organizations offered no incentive to data-entry personnel to get data quality right'. As a result, he believed that such issues needed to be tackled before undertaking a data-warehousing initiative.

The Information Architecture Manager of Rover Group stated that, 'in the teradata data-mart initiative, source-data quality issues were only discovered six months after they occurred, and the organization cannot do anything about catching back the data, because it is lost'. He further revealed that:

> On initiating the EDW project, a great deal of attention was paid to the quality of the data residing on the data marts. Therefore, an examination process was undertaken before the data was loaded onto the warehouse to ensure the quality was the best it could possibly be.

However, it took one-third of the project time frame to analyze the EDW source-data quality, involving end users and systems professionals.

A flexible enterprise data model

Even if project implementation is incremental, the data models on which a data warehouse is designed need to be consistent for every iteration of the project. Thus, representing a corporate-wide view (long-term) as opposed to a specific business-unit view (short-term) is necessary. In addition, business processes change over time, and these changes need to be reflected in the data-model design. Therefore, the organization has to think through the priority elements of the data model in advance, so that the initial design can allow for incremental and therefore manageable changes, to ensure flexibility.

Within BankCo Group there was an 'ideal' and a 'reality' in relation to the data model on which the client customer database was designed. The enterprise-wide data model – business reference model (BRM) – is a highly structured object-oriented model with numerous relationships between the objects. However, the physical model, a DB2 central database from which the data is sourced, represents a highly denormalized relational model, for performance reasons. The Group IT Project Director pointed out that 'a conflict existed between the "ideal" and the "reality"'! From a strategic point of view, the organization wanted to follow BRM. However, from a project point of view the DB2 model was followed, due to the sourcing of the data from the DB2 database'. The Group IT Project Director believed that:

> This option related to a 'short-term' view on behalf of the organization's warehousing implementation. While data mart 'spin-offs' are at present not an issue, they may be in the future, which will entail considerable redesign and restructure of the data model, in that the BRM was not followed.

Within Rover Group, the teradata data-mart initiative was modelled on entity relationship modelling (ERM), based on normalization. However, with the introduction of the EDW initiative, a hybrid of dimensional modelling, ERM (normalization) and denormalization was undertaken as the data-modelling technique. The Information Architecture Manager of Rover Group Ltd. believes that:

> Entity Relationship Modelling normalization is a great technique for reducing data redundancy, and a great technique for ensuring an optimum database design for flexibility etc. However, it is the worst possible technique for ensuring a queryable database. The hybrid data model adopted for the EDW initiative is easily updated, easily extensible, and easily changeable to represent business change.

Data stewardship

In the implementation of a data-warehousing project, the organization will identify problems relating to, for example, data security, data ownership and sensitivity, and lack of end-user experience in specifying queries. All of the organizations studied identified that, at a local level, data ownership and sensitivity were not considered. However, at a global level, this factor is one of the biggest problems encountered by the organization. Consequently, in an environment in which data is accessed and shared across business units, the role of a data steward is vitally important.

Within Bank of Ireland, data ownership was not really an issue, according to a project leader, because 'nobody wanted to own the data that existed on the legacy systems'. However, there is 'a certain degree of sensitivity around one business area having access to another business area's data'. The Group IT Project Director of BankCo stated that, 'from a business perspective, data sensitivity was not an issue, due to the fact that all of the source data for the CCD was generated by card services, even though it was processed externally'. Therefore, the data was not being shared across different business units, and consequently BankCo experienced fewer problems.

The Global Practice Manager of OilCo stated that 'one of the biggest problems encountered by the organization was the issue of data sensitivity'. He pointed out that 'in relation to the hierarchy of dimensions within the organization, ownership of the data model has to be firmly with the business who are driving the products of the business'. Similarly, Rover Group implemented a process of data stewardship involving one data steward per business unit, across all five of the manufacturing business units. The Information Architecture Manager stated:

> the role of the data steward is clearly defined as being the business steward of the data; assuming responsibility for assuring the quality of the data. It is not the steward's job to put the data quality right, but if a problem is discovered, there is a plan put in place to inform those whose job it is, to amend the data quality. Furthermore, the data stewards provide a definition of the data, along with identifying where the data is within the business, because sometimes the organization does not know.

A long-term plan for automated data extraction methods and tools
The volume of data to be extracted from source systems can experience extreme growth rates as the warehouse evolves and matures. Automated products that speed up the loading of the data onto the data warehouse are beneficial, and need to be considered early in the project lifecycle.

Initially, within Rover Group, there was some manual loading of data onto the teradata data marts. However, with the introduction of the EDW initiative, data warehouse loading was automated. In taking a long-term view of the requirements for an extract/acquisition tool, Rover identified that an appropriately selected tool pays for itself very quickly. The Information Architecture Manager noted:

> The hardware platforms influenced the choice of data-extract tools to be used in the EDW initiative. An organization basically has to have an extract tool which is certainly capable of going against Oracle on Unix, on a DEC Alpha, or on mainframe IBM DB2, plus the extract tool must be potentially extensible to run against any platform.

Within BankCo, Group IT spent a considerable amount of time deciding whether standard 'off-the-shelf' extract packages or 'in-house' *ad hoc* extract programs should be used for the project. The Group IT Project Director said that 'the project view was that as so many extract processes were already in place, it would be quicker to patch new processes into the existing extract programs, rather than ripping them all out and installing new tools, costing upward of £0.5 million'. Initially, Group IT could not justify the expenditure, within the project, for 'off-the-shelf' extract tools. However, according to the Project Director 'this decision is now being revisited, and although the organization did not initially have the resources, the option of implementing a standard off-the-shelf extract tool is now being seriously considered'.

Knowledge of data-warehouse compatibility with existing systems

The technology chosen for a warehousing initiative needs to show a level of compatibility and interoperability with that existing in an organization. Hardware and software choices (including the configuration of the 'box' in terms of the central processing unit (CPU), memory, disk etc.) are influenced by the source systems existing in the organization, and the configuration of such systems.

The data-warehousing project leaders of Bank of Ireland believe that platform configuration and integration is a vitally important area. They experienced difficulty making technological choices identified by solution vendors fit into the existing environment. They also believe that most of this difficulty could have been overcome by adequate attention to the issue of compatibility before implementation. The Global Practice Manager of OilCo International had a different experience. He believes that 'the choices of technologies like hardware, software applications and databases are irrelevant'. OilCo requires a 'commonality of technologies' based on a 'proprietary design' developed by the organization. The Global Practice Manager points out that 'even though the organization uses Oracle on NT, it wouldn't really matter if they used Informix and Cognos on Unix…no difference what so ever, just cost'; rather, 'it is important that an organization picks one technology, and once one has been chosen, the organization rules the others out; what an organization cannot have is seven technological choices'.

Hardware and software 'proof of concept'

A variety of technological choices exist for the implementation of a warehousing initiative, and an organization needs to ensure that the hardware and software infrastructure is free of conflicts. One possibility to ensure this is to establish a consulting partnership with the principal infrastructure vendors.

The data-warehousing project leaders of Bank of Ireland realized that no single vendor could satisfy all of the technological requirements, and formed strategic alliances with a number of vendors. A request-for-proposal (RFP) was issued to 15 vendors, with a 12-week pilot project undertaken to provide a 'proof of concept' of the proposed solutions.

External consultants were brought in for the analysis and design phase of the client customer database initiative within BankCo. However, a technology and strategy directive undertaken within BankCo Group IT raised concerns about the possible costs and functionality of the proposed solution. The internal IT Group consequently designed and implemented an organization-specific benchmark. This entailed visiting vendors and loading BankCo's data onto their platforms; they ran the systems with the CCD requirements in mind, and examined the results. Following this initiative a new technological solution was implemented.

Conclusions

The organizations involved in this study experienced problems with their initial project implementations, which were addressed in subsequent iterations of their data warehouses. This learning is captured in the foundation of an organizational prerequisites model – as summarized in table 12.2. The model presents decision-makers, responsible for implementing data warehousing, with a framework for internal assessment of the suitability of their organization for such infrastructures. The prerequisites cover a wide variety of factors, but it is clear that companies in this study experienced most difficulty with issues that are non-technological, as also illustrated by Kelly (1997). This raises questions about the desirability of implementing data-warehousing technology in organizational environments without first undertaking a comprehensive evaluation of these organizations. In effect, this approach justifies the development of an organizational-prerequisites model.

Table 12.2   Organizational prerequisites

1. A business-driven data warehousing initiative
2. Executive sponsorship and commitment
3. Funding commitment (budgeted and unexpected) based on realistically managed expectations
4. Project team with access to cross-functional project management and implementation experience
5. Attention to source-data quality
6. A flexible enterprise-data model
7. Data stewardship
8. A long-term plan for automated data extraction methods/tools
9. Knowledge of data-warehousing compatibility with existing systems
10. Hardware/software 'proof of concept'

This model differs from corporate-readiness models presented by other researchers (e.g. Boon, 1996; Wells and Thomann, 1995), and is not designed for use by data-warehousing consultants as part of an established implementation methodology. Rather, it is envisaged that it will be applied by organizations themselves. This study is both academic and exploratory, as called for by a number of researchers (Barquin, 1996; Widom, 1995). However, a more extensive study is still required, its purpose to verify and clarify our findings. In addition, a comprehensive method of organizational measurement is required to apply the model objectively. This research has laid a foundation, but further study is required to extend the use of the model into practice.

References

Babcock, C. (1995) 'Slice, dice and deliver', *Computerworld*, 29 (46), 129–132.

Barquin, R.C. (1996) 'On the first issue of the journal of data warehousing', *Journal of Data Warehousing*, 1 (1), 2–6.

Boon, C. (1996) 'Assessing corporate readiness for data warehousing', *Data Warehouse Report*, 7, 5–10.

DWN METIS (1997) *METIS Methodology Documentation Book – Release 2.3*, Data Warehouse Network.

Eckerson, W.W. (1995) 'The true nature of a data warehouse', *Oracle Magazine*, http://www.oramag.com/archives/15INDECK.html.

Finnegan, P., C. Murphy and J. O'Riordan (1999) 'Challenging the hierarchical perspective on information systems: implications from external information analysis', *Journal of Information Technology*, 14 (1), 23–38.

Gray, P. and H.J. Watson (1998) *Decision Support in the Data Warehouse*, The Data Warehousing Institute Series, Prentice Hall.

Gupta, V.R. (1997) 'An Introduction to Data Warehousing', http://www.dw-institute.com/pubsindex.htm.

Kelly, S. (1997) *Data Warehousing in Action*, Wiley.

Ladaga, J. (1995) 'Let business goals drive your data warehouse effort', *Health Management Technology*, 16 (11), 26–28.

Love, B. (1996) 'Strategic DSS/data warehouse: a case study in failure', *Journal of Data Warehousing*, 1 (1), 36–40.

Myers, M. (1995) 'Do you really need a data warehouse?' *Network World*, 12 (51), 26.

NCR (1996) 'The heart of a data warehouse', NCR Corp Online, http://www3.ncr.com/sdw/papers.html.

Park, Y.T. (1997) 'Strategic uses of data warehouses: an organization's suitability for data warehousing', *Journal of Data Warehousing*, 2 (1), 13–22.

Singh, H.S. (1998) *Data Warehousing Concepts, Technologies, Implementations and Management*, Prentice Hall.

Taha, Y., A. Helal and K.M. Ahmed (1997) 'Data warehousing: usage, architecture and research issues', *Microcomputer Applications*, 16 (2), 70–80.

Wells, D. and J. Thomann (1995) 'The keys to the data warehouse', *American Programmer*, 8 (5), 9–17.

Widom, J. (1995) 'Research problems in data warehousing', in *Proceedings of the International Conference on Information and Knowledge Management*, Seattle, WA.

13 Barriers to adoption of organizational memories: lessons from industry

Karma Sherif

Introduction

Organizational memory (OM) can be viewed as a repository of information gained from experience, made available to members of the organization for consultation. By retaining dynamic knowledge within an organization, members gain unlimited access to expertise beyond that of a human expert (Croasdell, Paradice and Courtney, 1997). Organizational learning is thus harnessed, not threatened, by personnel turnover (Stein and Zwass, 1995).

Most of the research in OM tends to focus on definitions of the term (Stein and Zwass, 1995; Walsh and Ungson, 1991) and on the content and types of OM (Argyris and Schön, 1978; Hall, 1984; March and Olsen, 1975; Walsh and Ungson, 1991). There have been few studies on the effects of OM on organizational effectiveness (El Sawy, Gomes and Gonzalez, 1986), the role of IT, and on the adoption and use of an OM and OMIS. Several researchers have stressed the role of IT in developing an OMIS to support the mnemonic functions of acquisition, retention, search, retrieval and maintenance. These functions serve as the basis for other effective functions, such as integration, goal attainment, pattern maintenance and adaptability (Walsh and Ungson, 1991). However, organizational learning becomes contingent on the acceptability and usability of organizational memories. With the focus on IT to capture, disseminate and maintain organizational knowledge, it becomes imperative for researchers and practitioners of OM to understand the belief system underlying the attitude of different stakeholders towards OMIS within organizations.

A review of the OM literature reveals that there is a paucity of studies to explain experiences with OM adoption. Researchers have alluded to the importance of personal attitudes in the capturing and sharing of individual knowledge as a conceivable source of problems (Stein and Zwass, 1995). Typical reported causes revolve around reluctance to share personal knowledge, or unwillingness to reuse the experience of others. As a result, little is known about why organizational members resist re-use of knowledge in OMIS, or what aspects of human nature defy the successful adoption of the technology. While researchers suggest that elements of organizational context are important (Vikas, Manz and Glick, 1998) these are rarely examined for their effect on the adoption of OM. Additionally, there is no empirical evidence to explain interactions among OM systems, the individuals involved and the organizational context. Experiences with previous technology implementations suggest that without understanding the nature of relationships that might exist between the technology and the organizational elements, including individuals, it will be hard to implement the technology and new approaches within organizations successfully.

This chapter thus focuses on understanding the individual and organizational beliefs underlying OMIS adoption, in an effort to inform theory and systems-development activities. We also aspire to provide managers with valuable insights on how to leverage knowledge assets. Rather than focusing on critical success factors, aspects that have been over-emphasized in the literature, this study addresses the concept of barriers to OMIS adoption. The focus stems from the belief that a considerable number of organizations implementing OMIS confront some level of barriers at either the individual or organizational level (Vikas, Manz and Glick, 1998). Without a clear assessment of the barriers and an identification of methods to cope with them, outcomes of the adoption processes will remain hard to interpret and prescriptive plans for OMIS adoption will not be comprehensive. The research questions addressed in this study are:

- Why do individuals and organizations constrain the adoption of OMIS?
- How can organizations overcome these barriers?

Research method

To ground theoretically an explanation of how and why organizations constrain the adoption of OMIS, this study focused on qualitatively analyzing the process of OMIS adoption. The grounded-theory methodology for qualitative research was chosen to guide data collection and analysis of cases studied. As a first step, conceptual categories were defined, to establish a context. These categories were drawn specifically from the OM literature; in particular, from studies related to adoption. Interview questions were designed around these categories, and data collected in the form of interview transcripts were classified under these categories. Initial classifications were compared among the different OMIS groups within the four cases, to help identify theoretical properties of the categories and relationships among them. Comparing similarities and differences among the different groups helped to define the scope of the theory, and also broadened its explanatory and predictive power (Eisenhardt, 1989). In keeping with the tenets of this methodology, the study alternated between data collection and analysis to determine whether new categories needed to be developed. The process followed was iterative, causing new categories to emerge as the data was re-examined and re-categorized. Repeated comparison of categories within the groups helped to identify relationships and formulate interesting hypotheses. During the iterative process of data analysis and collection, some hypotheses were dropped, others verified and new ones emerged. We followed this process to the saturation stage, i.e. when no new modifications were made during a comparison and when the number of categories collapsed to a shorter and more abstract list. A set of propositions was generated to crystallize the grounded theory. Each one of the propositions represents a hypothesis, the objectives being to provide a venue for future testing, and quantitative evidence to support or reject the theoretical construct.

While researchers embracing quantitative methods to test theories might not agree with the methodology used for this study, the author strongly believes that 'by studying organizations, scholars can build grounded theories incorporating new variables and insights as they increase their own expertise, and write up the result' (Daft and Lewin, 1993: p.ii). In particular, deduced theories have the tendency of intentionally or unintentionally swaying their followers away from seeing the social reality of the phenomena under study (Glaser and Strauss, 1967).

Research design

This study involves four organizations that adopted Lotus Notes as a collaborative tool for knowledge-creation and sharing. At all four sites, the technology was adopted to build a frame of reference for developers to utilize when collaboratively delivering solutions to customers. Data from the four sites was collected to identify the elements of organizational design that enable organizational learning from collaborative systems. The four case companies studied exist in three fundamentally diverse industries – oil and gas, telecommunications and software consulting. The names for all units studied and their respective organizations, have been masked to protect confidentiality. Specifically, the cases are:

- Case 1: the Energy Solution Group (ESG) at SCC – a leading software consulting firm. ESG develops accounting systems for customers in the energy industry. This group has realized the importance of capturing best practices and re-using them to develop applications quickly.
- Case 2: the Customer Billing Systems (CBS) at TCC – a worldwide telecommunications firm that provides local and long-distance services to customers worldwide. Several attempts have been launched within the organization to capture corporate knowledge and disseminate it among the different information-seekers within the organization.
- Case 3: an Oil and Gas Company (OGC) that operates worldwide. The department studied developed software solutions for refineries and chemical plant operations.

- Case 4: the client-server computing group (CCG) at ITS – a leading software consulting firm with offices in 13 US states. The client-server computing group provides solutions to telecommunications companies.

As suggested by other IT adoption studies (Markus and Robey, 1988; Orlikowski, 1993), we focused on two embedded units within the organization: individuals affected by the adoption process and the organizational context in which the concept is being applied. The study examined the individual beliefs of three sets of stakeholders identified by the literature – and supported by practitioners – as having the biggest influence on the adoption process. These are:

- contributors to OM
- users of OM
- upper management.

We also included elements of organizational structure in the research design, following the belief of many researchers in the field of organizational development (Myers, 1996; Mohrman, Cohen and Mohrman, 1995). In this area of research, it is strongly believed that KM initiatives will result in learning only when organizations intervene to modify elements of structure – such as division of labour, power structure, co-ordination mechanisms and networks of informal relationships. In this chapter, we focus on three main elements of organizational design drawn from previous research (e.g. DiBella and Nevis, 1998; Myers, 1996):

- strategies – including fit with organizational goals
- resources
- cultural issues – including receptivity to information sharing, re-use of knowledge and norms of collective achievement.

These constructs were used to guide the research – formulating a protocol for the interview. They were not taken as *a priori* explanations of the issues that underlie OM adoption (Eisenhardt, 1989; Kirsch, 1997); Glaser and Strauss (1967) warn against prior specification of constructs, because of the danger of forcing the constructs onto the data. However, we agree with Eisenhardt (1989), who states that:

> *A priori* specification of constructs can also help to shape the initial design of theory-building research. Although this type of specification is not common in theory-building studies to date, it is valuable because it permits researchers to measure constructs more accurately. If these constructs prove important as the study progresses, then researchers have a firmer empirical grounding for the emergent theory.

Data collection
The data-collection activity was primarily based on structured interviews. A set of open-ended questions was posed to each participant at the beginning of the interview. The aim was to allow participants to express beliefs freely, and in relation to their personal experiences. After the initial round of interviews, a new set of questions was added to the list to reflect additional concepts that emerged from the data. Follow-up interviews were conducted to collect data on emerging concepts that were not considered in the original interviews. This approach

is considered legitimate in grounded-theory methodology (Strauss and Corbin, 1990).

Archival data in the form of articles, promotional material and Web pages, was collected in addition to the interviews. This facilitated validation by triangulation. The variety of stakeholders interviewed provided a rich data-set with different levels of abstraction. Our goal was to slice vertically through each organization, obtaining data from multiple levels and perspectives.

Thirty-three interviews were conducted for the four cases. Twenty-nine of the interviews were taped and transcribed. At the request of the interviewees, the remaining four interviews were not taped. Extensive notes were taken during all interviews to mark contradictions with information gained from other sources, including the literature. Similarities were also marked.

Data analysis

The qualitative data-analysis software, QSR NUD*IST, was used to categorize the components of each interview. Transcribed interviews were imported into the package as text files. Subsequently, each interview was thoroughly examined and every sentence categorized under one or more of the emerging categories. This process of coding is known as open coding in grounded-theory methodology (Strauss and Corbin, 1990). In addition to coding, a contact summary form was prepared, so that the researcher could:

- specify the main issues drawn from this contact
- summarize the information collected under the research questions
- identify new concepts found salient, interesting, illuminating or important in the contact
- identify new target questions to be considered for the next contact at this site.

Issues emerged as interviews were being conducted and new cases were studied. Concepts were grouped into categories. Occasionally, new categories were added and others were regrouped when transcribed interviews were compared. After comparison of all interviews, a saturated list of categories was finalized. Data collected for each of these categories were compared across cases. The main focus was to compare and contrast the underlying issues that impact adoption of OM.

Research findings

In spite of the notable enthusiasm of top management for OMIS tools in all four organizations, there were inherent barriers within these organizations that constrained the adoption of these tools. The comparative analysis of the data revealed that barriers to the creation and use of an OMIS exist mainly in individual beliefs and misconceptions about the utility and ease of capturing expertise and disseminating it across organizational boundaries. Contrary to what has been suggested in the literature, cultural issues related to information sharing, collective achievement and tools defy traditional wisdom and support adoption. The major findings of the study are presented in figure 13.1. Barriers are indicated in the figure by negative symbols; positive symbols indicate concepts that support adoption.

Figure 13.1 **Barriers to OMIS adoption**

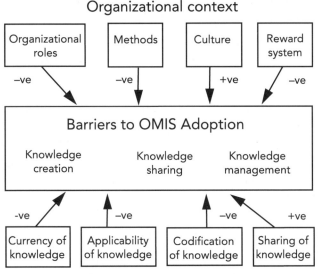

Organizational context

| Organizational roles | Methods | Culture | Reward system |

−ve   −ve   +ve   −ve

Barriers to OMIS Adoption

Knowledge creation   Knowledge sharing   Knowledge management

-ve   −ve   −ve   +ve

| Currency of knowledge | Applicability of knowledge | Codification of knowledge | Sharing of knowledge |

Stakeholder's beliefs

Individual beliefs

We found that there was surprising consistency in the belief structure of the four organizations. The beliefs were presented as a series of 'optimistic' and 'sceptical' convictions about OM and OMIS. In general, the stakeholders across the four organizations expressed a deep scepticism about knowledge codification (Sherif and Mandviwalla, 2000) when discussing the role of OMIS. The stakeholders believed that it is hard to capture experts' know-how, due to the difficulty of expressing and capturing tacit knowledge. For example, one user of the OM suggested:

> I just can't see how you're going to codify people's experience. It's just kind of an informal knowledge. There are some people that have worked in some project areas for a long time, so they have just become the domain experts, but we've never really documented that.

Similarly, one expert contributor to OM stated:

> My brain works in an unstructured manner. A lot of times there are just no reasons why I thought of a specific issue. I do not know how to explain to someone the way I go about making decisions, the way I go about solving problems.

Besides the uncertainty of codifying knowledge, stakeholders also expressed doubts about the currency of codified knowledge. Given the degree and frequency of change that organizations typically face, knowledge that can be captured and disseminated needs to be updated frequently. Most stakeholders – especially managers – did not believe that the economic cost of maintaining the repository would be justified. The belief is exemplified in the words of a manager at OGC:

> To me codified knowledge is static information, unless you update the repository; otherwise it's not accurate. That is why we keep documentation to a minimum. Unless you can guarantee that it is up-to-date, documentation is worthless. Unless you keep your knowledge assessment up-to-date, it's worthless. You can't count on it. So if it only happens once a year, I think why do it. It's not worth the trouble. And to me it would be hard to justify having a staff member that all he does on a year-around basis is to update everyone's knowledge. To me that's a waste of time.

Even if knowledge was periodically updated, stakeholders believe that it needs to be abstracted to allow its effective re-use. However, the lack of a formal methodology for synthesizing and aggregating the bulk of knowledge in the shared databases makes it hard for developers to learn from the experience of others outside their immediate group. This is especially true when there is no effort to consolidate different pieces of information to build a coherent domain model that members can rely on as a frame of reference. One developer explains the problem this way:

> A lot of the elements that comprise the database are very line-specific to [one of their customers]. We have made it available to some of the other projects and subsequently lost connection with those other projects with respect to how they are using that same database and how they are modifying it. Some effort could probably be spent to go and reconsolidate all the different copies of this that are out there and develop maybe a cohesive, complete version of the same database.

Overall, the beliefs surrounding the codification and currency of knowledge hosted by OMIS may lead organizations confronted with frequent change to be less motivated to invest time and resources in sustaining a structured reusable OMIS. As pointed out by a user:

> When an organization is changing so much, there's very little chance that certain processes that are in place will be carried over to the new organization. So the dynamics of an organization could also affect the stability of a knowledge library.

As a result of a lack of methodology to abstract knowledge, stakeholders attributed little value to idiosyncratic experiences, questioning their applicability to the range of a domain. Many stakeholders believed that codified knowledge would be so specific to the original contact that it would be useless in other contexts. Individuals articulated different (but related) thoughts on how the original contributor was needed in order for knowledge to be practically applied. A better system would be, as described by one manager:

> a mentoring process that goes on. Somebody gets really good at an area, then they take other people who are newer to it and they try and help them up the learning curve so it would be reasonably effective. But I've never seen anybody actually try and put an expert system in place to help other people to capture the knowledge of somebody else.

Contrary to the belief that an OMIS is of more practical benefit to decision-makers in accessibility to knowledge, the stakeholders interviewed in this study believed that, in the words of one user:

> with the hectic schedules, people don't have a lot of time to read over certain expertise in certain areas. If experts are needed on a project, they are going to be asked anyway to go work on that certain project and be available as a whole.

The main benefit that stakeholders attributed to the use of an OMIS was the ease of locating a source of expertise. Stakeholders saw OMIS as more reactive than proactive, enabling the soliciting of information from experts, rather than being a knowledge mine in themselves. This view is in alignment with the claim that organizational learning is a social phenomenon that is positively correlated with rich media. Accordingly, knowledge-seekers always felt the need for face-to-face communication to support learning from OMIS databases.

Stakeholders also expressed optimism about the personal value of knowledge-sharing. Unlike the suggestion in the literature regarding possible reluctance to share expertise (Stein and Zwass, 1995; Walsh and Ungson, 1991), data from all four sites confirmed that experts believed that knowledge-sharing would actually increase their value. One of the experts, a manager, believed:

> As time goes, experts' knowledge grows and you never really capture it all. You become more valuable when you've transferred that knowledge. You derive your sense of value from being able to learn quickly, being bright and very well adapted to a social environment.

Organizational context

Organizational development research argues that KM and sharing initiatives result in learning only when organizations intervene to modify elements of their structure – such as division of labour, power structure, co-ordination mechanisms and networks of informal relationships (Mohrman, Cohen and Mohrman, 1995; Myers, 1996). Data collected from the four sites supported these findings. Stakeholders suggested that the primary source of barriers to the development and use of OMIS is the lack of structural mechanisms to institutionalize the system.

First, the lack of defined roles and responsibilities to support the mnemonic functions of knowledge-creation and sharing cause stakeholders to question the organization's commitment to the whole initiative of actualizing an organizational memory. As one developer puts it:

> Management is never dedicated; I mean, if they really think something is important, they usually dedicate someone to the cause and make that part of their job description and review their performance on that particular topic if they really want something changed. They don't do that around here – they just throw it onto somebody else's platter, and it's just one of the twenty odd things you've got to do. And, if you get a client banging on your door, you're going to take care of the client, and you're not going to mess with that stuff.

With increasing workloads and the growing trend towards decentralization, the responsibility for consolidating information becomes an overhead. The lack of specific roles for KM causes OM stakeholders to view KM as an additional burden to existing workloads. Several interviewees justified their reluctance to spend time on abstracting information to support its use by other groups. For example, one user stated: 'I don't think people have time in some cases to share information unless they're in a close-knit functional group to communicate what's going on, to share in some of the things that are going on'. Similarly, in the words of a manager: 'We don't really allow that much time for developers to work on solutions so that they can be shared across the whole department'.

Another confounding problem is the lack of incentives for members of an organization to contribute to or use OMIS. The four organizations studied did not have any formal mechanisms for rewarding members who contributed information to knowledge bases to invigorate organizational learning. Although the organizational culture of all four sites nurtured a personal drive within developers to share information and contribute to organizational memories, the effort of transforming idiosyncratic experiences to meaningful cues is still localized. It becomes apparent that learning requires a motivation of both the knowledge-generators and the knowledge-users. As one developer explains:

> If we were set up to seriously invest in organizational learning, then part of the process would be providing incentives to both knowledge-creators and knowledge-users – because you need both. You need people to go out there and find the right information to take decisions, and you need people to take the time to take what they have and abstract it to make it re-usable and stick it into our repository.

A direct outcome of the lack of formal structure surrounding OMIS is the difficulty of accessing the right information. Stakeholders complained that, in some cases, they were not even aware of what was available. To illustrate, as specified by a manager:

> You've got distribution barriers. How do you make people aware that knowledge is out there and should be leveraged? How do you make that a part of their daily job, where they go out, and before they do anything around a particular area, they go out and look for things that they can leverage, rather than starting from scratch?

Organizations need to interject the right structure for the creation and sharing of knowledge. Although formal roles were believed to be critical to the actualization of organizational memory, one stakeholder suggested casual sessions or workshops where:

> you get people together to talk about the different solutions that they came up with [for a particular domain] and prompt them to synthesize it for future reference, instead of having snippets here and there which people don't seem to understand.

Thus, the main problem, as seen by the users of an OMIS, is the lack of an appropriate structure that defines a methodology for representing and managing knowledge, organizational roles and a reward system to motivate users to contribute to and re-use information residing in an OMIS. Unlike the suggestions in the literature, organizational culture was not believed to have played a role in the adoption of OMIS. In fact, all of the stakeholders interviewed in the four organizations asserted that their cultures fully supported information-sharing and knowledge-creation.

In other words, they expressed optimism about the organizational culture with respect to knowledge-sharing. At the same time, they questioned the cultural values of other organizations, as the words of one manager implies: 'I think that's a trait that we foster and nurture within our organization, with our people. I don't think sometimes the various customer sites I've worked in fully support it.'

Lessons learnt

Having uncovered the beliefs of OMIS stakeholders, it becomes obvious that the process of building an OMIS goes beyond the acquisition of tools. In fact, the most critical success factor is the recognition of the role of non-technical issues. Organizations need to assess the belief-system of prospective users of the OMIS, to reveal and cope with any possible misconceptions. In addition, organizations need to define an appropriate method for acquiring information, modelling it and developing knowledge assets. Roles need to be defined, and a reward system established. A summary of lessons learnt is presented below.

- Assess the need for an organizational memory.
- Make a business case for developing the OMIS, comparing the costs of not having a repository with the costs of having one. Present the results to all stakeholders – managers and decision-makers. The presentation should be in language that the stakeholder understands.
- Assess the receptivity of decision-makers to the idea and carefully study any concerns that might surface. Convey the reasons for adopting an OMIS and its importance to the organization as a whole.
- Depending on the organizational culture, determine the scope of the repository. The programme can start with a small pilot project to demonstrate the feasibility of building an OMIS. Stress the importance of learning from past experience.
- Determine the resources required to take the repository beyond a pilot study. Resources include funding, time and staffing.
- Assess the skills available, and determine the roles of creators and utilizers of the OMIS.
- Assess the currently adopted processes for decision-making and their compatibility with re-using past experience. Determine any necessary changes needed to adapt it to re-use. Convey to decision-makers the need for changing current methods, and get feedback regarding the applicability of the new methods.
- Promote the results achieved by projects. Aggregate the results in the form of lessons learnt that highlight both success factors and possible barriers.
- Make sure that decision-makers in different fields are aware of the available knowledge assets, and advantages associated with their use.
- Get feedback from decision-makers about the quality and use of knowledge in the repository.
- Remember that creating a shared organizational culture that fosters an OM is the only sustainable support for OMIS in today's continuously changing economy.

Conclusion

The literature on OM attributes the majority of barriers in the adoption of these systems to cultural beliefs. In a study of four organizations that adopted Lotus Notes to develop an OMIS, evidence from the data collected suggests that an organizational culture of information-sharing and collective achievement does not play a role in the adoption of OMIS. Data collected, however, suggests a number of misconceptions about knowledge residing in OMIS. Such beliefs regarding the feasibility of codifying expert knowledge, the currency of information stored in shared databases and the applicability of codified knowledge to different contexts, have caused members of the studied organizations to cut back on the necessary changes required to build an effective infrastructure to sustain the effort. At the organizational level, the lack of structural elements – such as methods to synthesize pieces of information and package knowledge into assets for re-use in different contexts, along with the lack of formal roles – caused stakeholders to question the commitment of the organization to OMIS adoption. In order to build organizational designs that support the development and usage of OMIS, organizations need to develop adoption strategies for educating members in ways of developing knowledge assets and the application of these assets to different contexts. Such training needs to go beyond simple tool introduction. It requires a strategy to cope effectively with the individual misconceptions that organizational members share and reinforce through organizational culture. It will also involve educating managers and employees on how to organize and disseminate re-usable knowledge. Additional structural elements include modifying organizational roles and restating job descriptions to stress the importance of knowledge-creation and sharing.

An interesting finding of the study is that the existence of barriers to an OMIS had no adverse effect either on decision outcomes like the cost, time and quality of a decision, or effect on organizational learning. The existence of mentoring systems to complement a semi-functional OMIS clearly mediated the negative effect of individual beliefs and environmental changes. In all four organizations there were active mentors that played the role of a human OM system. The project mentors taught developers certain ways of doing things; thus, information dissemination was more experience-based than just knowledge-based.

References

Argyris, C. and D.A. Schön (1978) *Organizational Learning: A Theory of Action Perspective*, Addison-Wesley.

Croasdell, D., D. Paradice and J. Courtney (1997) 'Using adaptive hypermedia to support organizational memory and learning', in *Proceedings of the Hawaii International Conference on Systems Sciences*, Maui, Hawaii.

Daft, R.L. and A.Y. Lewin (1993) 'Where are the theories for the 'new' organizational forms? An editorial essay', *Organization Science*, 4 (4), i–iv.

DiBella, A.J. and E.C. Nevis (1998) *How Organizations Learn: An Integrated Strategy for Building Learning Capability*, Jossey-Bass.

Eisenhardt, K.M. (1989) 'Building theories from case study research', *Academy of Management Review*, 14 (4), 532–550.

El Sawy, O., G.M. Gomes and M.V. Gonzalez (1986) 'Preserving institutional memory: the management of history as an organizational resource', *Academy of Management Best Paper Proceedings*, 37, 118–122.

Glaser, B.G. and A.L. Strauss (1967) *The Discovery of Grounded Theory: Strategies for Qualitative Research*, Aldine Publishing Company.

Hall, R.I. (1984) 'The natural logic of management policy making: its implications for the survival of an organization', *Management Science*, 30, 905–927.

Kirsch, L.J. (1997) 'Portfolios of control modes and IS project management', *Information Systems Research*, 8 (3), 215–239.

March, J.G. and J.P. Olsen (1975) 'The uncertainty of the past: organizational learning under ambiguity', *European Journal of Political Research*, 3, 147–171.

Markus, M.L. and D. Robey (1988) 'Information technology and organizational change: causal structure in theory and research', *Management Science*, 15 (5), 583–598.

Mohrman, S.A., S.G. Cohen and A.M. Mohrman (1995) *Designing Team-Based Organizations: New Forms for Knowledge Work*, Jossey-Bass.

Myers, P.S. (1996) *Knowledge Management and Organizational Design*, Butterworth-Heinemann.

Orlikowski, W.J. (1993) 'CASE tools as organizational change: investigating incremental and radical changes in systems development', *MIS Quarterly*, 17 (3), 309–340.

Sherif and Mandviwalla (2000) 'Barriers to actualizing organizational memories', in *Proceedings of the Hawaii International Conference on Systems Sciences*, Maui, Hawaii.

Stein, E.W. and V. Zwass (1995) 'Actualizing organizational memory with information systems', *Information Systems Research*, 6 (2), 85–117.

Strauss, A. and J. Corbin (1990) *Basics of Qualitative Research: Grounded Theory Procedures and Techniques*, Sage Publications.

Vikas, A., C. Manz and W.H. Glick (1998) 'An organizational memory approach to information management', *Academy of Management Review*, 23 (4), 796–809.

Walsh, J. and G.R. Ungson (1991) 'Organizational memory', *Academy of Management Review*, 16 (1), 57–91.

14 Understanding knowledge management solutions: the evolution of frameworks in theory and practice

C. W. Holsapple and K. D. Joshi

Introduction

In order to help understand KM phenomena, researchers have posited various frameworks, identifying concepts of interest, offering perspectives for guiding investigations, and providing languages for discourse. Here, we trace the evolution of KM frameworks from a disparate set, in which no one subsumes the others, toward an over-arching framework that describes KM phenomena in a relatively comprehensive and unified fashion. The early frameworks stemmed from the experiences and case studies of their authors. Building on these, a KM framework was synthesized through a process of evaluation and integration. The synthesized framework was then refined and extended through a Delphi process involving critiques and suggestions from an international panel of KM researchers and practitioners. The result is what we refer to as the collaborative KM framework. In tracing the evolution of KM frameworks, this chapter furnishes a wide-ranging picture of alternative viewpoints for shaping study, practices and advances in the KM field.

Representative frameworks

This section identifies and describes 10 representative KM frameworks posited during the 1990s. These frameworks vary in breadth and depth. Some attempt to characterize the whole KM phenomena, others focus on a particular aspect. The frameworks are presented here in chronological order of their appearance in the literature, and serve as a starting-point for the synthesized framework. As an introduction, the frameworks are presented in a brief, descriptive mode. Later in the chapter we discuss and analyze the frameworks, and begin to develop their ideas further. A more detailed discussion of these frameworks can be found in Holsapple and Joshi (1999a).

A framework of knowledge management pillars

Wiig's (1993) framework elements are classified into three categories, which he calls the pillars of KM. Each of these three pillars represents a set of functions needed for knowledge creation, manifestation, use and transfer. Table 14.1 lists the major functionalities contained within each of the pillars. Pillar I is concerned with exploring knowledge and its adequacy. It is comprised of several sub-elements, including survey and categorization of knowledge, analysis of knowledge, and the knowledge-related activities of elicitation, codification and organization of knowledge. The second pillar is concerned with appraising the value of knowledge and knowledge-related activities. The third pillar focuses on governing KM activity. This element consists of synthesizing knowledge-related activities; handling, using and controlling knowledge; and leveraging, distributing and automating knowledge.

Table 14.1   **Pillars of knowledge management** (adapted from Wiig, 1993)

Knowledge management components

Foundation
Broad understanding of knowledge:
- creation
- manifestations
- use
- transfer

Pillar I
- Survey and categorize knowledge
- Analyze knowledge and related activities
- Elicit, codify and organize knowledge

Pillar II
- Appraise and evaluate value of knowledge
- Knowledge-related actions

Pillar III
- Synthesize knowledge-related activities
- Handle, use and control knowledge
- Leverage, distribute and automate

A framework of knowledge conversion

Nonaka (1994) has advanced a model that characterizes the nature of 'knowledge conversion' during knowledge creation. This refers to situations in which knowledge is converted from one mode to another. The two modes of knowledge involved in conversion are tacit and explicit knowledge, the former being knowledge that cannot be easily verbalized and articulated, the latter knowledge that can be readily verbalized in a formal, systematic language (Polanyi, 1962).

As indicated in table 14.2, knowledge conversion occurs in four forms: socialization, externalization, internalization and combination. The transfer of tacit knowledge from one entity to the other is known as socialization. Combination is a process of creating new explicit knowledge from existing explicit knowledge. In Nonaka's model, externalization refers to a situation in which tacit knowledge is converted to explicit knowledge. The conversion of explicit knowledge into tacit knowledge is internalization. Through the interactions among these four conversion processes, organizational knowledge is created and transferred from individual to group to organizational levels.

Table 14.2   **Knowledge conversion framework** (adapted from Nonaka, 1994)

Knowledge management components

- Socialization (conversion of tacit knowledge to tacit knowledge)
- Internalization (conversion of explicit knowledge to tacit knowledge)
- Combination (conversion of explicit knowledge to explicit knowledge)
- Externalization (conversion of tacit knowledge to explicit knowledge)

A framework of core capabilities and knowledge-building

The KM framework proposed by Leonard-Barton (1995) consists of two major elements: organizational core capabilities and knowledge-building activities. As indicated in table 14.3, there are four knowledge-building activities and four core capabilities. The four knowledge-building activities are shared and creative problem-solving (to produce current products), implementing and integrating new methodologies and tools (to enhance internal operations), experimenting and prototyping (to build capabilities for the future), and importing and absorbing technologies from outside the firm. These four activities drive knowledge-creation and diffusion.

Knowledge-building activities are governed by organizational core capabilities. The four core capabilities included in this framework are: physical systems (competencies accumulated in material systems built over time, such as databases, machinery and software), employee knowledge and skills, managerial systems (organized routines directing

Table 14.3   **Core capabilities and knowledge-building activities** (adapted from Leonard-Barton, 1995)

Knowledge management components

Core capabilities:
- physical systems
- managerial systems
- employee skills and knowledge
- values and norms

Knowledge-building activities:
- problem-solving
- importing knowledge
- implementing and integrating
- experimenting

resource-accumulation and deployment, as well as creating the channels through which knowledge is accessed and flows – e.g. education, reward and incentive systems), and the organization's values and norms (determining the kinds of knowledge sought and nurtured and the kinds of knowledge-building activities tolerated and encouraged within an organization). The first two capabilities collectively represent the knowledge reservoir of an organization, the other two serve as knowledge-control or channelling mechanisms.

A model of organizational knowledge management

The KM model advanced by Arthur Andersen and APQC (1996) is comprised of three main elements: organizational knowledge, organizational KM processes, and factors that govern these processes.

These three elements along with their sub-elements are shown in table 14.4. According to this model, seven processes operate on an organization's knowledge in a cyclical fashion: create, identify, collect, adapt, organize, apply and share knowledge. The four organizational enablers that influence the execution of these KM processes are leadership, measurement, culture and technology. However, the model does not detail the nature of these enablers, nor does it characterize the nature of organizational knowledge resources or KM processes.

Table 14.4   **Organizational KM model** (adapted from Arthur Andersen and APQC, 1996)

Knowledge management components

Organizational knowledge

KM processes:

   Share → create → identify → collect → adapt → organize → apply → share

KM enablers:
- leadership
- culture
- technology
- measurement

A model of the knowing organization

Choo (1996) characterizes the notion of 'a knowing organization' using three processes 'linked as a continuum of nested information activities that define an organization which possesses the information and knowledge to act intelligently' (Choo, 1996). The model's three processes are sensemaking, knowledge-creation, and decision-making (see table 14.5).

During a sensemaking process, an organization tries to understand its changing environment. This process involves comprehending how people in the organization interpret information to deal with environmental uncertainty. During knowledge-creation, an organization produces new knowledge. This process involves understanding how information is transformed into new knowledge in an organization. The model views decision-making as a process concerned with understanding how an organization processes information to resolve task uncertainty.

Table 14.5 Model of the knowing organization (adapted from Choo, 1996)

Knowledge management components

Sensemaking (information interpretation)
Knowledge creation (information transformation)
Decision (information processing)

A model of intellectual capital

Leif Edvinsson of Skandia, Hubert Saint Onge of the Canadian Imperial Bank of Commerce, Patrick Sullivan of Intellectual Capital Management, and Gordon Petrash of Dow Chemicals developed a model of organizational knowledge resources referred to as intellectual capital. As identified in table 14.6, it consists of three elements: human capital, organizational capital and customer capital.

Human capital is the knowledge that each individual has and generates. Organizational capital is the knowledge that has been captured and institutionalized as the structure, processes and culture of an organization. Customer capital 'is the perception of value obtained by a customer from doing business with a supplier of goods and/or services' (Petrash, 1996). The nature of the interaction among these three components drives the financial outcomes (i.e. value) of an organization.

Table 14.6 Intellectual capital model (adapted from Petrash, 1996)

Knowledge management components

Human capital (individuals' knowledge)
Organizational capital (structure, process, culture)
Customer capital (customers' value perception)

A model of knowledge transfer

Szulanski (1996) has advanced a model to examine the internal stickiness of an organization. Internal stickiness is defined as the level of difficulty experienced in transferring knowledge within an organization. The focus of this study was on the transfer of organizational best practices. As shown in table 14.7, the model consists of two components, knowledge transfer stages and factors that influence knowledge transfer.

The knowledge-transfer stages are of four kinds: initiation, implementation, ramp-up and integration. The factors that impact difficulty of knowledge transfer are: characteristics of knowledge transfer (causal ambiguity and unprovenness); characteristics of the source of knowledge (lack of motivation and perceived unreliability); characteristics of the recipient of knowledge (lack of motivation, lack of absorptive capacity and lack of retentive capacity); and characteristics of the context (barren organizational context and arduous relationships).

The initiation stage of knowledge-transfer involves all events leading to a decision to transfer. This includes recognizing a need for knowledge, searching to satisfy that need, and exploring the feasibility of transferring knowledge identified to meet the need. The implementation stage of knowledge-transfer commences once a transfer decision is made. It encompasses the flow of knowledge resources from source to recipient, establishing social ties between recipient and source, customizing the transfer to suit recipient needs, and avoiding problems that may have been encountered in prior transfers. In the ramp-up stage of knowledge transfer, a recipient begins using the knowledge received. Here, the recipient tries to identify and solve unanticipated problems that arise in the course of using the knowledge, and satisfy post-transfer performance expectations. In the integration stage of knowledge transfer, transferred knowledge becomes institutionalized and routinely used.

Table 14.7 Model of knowledge transfer (adapted from Szulanski, 1996)

Knowledge management components

Knowledge transfer stages:
- initiation (recognize and satisfy knowledge need)
- implementation (knowledge transfer takes place)
- ramp-up (use the transferred knowledge)
- integration (internalize the knowledge)

Factors influencing knowledge transfer:
- characteristics of knowledge transfer (includes causal ambiguity and unproveness)
- characteristics of knowledge source (includes lack of motivation, perceived unreliability)
- characteristics of knowledge recipient (includes lack of motivation, absorptive and retentive capacity)
- characteristics of the context (includes barren organizational context and arduous relationships)

A model of knowledge management process

This model provides a description of the KM process in the KPMG Peat Marwick consulting firm (Alavi, 1997). In this model, KM is defined as the creation, leveraging and sharing of know-how and intellectual assets by all individuals across the firm in order to serve clients better. As listed in table 14.8, it consists of six KM elements that occur in a lock-step sequence: acquisition, indexing, filtering, linking, distribution and application. Acquisition refers to knowledge creation and content development through the distilling of experiences and lessons learned from client engagement projects, by collecting, synthesizing and interpreting a variety of information. The phases of indexing, filtering and linking are referred to as library-management activities; they include screening, classifying, cataloguing, integrating and interconnecting knowledge from internal

Table 14.8 KPMG knowledge-management process (adapted from Alavi, 1997)

Knowledge management components

- Acquisition (knowledge-creation and content development)
- Indexing
- Filtering
- Linking
- Distributing (packaging and delivery of knowledge in the form of Web pages)
- Application (using knowledge)

and external resources. Distribution involves packaging and delivering knowledge via Web pages (e.g. designing the appearance and organization of knowledge displays). The application phase is concerned with using knowledge that has been collected, captured and delivered to produce products and services.

A framework of intangible assets

The framework advanced by Sveiby (1997) aims to characterize the nature of organizational knowledge as intangible assets. As table 14.9 shows, the framework is comprised of three components: external structures, internal structures and employee competence. External structures include relationships with customers and suppliers, trademarks, brand names and reputation/image. Internal structures include models, concepts, patents, computer and administrative infrastructure and culture. Employee competence is comprised of skills and knowledge of an organization's individuals. Employees apply their skills and knowledge bases to a variety of organizational processes in order to create tangible or intangible assets. When the employees' knowledge bases are applied towards processes aimed at entities outside the organization, they are considered to produce external structures; if those efforts are directed inward, they are considered to produce internal structures.

Table 14.9   Intangible assets (adapted from Sveiby, 1997)

Knowledge management components

External Structures
Examples: brands, customer and supplier relationships

Internal Structures
Examples: management, legal structure, manual systems, attitudes, R&D, software

Employee Competence
Examples: education, experience

A framework of knowledge management stages

The framework developed by van der Spek and Spijkervet (1997) characterizes KM as a cycle of four stages: 'conceptualize', 'reflect', 'act' and 'retrospect'. The configuration of these stages, listed in table 14.10, is oriented toward a problem-solving cycle. The conceptualize stage focuses on accessing knowledge resources through researching, classifying and modelling existing knowledge. During the reflect stage, the conceptualized knowledge is evaluated, improvement requirements are established, and an improvement process is planned. The actions to improve the knowledge are taken during the act stage. This involves developing, distributing, combining and holding new knowledge. During the retrospect stage, results of the act stage are evaluated and compared with the previous actions. The four stages are influenced by internal and external developments. The former include culture, employee motivation, management, organization and IT. Although external influences are recognized as existing, examples of these factors are not specified.

Table 14.10 **A framework of knowledge management stages** (adapted from van der Spek and Spijkervet, 1997)

Knowledge management components

Conceptualize:
- draw up inventory
- analyze strong and weak points

Reflect:
- establish required improvement
- plan the improvement process

Act:
- develop
- distribute
- combine
- hold

Retrospect:
- evaluate results achieved
- compare old and new situation

Internal developments:
- culture
- employee motivation
- organizational adjustments
- management
- technology

External developments

A synthesized framework

This section summarizes a framework synthesized from this KM literature. It evolved through a two-step process. First, extant literature was studied and analyzed in an effort to identify fundamental dimensions of KM phenomena in organizations. As a result, three dimensions were identified that seemed essential to appreciating the full scope of the many writings. Together, they form an outline that can be used to categorize and compare elements of KM frameworks (Holsapple and Joshi, 1999a).

In the second step, this content (i.e. the categorization of KM elements), along with KM issues and concepts discussed elsewhere in the literature were integrated to create a unified, over-arching framework. This descriptive three-fold framework develops each of the dimensions in some detail by identifying factors to be considered (Holsapple and Joshi, 1997, 2001a).

Categorization of KM elements

The frameworks reviewed in the previous section vary in terminology. They differ in focus, reflecting variations in the primary intentions of their authors. They also differ in their origins, having been devised through various means and from various vantage points. Analysis of the frameworks suggests that the components of each are concerned with one or more of three basic dimensions: knowledge resources, KM activities that operate on these resources, and KM influences that facilitate and constrain the manifestation of these activities. The knowledge-resource dimension is concerned with characterizing an organization's knowledge resources. It is concerned with the question of how knowledge is embedded, stored, expressed and represented in an organization. What are the classes of knowledge and what are their attributes? The activity dimension is concerned with understanding operations on knowledge resources that can be performed by an organization's processors. It includes both elemental activities and composites of them. The influences dimension is concerned with the factors that guide, shape and limit the pattern of activities performed as KM continues to unfold within an organization.

No framework reviewed in the previous section fully covers all three dimensions in describing the nature of KM. However, each is concerned with at least one of these dimensions in its characterization of KM. Elements from these frameworks are categorized into the three dimensions, as shown in the second of the four columns in figure 14.1. Here, the frameworks are briefly compared and contrasted in light of the three dimensions.

Knowledge resources

Three of the frameworks explicitly address the knowledge-resources dimension by identifying various kinds of knowledge resources. Leonard-Barton (1995) identifies two types of knowledge resources: employee knowledge and physical systems (e.g. machinery or databases). The Petrash (1996) framework recognizes the employees and physical-knowledge resources identified by Leonard-Barton, but adds four additional knowledge resources: customers (referred to as customer capital), organizational processes, organizational structures and organizational culture. Sveiby's framework is similar. However, it incorporates customer capital within the notion of external knowledge resources, which includes knowledge resources other than customers (e.g. suppliers).

The other frameworks assume that knowledge resources exist insomuch as KM activities must operate on something. However, they do not focus on explicitly characterizing classes of knowledge resources. For instance, Nonaka's framework focuses on activities that operate on knowledge. It recognizes one attribute of knowledge, namely whether it is in a tacit or explicit form. However, unlike the three frameworks noted above, it is not concerned with attempting to identify different classes of knowledge resources.

Knowledge management activities

Most of the frameworks explicitly identify KM activities. Some frameworks treat these activities at a relatively elemental level, while others view activities at a higher level. The latter can be seen as composites of the former. For instance, the activities identified by Arthur Andersen and APQC, Wiig, van der Spek and Spijkervet, Alavi and Szulanski appear to be more elemental than those identified by Leonard-Barton, Choo and Nonaka. The higher-level activities seem to be comprised of some configuration of more elemental activities. For example, decision-making is an activity that may involve a subset of the more elemental activities identified by Arthur Andersen and APQC.

Knowledge management influences

Several frameworks explicitly recognize the influence dimension of KM. Such influences govern the execution of KM activities that operate on knowledge resources. Influences identified by the frameworks include: assessment and evaluation of KM activities and knowledge resources (Wiig; Anderson and APQC; van der Spek and Spijkervet), culture (Leonard-Barton; Arthur Andersen and APQC; Szulanski; van der Spek and Spijkervet 1997), employee motivation (Szulanski; van der Spek and Spijkervet), external development (van der Spek and Spijkervet), leadership (Arthur Andersen and APQC), managing (i.e. governing or administrating) knowledge manipulation activities and/or knowledge resources (Wiig; Leonard-Barton; Szulanski; van der Spek and Spijkervet), organizational adjustments (Szulanski; van der Spek and Spijkervet) and technology (Arthur Andersen and APQC; van der Spek and Spijkervet).

Szulanski's framework focuses on influences related to knowledge transfer, thus identifying influences very specific to the transfer of best practices within an organization. Other than this, only Leonard-Barton's characterization details and illustrates the influences it posits. The Anderson and APQC framework regards the influences it identifies strictly as KM enablers; impediments to KM are not identified. On the other hand, Szulanski's framework emphasizes influences that are impediments. Both Leonard-Barton and van der Spek and Spijkervet regard the influences they identify as being potential facilitators or potential barriers to an organization's conduct of KM.

The three-fold framework

The comparative examination of KM frameworks in terms of the three dimensions reveals that each, in its own way, contributes to an understanding of KM phenomena. It also reveals that no single framework subsumes all the others, that the knowledge-resources dimension has received relatively modest attention, and that there is no common or standard way of characterizing KM activities and influences. The categorization of KM elements in figure 14.1 gives a basis for a more unified, over-arching framework that attempts to:

- characterize an organization's knowledge resources in a more comprehensive manner than has heretofore been the case
- organize and consolidate knowledge manipulation activities in a way that not only describes each activity clearly and completely, but also identifies their inter-relationships
- identify the influencing factors in a relatively comprehensive and unified way.

The result of this effort at interpretive synthesis is a three-fold KM framework that characterizes knowledge resources that need to be managed, identifies and explains elemental activities involved in managing these knowledge resources, and recognizes factors that affect knowledge management (Holsapple and Joshi, 1997, 2001a). The three components of the synthesized framework are summarized in the third column of figure 14.1, and are reviewed below.

Knowledge-resource component

The knowledge-resource component is based on insights gained from categorization and evaluation of past KM frameworks, and KM concepts and ideas presented in other literature. Six primary types of organizational knowledge resources were identified and characterized in the synthesized framework. Knowledge can be stored, embedded or represented in an organization as any of six distinct kinds of resource:

- participants' knowledge
- culture
- infrastructure
- knowledge artefacts
- purpose
- strategy.

An organization also has access to knowledge existing in its environment, but which does not belong to the organization.

Let us examine each of these knowledge resources in turn:

- *Participants' knowledge.* An organization's participants can be human resources and/or material resources. They include employees and computer systems. Each participant has a reservoir of knowledge. Participants' knowledge becomes organizational knowledge when it is applied by participants as they perform their roles.
- *Culture.* An organization's values, principles, norms, unwritten rules and procedures comprise its cultural-knowledge resource. This knowledge establishes the basic assumptions and beliefs of an organization, which in turn controls and regulates organizational KM activities.
- *Infrastructure.* Infrastructure is a knowledge resource that determines formal structuring of work performed by both human and computer participants. It involves the roles that exist for participants to fill, relationships between these roles, and regulations that govern roles and their relationships (Holsapple and Luo, 1996).
- *Knowledge artefacts.* A knowledge artefact is an object that represents knowledge. Common examples of organizational knowledge artefacts are products (e.g. knowledge embedded in a manufactured television) and services (e.g. knowledge embedded in an advisory report for a client) that an organization sells, patent documents, video training tapes and books.
- *Purpose.* This knowledge resource reflects the reason for an organization's existence. It represents an organization's mission, vision, objectives and goals. Organizational strategies are directed and formulated on the basis of this knowledge.
- *Strategy.* Strategy is a knowledge resource that drives an organization's major activities, including its KM activities. It is comprised of plans for achieving purpose by using infrastructure, culture, participants' knowledge and artefacts, as well as other resources. These other organizational resources include human (e.g. individual and collective-knowledge-processors), material (e.g. computer-based processors) and monetary resources.
- *External sources.* An organization can augment and replenish its knowledge resources by acquiring resources that exist beyond its

Figure 14.1 KM evolution framework

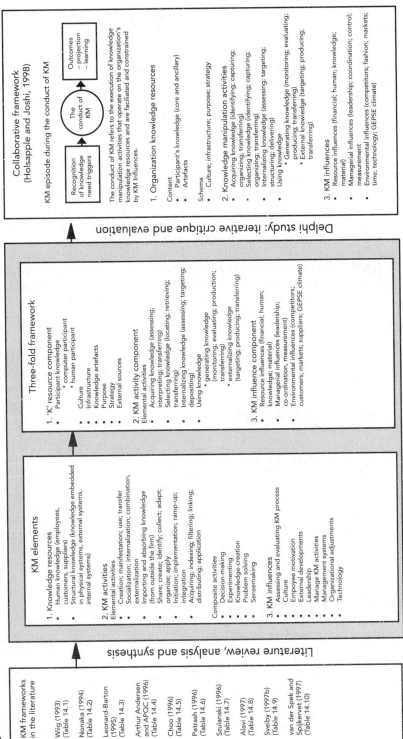

boundaries. Although not actually possessed or controlled by an organization, such knowledge may be thought of as a virtual knowledge resource.

Knowledge management activities component

Through a synthesis of elements existing in the literature, four activities for manipulating knowledge are identified: acquisition, selection, internalization and use of knowledge. These are summarized in the third column of figure 14.1, and are discussed below.

- *Acquiring knowledge.* This is the activity of accepting knowledge from outside the organization's boundaries and transforming it into a representation that can be internalized and used within an organization. Knowledge acquisition involves the sub-activities of extracting knowledge from external resources, interpreting this extracted knowledge, and transferring the interpreted knowledge for further manipulation by other activities.
- *Selecting knowledge.* This is the activity of extracting needed knowledge from the organization's extant knowledge resources and presenting it in a form appropriate to a requesting activity (i.e. to the acquisition, use or internalization activities). Selection involves the sub-activities of locating needed knowledge internally, retrieving the located knowledge, and transferring retrieved knowledge to an activity that needs it.
- *Internalizing knowledge.* This is an activity that alters the state of an organization's knowledge resources, typically based on knowledge that has been acquired or generated. Its sub-activities are assessing the knowledge to be internalized, targeting the assessed knowledge and depositing it as targeted.
- *Using knowledge.* This is the activity of manipulating existing knowledge to generate new knowledge or produce an externalization of knowledge. Existing knowledge used in generation can be the result of selection, acquisition or prior generation. Generation sub-activities are monitoring organizational knowledge resources and the external environment, evaluating selected or acquired knowledge, producing knowledge and transferring generated knowledge for subsequent externalization and/or internalization. Externalizing knowledge is the activity of using existing knowledge and other resources to produce organizational outputs. It involves the sub-activities of targeting, producing and transferring the output.

Knowledge management influences

The management of knowledge in an organization is influenced by a variety of factors. The third component of the three-fold framework identifies three classes of factor distilled from an analysis of influence elements discussed in the literature. As indicated in the third column of figure 14.1, these three classes of factor are resource influences, managerial influences and environmental influences.

- *Resource influences.* Organizational resources – either human, financial, knowledge or material – affect the way in which KM is conducted in an organization. For instance, financial resources could put a ceiling on the money spent on KM activities. Similarly, participants' KM skills, for example human resources or computer systems' processing capabilities, both constrain and facilitate KM activities. Each of the six classes of knowledge resource can constrain, shape or otherwise influence how the conduct of KM unfolds in an organization.

- *Managerial influences.* The management of knowledge is affected not only by the nature of various resources, but also by the manner in which these resources are deployed and utilized. This is where managerial influences on KM conduct come into play. Such influences govern the state of an organization's knowledge resources and the use of participants' KM skills in manipulating knowledge. As indicated in figure 14.1, the synthesized framework recognizes three types of managerial influences: leadership, co-ordination and measurement.

  Characteristics of the leader of a KM initiative can have a significant impact on how KM is performed and what its outcomes are. In today's knowledge-based organizations, successful leaders are those who can effectively manage organizational knowledge resources and KM activities. They create conditions that foster participants' use and cultivation of KM skills, that enable and encourage participants' contributions of individual knowledge resources to the organizational knowledge base, and that furnish convenient, timely access to needed knowledge resources.

  Co-ordination is concerned with harmonizing an organization's activities by bringing proper resources to bear at appropriate times, and ensuring that they correctly relate to each other as activities unfold (Holsapple and Whinston, 1996). Examples of co-ordination issues include alignment of participants' knowledge with strategy, diffusion of knowledge among participants, structures governing which knowledge-manipulation activities are undertaken under varying circumstances, the allocation of financial resources to KM activities, and the assignment of participants to infrastructure roles. The conduct of KM in an organization is strongly influenced by how such issues are addressed.

  A third kind of managerial influence stems from the installation of mechanisms for measuring KM within an organization. This involves assessing, evaluating and valuing knowledge resources and KM activities. It gives management the means for gauging the status of knowledge resources, processors and projects, and a basis for assessing KM outcomes. As such, measurement is a foundation for co-ordinating and leading KM initiatives.

- *Environmental influences.* Aside from internal factors, forces from outside an organization can affect the conduct of KM in the organization. As shown in figure 14.1, external influences identified by the synthesized framework are competition, customers, markets, suppliers and the GEPSE (governmental, economic, political, social and educational) climate.

A collaborative KM framework

The development process for the synthesized framework was necessarily interpretive. Although the aim was to ensure accurate analysis, proper categorization and unified synthesis of previous KM works, oversights and errors were possible. A collaborative effort was launched to improve on the original synthesized framework (Holsapple and Joshi, 1998). This involved a Delphi study to ascertain where the synthesized framework fell short, and to iteratively revise it to address those shortcomings. An international panel of over 30 scholars (see chapter 14 appendix) collaborated in this effort. Their diverse perspectives, critiques, suggestions and insights are reflected in the collaborative KM framework presented here, and summarized in the right-most column of figure 14.1. Here, the description of this framework is necessarily brief. For a more detailed treatment, refer to Holsapple and Joshi (1998, 1999b, 2001b, 2001c).

The conduct of knowledge management

The synthesized framework makes no explicit mention of the context or outcome of KM. However, KM does not occur in a vacuum; nor is it without outcomes. The collaborative KM framework directly characterizes both the content and outcomes of an organization's conduct of KM.

The conduct of KM in an organization refers to the application of knowledge-manipulation skills to certain activities that operate on the organization's knowledge resources. The collaborative framework calls these knowledge manipulation instead of KM activities, since the latter has a broader meaning. Knowledge management conduct (KMC) is both facilitated and constrained by various KM influences that govern the fashion in which it unfolds in an organization. Moreover, KMC unfolds on a continuing basis as a pattern of inter-related KM episodes. As indicated in the fourth column of figure 14.1, each KM episode (KME) is triggered by a knowledge need, and culminates when that need is satisfied. Examples of KMEs include the composite KM activities shown in the second column of figure 14.1: decision-making, problem-solving, experimentation and innovation. KMEs can be considered at higher or lower levels of resolution. They can be nested and may overlap. By satisfying knowledge needs, KMEs result in two outcomes: learning and projection. Organizational learning is a process whereby an organization's knowledge resources are modified. Projection is a process whereby organizational resources are released into the working environment.

Knowledge management influences

The three main classes of influence factors identified in the synthesized KM framework are unaltered. However, the collaborative KM framework adds new elements to the managerial and environmental influence classes. It also develops the factors and their relationships in greater depth, as described by Holsapple and Joshi (1998, 2001b). Let us examine the developments in more detail.

- *Managerial influences.* These influences manifest themselves through the administration of KM. As shown in figure 14.1, the framework categorizes these influences into four main factors: exhibiting KM leadership, co-ordinating KM conduct, controlling resources used in

KM conduct, and measuring processes and outcomes of KM conduct. The control component is a new addition to the list of managerial influences. Although the notions of leadership, co-ordination, control and measurement are not unique to KMC, their execution in this context may require special attention and techniques.

- *Leadership*. This heads the managerial factors influencing KM application. Core competencies for effective leaders of knowledge-intensive organizations are the ability to be a catalyst (e.g. by mentoring), a co-ordinator, an evaluator and an exerciser of control.
- *Co-ordination*. KM within an organization can be left to serendipity, or can be planned and structured as an organized initiative. The planned approach requires co-ordination within and across KMEs, in the identification and sequencing of knowledge manipulation activities, and assessment of the nature of knowledge resources needed for KM use. Co-ordination involves the marshalling of an adequate level of skill in manipulation activities, the temporal arranging of those activities (both within and across KMEs), and the integration of knowledge processing with other organizational operations.
- *Control*. This managerial influence factor is concerned with the protection and quality of knowledge resources, knowledge-processors and the processes occurring in KMEs. Protecting knowledge resources from loss, obsolescence, unauthorized exposure, unauthorized modification and erroneous assimilation is crucial for the effective conduct of KM. The same is true of knowledge-processors and KME processes. The quality notion is concerned with ensuring that knowledge resources have sufficient validity and utility. The same holds for processors and processes.
- *Measurement*. The procedures and policies established in assessing knowledge resources, processors and processes can influence the conduct of KM and its outcomes. Measurement involves the evaluation of knowledge resources: KM leadership, co-ordination and control; knowledge-processor performance; and knowledge-manipulation performance. It gives a basis for: the identification and recognition of value-adding resources and activities; awareness of problem areas and disturbances; assessment and comparison of alternative means for performing knowledge-manipulation activities; and an understanding of the impact of KMC results (i.e. learning and projection) on overall organizational performance.

- *Resource influences*. The existence of four resource influences remained unchanged. However, the characterization of knowledge resources underwent substantial revision, as described in the knowledge-resources section below.
- *Environmental influences*. The collaborative framework's characterization of environmental influences includes competition, fashion, markets, technology, time and the GEPSE climate. Two elements from the synthesized framework – suppliers and customers – belong to the collaborative KM framework's resource dimension. Fashion, time and technology are additions to the class of environmental influences. Although an organization has little control over environmental

influences, if appropriately handled, the environment can present opportunities for improving KMC. It certainly presents a variety of challenges.

Knowledge manipulation activities

It is through the execution of knowledge manipulation activities that learning and projection take place. The names for the four major knowledge activities (acquisition, selection, use and internalization) remain unchanged in the collaborative framework, but their characterizations have undergone modification, especially in their sub-activities:

- *Acquiring knowledge.* This is the identification of knowledge in the organization's environment and transforming it into a representation that can be internalized or used within an organization. Sub-activities involved in acquiring knowledge are identifying appropriate knowledge in external sources, capturing identified knowledge, organizing the captured knowledge, and transferring this organized knowledge.
- *Selecting knowledge.* This is the identification of needed knowledge within an organization's existing knowledge resources and its presentation in a form appropriate to an activity that needs it (i.e. an acquiring, using or internalizing activity). This activity is analogous to acquisition, the main distinction being that it manipulates resources already existing in the organization rather than those in the environment. Sub-activities involved in selecting knowledge are identifying appropriate knowledge within the organization's existing resources, capturing the identified knowledge, organizing the captured knowledge, and transferring organized knowledge to an appropriate activity.
- *Internalizing knowledge.* The collaborative KM framework views internalizing as an activity that alters an organization's knowledge resources based on acquired, selected or generated knowledge. It receives knowledge flows from these activities and produces knowledge flows that impact on the organization's state of knowledge. Internalizing knowledge is a culminating activity in organizational learning. Sub-activities involved in internalizing knowledge are assessing and valuing knowledge to be internalized, targeting knowledge resources that will receive the knowledge, structuring knowledge, and delivering knowledge representations as targeted.
- *Using knowledge.* This is the application of existing knowledge to generate new knowledge or produce an externalization of knowledge. Where the activity of using knowledge exists, there is the possibility that organizational learning is innovative and adds value. Generation is an activity that produces knowledge by processing existing knowledge, where the latter has resulted from selection, acquisition or prior generation. Sub-activities involved in generating knowledge are monitoring the organization's knowledge resources and the external environment by invoking selection or acquisition activities, as needed, evaluating selected or acquired knowledge for utility and validity in the production of knowledge, producing knowledge from a base of existing knowledge, and transferring the produced knowledge for externalization or internalization. Externalizing knowledge

involves using existing knowledge to produce organizational outputs. It yields projections, or embodiments of knowledge in outward forms, for external consumption. Sub-activities involved in externalizing knowledge are targeting, producing and transferring the output.

Knowledge resources

The collaborative KM framework has a structured taxonomy for classifying an organization's knowledge resources. The taxonomy is based on the basic premise that some organizational knowledge resources depend on the organization for their existence, whereas others can exist separately from the organization to which they presently belong. The former are called schematic resources, the latter content resources. Schematic resources form the basis for attracting, arranging and deploying content resources that, in turn, instantiate and enrich the frame of reference provided by schematic resources. As illustrated in the fourth column of figure 14.1, the collaborative KM framework identifies four schematic resources: culture, infrastructure, purpose and strategy. Content resources are comprised of participants' knowledge and artefacts. Here, we confine our discussion of knowledge resources to the two high-level categories: content and schematic resources. More detailed descriptions can be found in Holsapple and Joshi (1998, 2001c).

As mentioned, there are two classes of content resources in which an organization's knowledge is represented: participants' knowledge and artefacts. The primary distinction between participants' knowledge and artefacts lies in the presence or absence of knowledge-processing abilities. Participants have skills that allow them to manipulate their own repositories of knowledge. Artefacts have no such skills. An organization's participants include employees, customers, suppliers, partners, consultants and computer systems. These participants can be classified as core participants and ancillary participants. An organization's employees and computer systems are the core participants. An organization's customers, suppliers, partners, consultants and external computer systems are considered ancillary participants.

Schematic knowledge is represented in the workings of an organization, manifesting through its behaviour. Although perceptions of such knowledge may be represented (more or less accurately) in artefacts or participants' memories, schematic knowledge exists independent of these perceptions and independent of any single participant or artefact. The four classes of schematic knowledge resources are inter-related, and good fits among them are important. However, none can be characterized solely in terms of the others.

Summary and conclusion

Frameworks are useful in understanding and studying KM phenomena. This chapter traces an evolution of KM frameworks, culminating in a collaboratively developed KM framework that gives a relatively unified and comprehensive view of KM phenomena. Practitioners, researchers, teachers and students can adopt whichever KM framework suits their needs and tastes, whichever identifies the issues and parameters relevant to their interests. Each framework is a candidate for further development or modification by these users. Each can serve as a starting-point for the devising of prescriptions about how KM should be accomplished, or for the better appreciation of the relationship between KM and organizational performance. For instance, as an extension of this work, the collaborative framework is the basis for further research that identifies KM activities that can serve as means for achieving competitive advantage (Holsapple and Singh, 2001). Moreover, this overarching framework and discussion serves as a theoretical foundation for other chapters in this book.

References

Alavi, M. (1997) 'KPMG Peat Marwick U.S.: one giant brain', Harvard Business School Case, 9-397-108, Rev. July 11.

Arthur Andersen and APQC (American Productivity and Quality Center) (1996) *The Knowledge Management Assessment Tool: External Benchmarking Version*, Arthur Anderson/APQC.

Choo, C. (1996) 'An Integrated Information Model of the Organization: The Knowing Organization', December 7. http://www.fis.utoronto.ca/people/faculty/choo/FIS/KO/KO.html1#contents.

Holsapple, C. and K.D. Joshi (1997) 'Knowledge management: a three-fold framework', Kentucky Initiative for Knowledge Management, Research Paper No. 104, College of Business and Economics, University of Kentucky, KY.

— (1998) 'In search of a descriptive framework for knowledge management: preliminary Delphi results', Kentucky Initiative for Knowledge Management, Research Paper No. 118, College of Business and Economics, University of Kentucky, KY.

— (1999a) 'Description and analysis of existing knowledge management frameworks', in *Proceedings of the Hawaiian International Conference on System Sciences*, Maui, Hawaii, January.

— (1999b) 'Knowledge manipulation activities: results of a Delphi study', Kentucky Initiative for Knowledge Management, Research Paper No. 127, College of Business and Economics, University of Kentucky, KY.

— (2001a) 'Knowledge management: a three-fold framework', *The Information Society*.

— (2001b) 'An investigation of factors that influence the management of knowledge in organizations', *Journal of Strategic Information Systems*.

— (2001c) 'Organizational knowledge resources', *Decision Support Systems*.

Holsapple, C. and W. Luo (1996) 'A framework for studying computer support of organizational infrastructure', *Information and Management*, 31 (1), 13–24.

Holsapple, C. and M. Singh (2001) 'The knowledge chain model: activities for competitiveness', *Expert Systems with Applications*.

Holsapple, C. and A. Whinston (1996) *Decision Support Systems – A Knowledge Based Approach*, West Publishing Company.

Leonard-Barton, D. (1995) *Wellsprings of Knowledge*, Harvard Business School Press.

Nonaka, I. (1994) 'A dynamic theory of organizational knowledge creation', *Organization Science*, 5 (1), 14–37.

Petrash, G. (1996) 'Dow's journey to a knowledge value management culture', *European Management Journal*, 14 (4), 365–373.

Polanyi, M. (1962) *Personal Knowledge: Towards a Post-Critical Philosophy*, Harper Torchbooks.

Sveiby, K. (1997) *The New Organizational Wealth*, Berrett-Koehler.

Szulanski, G. (1996) 'Exploring internal stickiness: impediments to the transfer of best practice within the firm', *Strategic Management Journal*, 17, 27–43.

van der Spek, R. and A. Spijkervet (1997) 'Knowledge management: dealing intelligently with knowledge', in *Knowledge Management and its Integrative Elements* (eds J. Liebowitz and L. Wilcox), CRC Press.

Wiig, K. (1993) *Knowledge Management Foundations*, Schema Press.

Appendix:
Delphi panelists (name and affiliation)

Debra Amidon, ENTOVATION International Ltd, USA
Sulin Ba, University of Southern California, USA
Thomas J. Beckman, George Washington University and IRS, USA
Kesper Deboer, Andersen Consulting, USA
Marc Demarest, The Sales Consultancy, USA
Alain Godbout, Godbout Martin Godbout & Associates, Canada
Valerie Cliff, ICL Enterprise Consultancy, UK
Ming Ivory, James Madison University, USA
Linda Johnson, Western Kentucky University, USA
Mark A. Jones, Andersen Consulting, USA
Sam Khoury, Dow Chemical Company, USA
Kai Larsen, Center for Technology in Government, USA
Dirk Mahling, University of Pittsburgh, USA
Eunika Mercier-Laurent, EML Conseil – Knowledge Management, France
Philip C. Murray, Knowledge Management Associates, USA
Brian Newman, Newman Group and KM Forum, USA
David Paradice, Texas A&M University, USA
Gordon Petrash, Dow Chemical Company, USA
Dave Pollard, Ernst & Young, Canada
Larry Prusak, IBM Corporation, USA
David Skyrme, David Skyrme Associates Ltd, UK
Charles Snyder, Auburn University, USA
Kathy Stewart, Georgia State University, USA
Karl Sveiby, Sveiby Knowledge Management, Australia
Robert Taylor, KPMG Management Consulting, UK
Karl Wiig, Knowledge Research Institute, Inc., USA
Andrew Whinston, University of Texas, Austin, USA
Fons Wijnhoven, University of Twente, Netherlands
Dennis Yablonsky, Carnegie Group, Inc., USA
Michael Zack, Northeastern University, USA
One participant preferred to remain anonymous

Index

Accenture 27
active support for KM 147, 159
  see also KnowMore
activities of KM, *see* knowledge
  management: activities
ADAPT 50
Addenbrooke's Hospital NHS
  Trust 75
ADONIS 149, 156–7
agent-based retrieval 5, 40–7,
  136–41, 152–6
  see also recommender systems
Alta Vista 136
Amalthaea 133
Amazon 40–1
Andersen Consulting 27, 134, 225
Annotate 8, 129, 131–2, 134–143
  benefits of annotations 139
  evaluation 140–2
  hybrid documents 139
  icon legend 137–8
  KM processes 135, 139
  query interface 136, 141
  retrieval interface 136–7, 141
  session-data store 140
  structure of annotation 135–6
  see also waterfall model for
    document management
architectures for KMS 4, 7–8, 28,
  97–175
  see also design of KMS
Ariadne's Thread 58–60
  development 58–9
  problems 59
  see also Sigma; SigSys
ARIS 158
Arthur Andersen 27
artificial intelligence (AI) 54

ASCII 139, 143
associative trails 133
Autonomy 2
Autonomy Nordic 41

Bank of Ireland 197–8, 201, 202,
  203, 205, 207
BankCo Group 200, 201, 202,
  203, 205, 206, 207
barriers to information retrieval
  68, 218
benefits of KMS 2–3, 25–6
  annotations 139
  clinical practice 77–8, 79–80
  customers and business
    partners 29
  measuring 27, 74–8, 203
  recommender systems 47
  see also knowledge
    management: benefits
BIDS ISI search 181–4
black boxes in KM 188, 191
BMW Group 199
BPMS 158
BPR 1, 123, 206
  people management 180, 184,
    188, 192
  see also business engineering;
    enterprise modelling;
    process modelling
browser, *see* Web browser
BSCW 132
budgets for KMS 24
business bus 114
business engineering map 123–4
Business Objects 2
business process reengineering,
  see BPR

Canadian Imperial Bank of
    Commerce 226
capacity for effective action 16
Central Intelligence Agency
    (CIA) 2
Centre for Clinical Informatics 74
CERN Web editor 133
characteristics of KMS 23–4
chief knowledge officer (CKO)
    189
Ciba Geigy 113
client customer database (CCD)
    initiative 200, 202, 206
codification of knowledge 188,
    191, 225–6
  application of codified
    knowledge 216–17
  problems 215–16, 220
  tacit vs explicit 3, 37, 191
  tools 189
  traditional 15, 36
  see also externalization of
    knowledge
Cognos 2, 207
collaborative KM framework
    236–40
combination of knowledge 128,
    135, 224, 233
Commander 198
Competence Centre 'Data
    Warehousing Strategy' (CC
    DWS) 126
competitive advantage from KM
    2, 82, 179, 181
  data warehousing 195
  knowledge sharing 17–18, 52
  organizational resources 1–2
  tacit knowledge 38, 47
competitive pressures 1, 146
computer-supported co-
    operative work 135, 147
concerns for KMS 22–3
confidence score 137
contributions of KMS
    participants 218
  anonymity 57, 60, 61, 139, 140
  authentication 140, 163
  co-operation 140–2
  economic analysis 141–2
  free ridership 141
  recognition 138, 217

risks 38, 45–6, 52–3
virtual organizations 60–1
WaX ActiveLibrary 69–70
  see also incentives for KMS
    participants
Coopers & Lybrand 50
core capabilities and knowledge
    building activities 224–5
corporate memory 147
cost-performance of technology
    1, 64–5
critical success factors 27
  data warehousing 201–8
  OMIS 219
CSCW, *see* computer-supported
    co-operative work
CSVTool 165–6
cultural fit 29
currency of knowledge 215–16

DaimlerChrysler 113
data 16–17
data-extraction methods and
    tools 206–7
data marts 7, 117–18, 121,
    199–200, 204–6
data stewardship 122–3, 205–6
data warehousing 8, 9, 195–208
  architecture 117–18
  challenges 118–19, 174–5
  costs 129
  customer support 171
  decentralized organizations
    113, 116–26
  enterprise readiness 196–7
  ETL (extraction, transformation
    and loading) processes 117
  failure 196, 200
  implementation: case studies
    197–201
    see also Bank of Ireland;
    BankCo Group; OilCo
    International; Rover Group
  measurement systems 162–75
  organizational prerequisites
    201–8
  business-drivers 202
  compatibility 207
  data extraction methods and
    tools 206–7
  data quality 204

data stewardship 205–6
executive sponsorship and commitment 202
flexible enterprise data model 205
funding commitment 203
project team 203–4
proof of concept 207
significance 117, 162, 195
strategy 119, 199, 202
see also data marts; LUCOS; management middleware
DB2 205
decentralized organizations 6, 7, 49–61, 112–26
see also federated organizations; management holdings
decision support
clinical 66, 68, 75
data warehousing 117, 195, 198
insurance 148
purchasing 149–52
decision support systems (DSS) 15, 28, 98, 110
Deloitte & Touche 27
Delphi study of KM 236–40, 242
design of KMS 4, 7–8, 28
clinical interface 66–8
communication mediums 60
data models 205
data warehousing 161–75, 198
decentralized organizations 112–26
KM support systems for document collections 129–43
multi-perspective KMS 97–110
recommender systems 42–6, 146–59
trusted distribution 71
users 29
see also architectures for KMS
destruction of documents 132
DFKI 148
document management 8, 53, 129–43, 158
see also waterfall model for document management
document marketing on the Web 133
document type definition (DTD) 138

document workflow 132–3
documents as knowledge bases 130–3
domains of knowledge 25
DOW Chemicals 226
downsizing 1
Dublin Core 132

Edvinsson, Leif 226
empowerment 1
enterprise data warehouse (EDW) initiative 199–200, 204, 205, 206
enterprise modelling 7, 98, 101–8, 205
entity relationship modelling (ERM) 205
epistemology of knowledge 16, 49
Ernst & Young 27
espoused theory 45
evolution of information systems 15
Excite 136, 137, 138
executive information systems (EIS) 15, 21, 28, 112, 118–19, 120
see also WaX ActiveLibrary
executive sponsorship and commitment 202
expert systems 21, 84, 88, 98, 110, 147
extensible markup language, *see* XML
externalization of knowledge 128, 135, 139, 224, 234, 238–9
problems 37–8
recommender systems 40, 45, 46–7
virtual organizations 6, 54
see also codification of knowledge

failure of KMS 9–10, 18, 59
see also data warehousing: failure; knowledge management: failure
federated organizations 8, 140, 142–3
information islands 130, 133
see also decentralized

organizations; homogeneous
    organizations
Fidelity Inc. 189
file conversion filters 132
file transfer protocol (FTP) 28,
    142
flexibility, *see* organizational
    flexibility
Ford 199
frameworks for KM, *see*
    knowledge management:
    frameworks
free riders 141
full-text search 133–4, 135, 136,
    139, 141
    see also keywords
funding commitment 203

Gantt charts 169, 172–3
Gartner Group 28
General Motors 189
general practitioner (GP) 6,
    65–80
GENIE 198–9
GEPSE climate 233, 235
German Federal Ministry for
    Education and Research
    159
global survey 18–19
globalization 1, 6, 109, 113, 195
GQM 168
granularity of information, *see*
    information: granularity
GrapeVine 130
grounded theory approach 42,
    211–12, 213–14
groupware 59, 61, 134, 140
    firm usage 186
    Web integration 132–3
    see also Lotus Notes; SigSys
growth of KMS 26–7

healthcare 6, 64–80
heterogeneous data sources 117,
    134, 147, 152, 161–2, 195
heterogeneous organizations 7,
    112–26
Hewlett Packard 2, 189
Hoechst 113
human brain 64
human knowledge 64

human resource management
    (HRM), *see* people
    management
Hummingbird 2
HyperNews 136
hypertext 66, 67, 97
hypertext markup language
    (HTML) 59, 70, 73, 132, 139,
    143
hypertext transfer protocol
    (HTTP) 114, 132, 163, 164

incentives for KMS participants
    27, 40, 41, 47, 84, 129
    annotations 140
    Ariadne's Thread 59
    economic analysis 140–2
    federated organizations 134
    law firms 85, 86–7
    management holdings 116, 125
    OMIS 218
    see also contributions of KMS
        participants
indexing knowledge 43, 67, 69,
    138, 158
influences on KM, *see*
    knowledge management:
    influences
information 28
    clinical sources 71–3
    definition 16–17, 83, 99
    granularity 74, 78, 118
    overload 6, 20, 23, 28, 65–6
    reformatting 73–4
    retrieval 68–9
    sources 71–3
    see also barriers to information
        retrieval; knowledge
information systems and KMS
    98–101, 103–4, 107–8, 110,
    115–16
Informix 207
initiators of knowledge
    management systems 23–4
InKoNetz 50
innovation 1, 123
    black box 199
    knowledge 180, 190
    law firms 85
Institute of Operations
    Management (IOM) 185

insuremarket.com 115
intangible assets framework 228
intellectual capacity 64
intellectual capital 182–4 188–9
  model 226
Intellectual Capital Management
  226
intelligent agents, *see* agent-
  based retrieval
International Standards
  Organization (ISO) 120
Internet 28, 68, 72, 142–3
  access to systems 57, 163, 170
Intel 2
internalization of knowledge 17,
  28, 128, 135, 224, 233, 234,
  238
intranets 84, 121, 163
  document management 131–4,
    143
  importance in KMS 25, 28
  KMS budgets 24
  limitations in KM 191
  ontologies 158
  Volvo 41, 46–7
Invention Machine 2

Java 130, 156–7, 170
Java database connection (JDBC)
  156
just-in-time knowledge 65

key performance indicators
  (KPIs) 204
keywords
  alternatives 40, 42, 43, 44
  conceptual 69
  search 73, 133–4, 136, 137, 138
  see also full-text search
KITs 148–57
  definition 153–4
  processing 155–6
  support specification 154–5
knowing organization: model
  225–6
knowledge 16–17, 28, 49, 83,
  98–100, 128
  coded 36, 54
  conceptual 54
  corporate 99–100
  cultural 36, 232

embedded 3, 36, 83, 190, 191,
  232
embodied 36, 188
embrained 36
encultured 36
events 54
experience-based 54
explicit 3, 17, 36–8, 53–4, 83,
  128, 190, 223–4
  process 54, 124
  social 54
tacit 3, 5, 17, 36–9, 53–4, 83, 128,
  223–4
  activating 40, 44–7, 135
  distal terms 39, 44–5
  limitations of IT 190–1
  problems in codification 215
  professional interests 5, 38–9,
    46
  proximal terms 39, 44–5
  see also information; knowledge
    resources
knowledge-based view of the
  firm 2, 36, 179, 180–1
knowledge chart 130
knowledge codification, *see*
  codification of knowledge
knowledge conversion 53–4,
  190–1
  framework 223–4
  see also combination of
    knowledge; externalization
    of knowledge; internalization
    of knowledge; socialization
    of knowledge
knowledge integration 147
knowledge integrator 116, 125
knowledge-intensive tasks, *see*
  KITs
knowledge management
  activities 230, 231, 233, 234, 236,
    238–9
  aims 147
  barriers 9, 197, 231
    clinical practice 68
    law firms 85, 92
    organizational memory
      214–20
    tools-based approaches 190–1
  benefits 84, 92, 116
  conduct 236–9

decision-making 225
  clinical 6, 66, 75, 77
  decentralized 7
  processes 219
defining 17, 83, 97, 180–1
Delphi study 236–40, 242
diffusion 188, 189, 192
disciplines 2, 83, 99, 100, 213
elements 229–30
emergence in the literature
  181–4
failure 3, 38, 116
frameworks 222–40
  collaborative framework 233,
    236–40
  core capabilities and
    knowledge-building 224–5
  intangible assets 228
  intellectual capital 226
  KM stages framework 228–9
  knowing organization 225–6
  knowledge conversion 223–4
  knowledge transfer 226–7
  KPMG KM process model
    227–8
  organizational KM model 225
  pillars of KM 223
  synthesized framework
    229–35
  three-fold framework 231–5
importance 181
influences 231, 234–5, 236–8
interdisciplinary perspective 9
maintenance of knowledge 109
organizational structure 213,
  217–8, 220
perspectives 2, 9, 37, 86
  culture-based 20–1, 88
  information-based 20–1, 83, 88
  technology-based 20–1, 36, 88,
    179–80, 182–4, 188–91
policies 140, 143
quality of knowledge 108–9,
  130, 138, 204
required capabilities 21–2
resources 234–5
strategy 18, 28, 29, 61, 220
technologies 16, 21–2, 24–5, 84,
  97–8, 179
see also intellectual capital;
  knowledge conversion;

knowledge re-use;
  knowledge sharing; learning
  organization; people
  management in KM
knowledge management
  conduct (KMC) 236–9
knowledge management episode
  (KME) 236–9
knowledge network 129, 143
knowledge resources 230, 231,
  232, 233, 239
knowledge retrieval 68–9
  barriers 68
  WaX ActiveLibrary 69
  see also agent-based retrieval;
    recommender systems
knowledge re-use 102–3, 106–7,
  216–17, 218, 219, 220
  corporate knowledge 100
  problems 216
  see also knowledge manage-
    ment; leveraging knowledge
knowledge scorecard 124–5
knowledge sharing 6, 22, 27, 86
  communication channels 18, 50,
    53, 99–100, 101
  increased value of the
    individual 217
  organizational benefits 2
  organizational culture 3, 21, 53,
    86, 89–90, 116, 218–19
  people management 185, 186–8
  problems 38, 134, 191
  role of organizations 128–9
  structures 217, 218, 220
  virtual organizations 49, 52, 55–61
  see also knowledge conversion;
    knowledge management;
    knowledge transfer
knowledge transfer 60, 83, 233
  federalist organizations 134
  increased personal value 217
  information retrieval facilities
    130
  law firms 85, 86, 87, 89, 90–1
  methods 17–8
  model 226–7
  tacit knowledge 38, 190
  see also knowledge conversion;
    knowledge management;
    knowledge sharing

knowledge visualization 130,
138, 169–70
knowledge work systems 84
KnowMore 8, 148–159
  architecture 152–3, 156–7
  enabling functionality 151–2
  example: purchasing a graphics
    card 149–51
  future development 157–9
  processing KITs 155–6
  see also KITs
KPMG Peat Marwick 27, 28
  KM process model 227–8

LaLiberte 136
Land Rover 199
law firms 6–7, 82–110
  barriers to KM 85, 92
  culture 84, 89–90
  IT use 85, 88–9, 90
  knowledge management 82,
    85–3
  partners 87
  research model 86–7
  size 91, 93
  types of knowledge 85, 90, 91–2
lean management 146
learning organization 189–90, 192
  emergence of discourse 181–4
  see also organizational memory
leveraging knowledge
  annotations 139
  benefits 3, 181
  data warehousing 195
  importance of tools 189
  leverage points 27
  see also knowledge
    management; knowledge
    re-use
Lotus Domino 130, 134
Lotus Notes 9, 130, 134
  barriers to adoption 140, 214–20
  cost 24
  firm use 186
  information sharing 18
  see also groupware
LUCOS 161, 163–75
  architecture 163–70
  deployment 170–1
  Excel metrics information
    exchange (EMIX) 166

external data modules 165–6
measurement design tool
  (MeTo) 167–8
metrics server (MESS) 163–5
pilot study 171–5
  challenges 174–5
  user reactions 173–4
Project metrics information
  exchange (PMIX) 166
toolset 163
visualization client applet
  (ViCA) 169–70
Lufthansa 113

Machine Learning and
  Knowledge Acquisition from
  Texts 158
Macintosh 130
management consultancy 18, 24,
  26–7, 134, 140, 158, 227
  promoters of KM 188
management control 161
management holdings 113–16
  globalization 113
  goals 113
  performance indicators 115
  reporting systems 115–16
  service integrators 114
  service providers 114
  see also decentralized
    organizations; federated
    organizations
management information
  systems, *see* MIS
management middleware 7, 113,
  116
  business view 122–25
  organizational integration 125
  technological view 121
  see also data warehousing
Mannesmann 113, 115
market for knowledge
  management systems 2
McDonald's 15
McKinsey & Co. 27
measurement systems 8, 161–75
  data 161–2
  designing measures 167–8
  see also LUCOS
media richness theory 60
medical knowledge 64–5

MEDLINE 68
MEMO 101–2
  see also enterprise modelling
merger and acquisition 7, 112,
  125
Microsoft Excel 166
Microsoft PowerPoint 132
Microsoft Project 166, 171
Microsoft Word 132
MIS 15, 28, 118–19, 198
MSWWF 50
multi-perspective enterprise
    modelling, *see* MEMO; multi-
    perspective KMS
multi-perspective KMS 101–8
  conceptual background 102–4
  conceptual-level layer 105–7
  interface-level layer 107–8
  meta-level layer 104–5

National Health Service (NHS)
    67, 69, 71, 72, 75
nature of the workforce 1, 191
NCSA Mosaic 133
network-like organizations 49
neural networks 41, 84
new product development
    (NPD) 161–2
NHSNet 67, 68
Novartis 113
NRW 50

object definition language (ODL)
    107
object models 104–8
object-oriented languages 107
ODBC 165
office automation systems 84
OilCo International
    (pseudonym) 198–9, 201, 202,
    204, 206, 207
OLAP 118
OMIS 54, 103, 147–53, 214–20
  adoption research 210–11
  barriers 214–20
  case studies 212–19
  software 97–8
  success factors 219
  see also organizational memory
online analytical processing, *see*
    OLAP

ontologies 97, 152, 153, 157–8
  document collections 130, 132,
    133–4, 143
open database connectivity, *see*
    ODBC
open systems interconnect (OSI)
    120
Oracle 206, 207
organizational capability 1–2
organizational complexity of
    KMS 27
organizational culture 61, 84,
    89–90
  see also knowledge sharing:
    organizational culture
organizational flexibility 1, 6, 18,
    52, 180–1
organizational KM model 225
organizational learning, *see*
    learning organization
organizational memory 3, 6, 54,
    61, 97
  actualizing 217–18
  definition 210
  effectiveness 210–11
  properties 147
  see also OMIS
organizational memory
    information system, *see*
    OMIS; organizational
    memory
organizational prerequisites
    model for data warehousing
    201–8
organizational structure, *see*
    knowledge management:
    organizational structure
outsourcing 1

people management in KM 8,
    180–92
  importance in practice 185–8
  tacit knowledge 190–1
performance measurement 8,
    161–75
Petrash, Gordon 226
Phoenix Consortium 199
pillars of KM 223
PriceWaterhouseCoopers 27
process knowledge scorecard
    124

process modelling 102–8, 148–9
  see also ADONIS
professional services 18, 24, 26–7
project management 8, 26
  data warehousing projects
    203–4
  software development 170–5
ProQuest Direct (PQD) search
    181–4
psychological needs of clinicians
    79

QSR*NUDIST 214
quality of knowledge, *see*
  knowledge management
Quicken 115

recommender systems 5–6, 37,
    40–7, 135
  definition 40
  externalizing tacit knowledge
    40
  levels of knowledge 46
  prototype 41, 42–4
    benefits 40, 47
    user reactions 42–4
  push and pull 40–1
  see also agent-based retrieval;
    Annotate; KnowMore
reference models 119–20
  business reference model
    (BRM) 205
  schematic hierarchy 122–3
request for proposal (RFP) 207
requirements of KMS 100–1
resource-based view of the firm
    1, 188
responsibility
  knowledge 22–3, 23–4, 59, 73,
    74, 109, 122–3, 125, 189, 217
  organizational 1
return on investment (ROI) 115
Robins, Kaplan, Miller and
    Ciresi 87
Rosenbluth International
    Alliance 50
Rover Group 199–200, 201, 203,
    204, 205, 206

Saint Onge, Hubert 226
SAir Group 113

Sandoz 113
Schelling diagram 141, 142
search, *see* full-text search,
    keyword search
security 22–3, 59, 205
  authentication 70
  distribution 70–1
  integrity 70
  non-repudiation 70
self-adaptiveness 147
semantics 117, 122
  clinical use 69
  corporate level 100
  documents 130, 135, 139, 143
  enterprise modelling 7, 100,
    102, 103–4, 105–6, 107–8
  information theory 99
  modification 100
  understanding 101
SGML 107
Shell Oil 2
Sigma 6, 54–61
  communication 57, 60
  network of expertise 56
  organizational culture 56, 57,
    60, 61
  organizational structure 55
  SIK 54, 58–9
  virtual organization 55
  see also SigSys; virtual
    organization
SigSys 6, 54–61
  future development 59–60
  limitations 57
  media choice 60
  usage patterns 57
  see also Ariadne's Thread
Skandia 226
socialization of knowledge 128,
    135, 139, 224
Society of Motor Manufacturers
    and Traders 199
software agents, *see* agent-based
    retrieval
software development 171–5
stages of KM model 228–9
standard graphic markup
    language, *see* SGML
standard query language (SQL)
    164–5, 169, 174, 175
strategy modelling 104

strategy of the organization 1
  business engineering 123
  data warehousing initiatives
    202
  knowledge resource 232
  knowledge scorecards 123–5
  understanding strategy using
    corporate knowledge 99
Sullivan, Patrick 226
Swiss Department of Defence
  126
Swissair 113
Sybase's Enterprise Data Studio
  164
System W 198

technological change 1, 6
theory-in-use 45
TKGL 85–6
total quality management 1
transmission control protocol/
    Internet protocol (TCP/IP)
    114, 157, 164

unified modelling language
    (UML) 104, 107
University of Cambridge 79
University of St Gallen 126
Unix 130 206, 207
Usenet 136
user participation 61

VIRTO 50
virtual organization 6, 49–61
  business models 50
  challenges for knowledge
    management 52–4
  definition 50
  flexibility 49, 50
  knowledge organization 52
  knowledge sharing 60–1
  organizational culture 53, 61
  team-oriented 50–2
    challenges 52
    enabling factors 52
    tasks for KM 53
    trust 52–3

Volvo 5, 36–47
  intranet 41

Walden Paddlers 50
waterfall model for document
    management 8, 131–2
WaX ActiveLibrary 6, 66–80
  audit trail 68, 78
  browsing performance 66–7
  Cambridge pilot study 75–9
  choice of content 71
  clinical outcomes 80
  evaluation 74–8
  information
    granularity 74, 78, 118
    reformatting 73–4
    retrieval 68–9
    sources 71–3
  interface design 66–8
  objectives 66
  patient management 6, 77, 80
  security 70–1
  structure of knowledge 69
  text editor 68, 70
  user reactions 77–8, 79
  WaX books 67–8
    approval 74
    creation 69–70
    trust 70–1
WaX Info Limited 79
Web browser 59, 150, 170
  editors 132–3
  growth of KM 2
  performance 66–7
  use in KMS 25
Web full-text search, *see* full-text
    search
WFTS, *see* full-text search
Windows NT 130, 207
work process definition
    language (WPDL) 107
Workflow Management
    Coalition (WfMC) 107, 120,
    153

Xerox 38–9
XML 114, 138, 139